NEW STATESMANSHIP

An Anthology selected by
Edward Hyams

New Statesmanship

AN ANTHOLOGY

SELECTED BY

Edward Hyams

Essay Index Reprint Series

 BOOKS FOR LIBRARIES PRESS
FREEPORT, NEW YORK

INTERNATIONAL STANDARD BOOK NUMBER:
0-8369-1891-6

LIBRARY OF CONGRESS CATALOG CARD NUMBER:
72-128281

PRINTED IN THE UNITED STATES OF AMERICA

Authors

Illustrations in the Text

Anthologist's Preface

I offer no introduction to this collection. The proper introduction is the companion volume to this one, The New Statesman: The History of the First Fifty Years 1913–1963. *Or perhaps I should say that this Anthology is an illustration to the History; that, in fact, is what it is meant to be. This statement calls for a word of explanation.*

An anthologist is guided in his choice either by his own taste; or by the requirements of received taste; or by a theme. I have been guided, more or less, by a theme. The theme is what I call 'new statesmanship'. This is a certain state of mind. New statesmanship is hard-minded and soft-hearted. With sympathy, it seeks to improve the general lot; but it seeks to do so intelligently. In its journalistic manifestation, moreover, it seeks to do so . . . yes, the word is entertainingly.

In making my choice – and the New Statesman *volumes from 1913–1963 contain well over 100 million words by almost every notable English and many foreign writers of the whole period – I have tried to pick out works of prose, poetry and drawing which are firstly representative new statesmanship; secondly, entertaining; thirdly, good examples of their authors' journalistic work. I do not pretend to have applied this rule of three with severity; I have sometimes allowed my own taste to modify a choice; and sometimes my feeling that a particular piece of work will interest or amuse the reader in any case.*

In one respect the choice I have made is necessarily invidious: I have left out a lot of work which is as good as, in some cases better than, work which I have included, Richard Crossman's, notably. The reason was this: very few book reviews, even at a high critical level, and very few political reviews, even at the level set by a Harold Laski or a Richard Crossman, remain interesting after the book reviewed or the political policy or crisis discussed have ceased to be interesting. My choice, then, was limited to those pieces which are more or less timeless, and even then I have broken the rule in several cases.

The articles are arranged in chronological order.

Edward Hyams

WHAT seemed to its founders to be the New Statesman's greatest asset in its first years was the service of George Bernard Shaw. But Clifford Sharp, the young Editor during the first sixteen years of the paper's life, found it difficult and finally impossible to handle Shaw. Comic theatre does not make sound journalism and Shaw was apt to be careless about facts. Typical of his high spirits as a New Statesman contributor is his treatment of the Marconi shares scandal: Cabinet Ministers had been accused by the Chestertons of buying shares in a company whose fortunes they were about to make by allowing it an immensely valuable concession.

Wireless Indignation   ## Bernard Shaw

It is impossible to let the curtain fall on the Marconi Comedy without a murmur of appreciation. We are an incorrigibly intemperate and ridiculous people in our cups of virtuous indignation. We are a nation of governesses. In vain did Macaulay try to cure us by a classic passage. We do it again and again. Just consider the course of the epidemic in this Marconi business. First it was suggested that Cabinet Ministers are speculating in Marconis; that they have relatives who are speculating in Marconis; that they are Jews; that their relatives are Jews; that the Jewish race exists only to speculate in Marconis; and, by implication, that no Englishman could, without a dastardly betrayal of his country, soil his hands with a Marconi share certificate. A frantic campaign of horror and vituperation followed. The *National Review* and the *New Witness* promptly set about the task of cleansing the Augean stable. The intolerable notion that a member of the Government could have a financial interest in anything was repudiated. Mr Herbert Samuel, being a Jew, was despoiled of his 'Mister', and became simply Samuel, like the Old Testament hero, but in a less complimentary sense. England was represented as bound hand and foot in the power of a gang of unscrupulous and corrupt financial adventurers. Those who live in glass-houses should not throw stones, it is said. We do not endorse the precept. Nothing but living in a glass-house and taking all the risks of stone-throwing before you begin it yourself can justify such a method of warfare: the man who throws stones from a bomb-proof casement is clearly no sportsman. But it is none the less amusing when the first pane that cracks is the window of the man who opens fire. As it happened, the proprietor of the paper that led the attack on the Jews and on Cabinet speculation was the first to retire from the fray in the hands of the police. We do not prejudge his case, and we wish him a safe deliverance: still, we cannot help smiling.

But his young lions were not to be baulked of their prey. The paper, under a slightly new title, held on manfully; and the young lions – very able lions, too – let themselves go as they had never let themselves go before. No defence was offered; and for the moment it looked as if they had got Ministers 'on the run'.

Then came the reaction. Sir Rufus Isaacs made an eloquent and memorable speech in the House from which his Party inferred that never in the whole course of a financially blameless life had he or any other member of the Government trafficked in anything known to the Stock Exchange. As to British Marconis – what did we take him for? It was crushing: it was magnificent. The Marconi Committee laid hands on Mr Maxse's no-longer-young lion, and took him in a pit and tamed him, and extracted from him a confession that he knew not what he wrote, but only believed what he was told. All England thrilled with virtuous indignation next day. The *Manchester Guardian*, the very citadel of the old English Press now that *The Times* is only 'the new journalism', headed the rush with a surpassing outburst of scornful invective, in which the tamed lion was held up and flung down and trampled on. After that, Ministers had such haloes of financial integrity set round their brows as were never lit up before by any sane paper. It looked now as if Sir Rufus had Mr Cecil Chesterton and Mr Belloc very hard on the run indeed, and that Mr Maxse must presently sleep in the Clock Tower.

But fancy the feelings of poor Sir Rufus and Mr Lloyd George and Lord Murray of Elibank! They had Marconi shares in their pockets all the time. It is true they were American Marconis; and if Sir Rufus and the *Manchester Guardian* had only drawn their virtuous indignation mild, the distinction might have saved the situation. But it had been drawn with such a raging head to it that Sir Rufus had come to be deemed incapable of even South Pole Marconis. Sir Rufus himself felt the need for some excuse. And the excuse was that he had lost by his deal, and involved Mr Lloyd George in the loss. But even the faithful *Guardian* could not pretend to believe that Sir Rufus had bought the shares with the intention of losing by them.

In the *Nation*, Mr Massingham, who supports the Government only on condition that he is not to be let in or trifled with, set his visage grimly upon Sir Rufus and said, in effect, 'You know what I think of the transaction.' Mr Lloyd George, who, as it presently turned out, had not done so badly after all, declared that he had only £400 a year to look forward to in his old age; that his speculation was an investment; and that if anybody raked up what he said about the Chamberlains and Kynochs he would make the Opposition wish it had never been born. And, calm amid all the recriminations and threats and altercations and excuses, Mr Samuel, the Jew, totally guiltless of any sort of Marconis whatever, annexed all the knocked-off haloes and added them to his own.

It is an amusing and silly business. It begins by an attempt to show that there is nothing to choose between a modern Cabinet Minister and Titus Oates. This provokes a counter-demonstration that there is nothing to choose between a modern Cabinet Minister and George Washington. The Party organs intervene to explain that the Titus Oates theory is correct when their side is in opposition, and the George Washington one when their side is in office. When the affair has reached an unbearable pitch of absurdity, Sir Rufus and Mr Lloyd George inform the public that they are neither Titus nor George, but simply Rufus and David. And the incident closes in frightful disillusion, because it began in deliberately manufactured illusion. Such is English public life!

For ourselves, if you ask us should a Cabinet Minister hold shares in commercial concerns, we reply: Of course not. And if you ask us further how a Cabinet Minister is to provide for his family and his old age except by commercial investments, we reply that we do not know, and neither does he. That is one of Commercialism's little ironies, and one of the reasons why we are out to get rid of Commercialism.

12 April 1913

A number of D. H. Lawrence's early short stories appeared in the New Statesman.

The Fly in the Ointment   D. H. Lawrence

Muriel had sent me some mauve primroses, slightly weather-beaten, and some honey-suckle-twine threaded with grey-green rosettes, and some timid hazel catkins. They had arrived in a forlorn little cardboard box just as I was rushing off to school.

'Stick 'em in water!' I said to Mrs Williams; and I left the house. But those mauve primroses had set my tone for the day. I was dreamy and reluctant; school and the sounds of the boys were unreal, unsubstantial;

beyond these were the realities of my poor winter-trodden primroses and the pale hazel catkins that Muriel had sent me. Altogether, the boys must have thought me a vacant fool; I regarded them as a punishment upon me.

I rejoiced exceedingly when night came, with the evening star, and the sky flushed dark blue, purple over the golden pomegranates of the lamps. I was as glad as if I had been hurrying home to Muriel, as if she would open the door to me, would keep me a little while in the fireglow, with the splendid purple of the evening against the window, before she laughed and drew up her head proudly and flashed on the light over the tea-cups. But Eleanor, the girl, opened the door to me, and I poured out my tea in solitary state.

Mrs Williams had set out my winter posy for me on the table, and I thought of all the beautiful things we had done, Muriel and I, at home in the Midlands, of all the beautiful ways she had looked at me, of all the beautiful things I had said to her – or had meant to say. I went on imagining beautiful things to say to her, while she looked at me with her wonderful eyes from among the fir boughs in the wood. Meanwhile, I talked to my landlady about the neighbours.

Although I had much work to do, and although I laboured away at it, in the end there was nothing done. Then I felt very miserable, and sat still and sulked. At a quarter to eleven I said to myself: 'This will never do', and I took up my pen and wrote a letter to Muriel: 'It was not fair to send me those robins' – we called the purple primroses 'robins', for no reason, unless that they bloomed in winter – 'they have bewitched me. Their wicked, bleared little pinkish eyes follow me about, and I have to think of you and home, instead of doing what I've got to do. All the time while I was teaching I had a grasshopper chirruping away in my head, as if it were midsummer there, and the arithmetic rattled like the carts on the street. Poor lads! I read their miserable pieces of composition on "pancakes" over and over, and never saw them, thinking "the primroses flower now because it is so sheltered under the plum-trees – those old trees with gummy bark." You like biting through a piece of hard, bright gum. If your lips did not get so sticky . . .'

I will not say at what time I finished my letter. I can recall a sensation of being dim, oblivious of everything, smiling to myself as I sealed the envelope; of putting my books and papers in their places without the least knowledge of so doing, keeping the atmosphere of Stretley Mill close round me in my London lodging. I cannot remember turning off the electric light. The next thing of which I am conscious is pushing at the kitchen door.

4

The kitchen is at the back of the house. Outside in the dark was a little yard and a hand's breadth of garden, backed by the railway embankment. I had come down the passage from my room in the front of the house, and stood pushing at the kitchen door to get a glass for some water. Evidently the oilcloth had turned up a little, and the edge of the door was under it. I woke up irritably, swore a little, pushed harder, and heard the oilcloth rip. Then I bent and put my hand through the small space to flatten the oil-cloth.

The kitchen was in darkness save for the red embers lying low in the stove. I started, but rather from sleepy wonder than anything else. The shock was not quite enough to bring me to. Pressing himself flat into the corner between the stove and the wall was a fellow. I wondered, and was disturbed; the greater part of me was away in the Midlands still. So I stood looking and blinking.

'Why ?' I said helplessly. I think this very mildness must have terrified him. Immediately he shrank together, and began to dodge about between the table and the stove, whining, snarling, with an incredibly mongrel sound:

'Don't yer touch me! Don't yer come grabbin' at me! I'll hit you between the eyes with this poker. I ain't done nothin' to you. Don't yer touch me, yer bloody coward !'

All the time he was writhing about in the space in which I had him trapped, between the table and the stove. I was much too dazed to do anything but stare. Then my blood seemed to change its quality. I came awake, sick and sharp with pain. It was such a display as I had seen before in school and I felt again the old misery of helplessness and disgust. He dared not, I knew, strike, unless by trying to get hold of him I terrified him to the momentary madness of such a slum-rat.

'Stop your row!' I said, standing still, and leaving him his room. 'Shut your miserable row! Do you want to waken the children ?'

'Ah, but don't you touch me; don't you come no nearer!'

He had stopped writhing about, and was crouching at the defensive. The little frenzy, too, had gone out of his voice.

'Put the poker down, you fool' – I pointed to the corner of the stove where the poker used to stand. I supplied him with the definite idea of placing the poker in the corner, and in his crazy witless state he could not reject it. He did as I told him, but indefinitely, as if the action were secondhand. The poker, loosely dropped into the corner, slid to the ground with a clatter.

I looked from it to him, feeling him like a burden upon me, and in some way I was afraid of him, for my heart began to beat heavily. His own indefinite clumsiness, and the jangle of the poker on the hearth, and then my sudden spiritual collapse, unnerved him still more. He crouched there abjectly.

I took a box of matches from the mantelpiece and lit the gas at the pendant that hung in the middle of the bare little room. Then I saw that he was a youth of nineteen or so, narrow at the temples, with thin, pinched-looking brows. He was not ugly, nor did he look ill-fed. But he evidently came of a low breed. His hair had been cut close to his skull, leaving a tussocky fringe over his forehead to provide him with a 'topping', and to show that it was no prison crop which had bared him.

'I wasn't doin' no harm,' he whined resentfully, with still an attempt at a threat in his tones. 'I 'aven't done nuffin' to you; you leave me alone. What harm have I done?'

'Be quiet,' I said. 'You'll wake the children and the people.'

I went to the door and listened. No one was disturbed. Then I closed the door and pulled down the wide-opened window, which was letting in the cold night air. As I did so I shivered, noting how ugly and shapeless the mangle looked in the yard, with the moonlight on its frosty cover.

The fellow was standing abjectly in the same place. He had evidently been rickety as a child. I sat down in the rocking chair.

'What did you come in here for?' I asked, almost pleading.

'Well,' he retorted insolently. 'An' wouldn't you go somewhere if you edn't a place to go to of a night like this?'

'Look here,' I said coldly, a flash of hate in my blood; 'none of your chelp.'

'Well, I only come in for a warm,' he said, afraid not to appear defiant.

'No you didn't,' I replied. 'You came to take something. What did you want from here?' I looked round the kitchen unhappily. He looked back at me uneasily, then at his dirty hands, then at me again. He had brown eyes, in which low cunning floated like oil on the top of much misery.

'I might 'a took some boots,' he said, with a little vaunt.

My heart sank. I hoped he would say 'food'. And I was responsible for him. I hated him.

'You want your neck breaking,' I said. 'We can hardly afford boots as it is.'

'I ain't never done it before! This is the first time —'

'You miserable swine!' I said. He looked at me with a flash of rat-fury.

'Where do you live?' I asked.

'Exeter Road.'

'And you don't do any work?'

'I couldn't never get a job – except – I used to deliver laundry –'

'And they turned you off for thieving?'

He shifted and stirred uneasily in his chair. As he was so manifestly uncomfortable, I did not press him.

'Who do you live with?'

'I live at home.'

'What does your father do?'

But he sat stubborn and would not answer. I thought of the gangs of youths who stood at the corners of the mean streets near the school, there all day long, month after month, fooling with the laundry girls and insulting passers-by.

'But,' I said, 'what are you going to do?'

He hung his head again and fidgeted in his chair. Evidently what little thought he gave to the subject made him uncomfortable. He could not answer.

'Get a laundry girl to marry you and live on her?' I asked sarcastically.

He smiled sicklily, evidently even a little bit flattered. What was the good of talking to him?

'And loaf at the street corners till you go rotten?' I said.

He looked up at me sullenly.

'Well, I can't get a job,' he replied with insolence. He was not hopeless, but, like a man born without expectations, apathetic, looking to be provided for, sullenly allowing everything.

'No,' I said; 'if a man is worthy of his hire, the hire is worthy of a man – and I'm damned if you are a man!'

He grinned at me with sly insolence.

'And would any woman have you?' I asked.

Then he grinned slyly to himself, ducking his head to hide the joke. And I thought of the coloured primroses and of Muriel's beautiful pensive face. Then of him with his dirty clothes and his nasty skin! Then that, given a woman, he would be a father.

'Well,' I said, 'it's a knock-out.'

He gave me a narrow, sleering look.

'You don't know everyfin,' he said in contempt. I sat and wondered. And I knew I could not understand him, that I had no fellow feeling with him. He was something beyond me.

'Well,' I said helplessly, 'you'd better go.'

I rose, feeling he had beaten me. He could affect and alter me; I could not affect nor alter him. He shambled off down the path. I watched him

7

skulk under the lamp-posts, afraid of the police. Then I shut the door. In the silence of the sleeping house I stood quite still for some minutes, up against the impassable fact of this man, beyond which I could not get. I could not accept him. I simply hated him. Then I climbed the stairs. It was like a nightmare. I thought he was a blot, like a blot fallen on my mind, something black and heavy out of which I could not extricate myself.

As I hung up my coat I felt Muriel's fat letter in my pocket. It made me a trifle sick. 'No!' I said, with a flush of rage against her perfect, serene purity, 'I don't want to think of her.' And I wound my watch up sullenly, feeling alone and wretched.

16 August 1913

New statesmanship in war entailed avoiding chauvinistic excesses and keeping one's head. But this must not also entail blinking the facts about the Germans even if one did not join in the hymn of hate. Havelock Ellis discussed the enemy in a thoroughly new statesmanly spirit three months after the outbreak of World War I.

Why the Germans are not Loved   Havelock Ellis

It may seem a futile question to discuss. '*Circumspice,*' one may be told, is the answer; you have only to look around Europe; there is no need for discussion. Yet there is a certain interest in discussing this attitude of the world towards Germans when we realize that it is two thousand years old. To seek to exacerbate passions that are already acute would be an unworthy task. The Germans are a great factor in the world's life; they will not be exterminated, whatever happens; they even have a large part – as they like to remind us – in our own blood. We shall still have to live in the world with them, and may as well try to understand them. If the world has not loved them, that is scarcely matter for exultation.

In Germany itself this attitude of the world is not unrealized; indeed, it is often morbidly exaggerated. Thoughtful Germans have from time to time anxiously pondered over the problem. One such attempt to elucidate the matter, made a few years ago, seems worth bringing forward, because the events of today serve to put it in a new light. Professor Georg Stein-hausen speaks with high authority. He is at the very centre of that 'Kultur' we now hear so much about. He is, indeed, its historian as well as the editor of the *Archiv für Kultur-Geschichte*. Steinhausen's *Geschichte des Deutschen Kultur* is deservedly a classic work, and his monographs on the German mediaeval merchant and other similar subjects are highly valued. Moreover, Professor Steinhausen, even in discussing so delicate a topic as the world's estimate of Germans, is reasonable and fair-minded; not, indeed, setting himself in opposition to the current attitude of his own people, but representing that attitude in a temperate and scholarly spirit. Although a Prussian, he is not of the school of Treitschke and Bernhardi. As he wrote at the conclusion of the latest edition of his 'History' last year, he looks for a reaction against the excessive materialism of modern Germany. He desires for his country a civilization of finer quality, for Germany still lacks, he remarks, what the French, the English, even the Dutch, have achieved – an evolved spirit of civilization, an independent art of living, a high *Lebenstil*. What such a man has to say is better worth hearing than the fanatical and less typical utterances of extremists, so wearisomely dinned into our ears of late.

'There is no people so unloved as we are. Why is it?' he asks. (He is writing, it must be remembered, five years ago, in the *Deutsche Rundschau* for December 1909, and January 1910.) Germany's position in the world reminds him of England's a century ago when she attacked unprotected Denmark, though he hastens to qualify this remark by adding that Germany has no such crime on her conscience; 'Germany's policy is the most peaceful and well-meaning in the world.' Steinhausen finds a partial answer to his question in the reflection that the reputation of nations is chiefly founded on their exterior qualities, and the good qualities of the German are interior. Even Tacitus, he remarks, who admired the courage and chastity of the Germans, regarded them as drunken and violent barbarians. Their cunning also impressed the Romans, and their aptitude for lying, as Velleius Paterculus records. In the fifth century the Goths, whose original home was Prussia, were for Salvianus *'Gothorum gens perfida.'* Their frenzy of drunkenness has been specially noted from the first and all through, often with gluttony in addition. Gregory of Tours gave a disgusting picture of their drinking habits, so also Venantius Fortunatus and a long succession of writers, down, it may be said, to the present. Their uncleanliness also impressed Salvianus and others, while Sidonius complained that their women reeked of onions.

Steinhausen is not, however, inclined to rely exclusively on the mere exteriority of the Germans' bad traits. He finds another explanation, which had, indeed (as he fails to mention), already been put forward by Nietzsche: Europeans are the legatees of the ancient Roman Empire, and have thus

'Dogs, do you want to live for ever?' – Frederick the Great to his hesitant guards, 1757.
by Vicky [10 Nov. 1961]

inherited its profound horror of the Teutonic barbarians who in successive waves rolled over their civilization. The Goths from Prussia who sacked Rome in 410, but spared the sacred places, were far outdone in the perpetration of horrors by their descendants who accompanied Charles of Bourbon to the later sack of Rome in 1527; and still later, in the Thirty Years' War, the troops of Mansfeld, which were a terror to their enemies, were a still greater terror to their friends. This view of the matter seems, indeed, to flash across Professor Steinhausen as he proceeds with his argument. The Rhinelander, he says, as well as the German of the South-West, looks down on the East German as half a barbarian, and the Rhinelander and South-West German occupy a region of ancient Roman civilization.

It is natural, therefore, that the Latin races of today, who are still closer to ancient civilization, should grow impatient when they hear Gobineau and Houston Chamberlain declare that the German is the salt of the earth and European civilization a Teutonic creation, declaring on their side that civilization is a Mediterranean product, and that the Germans have merely been a destructive element. Such a criticism, the fair-minded Steinhausen admits, is in part not unjust. The Germans had their own sources of culture, and the modern world owes to the Germans (in the wide sense, including the English*) much, and not of the worst, that it possesses. But this debt to Germany only began in the middle of the eighteenth century. It has proceeded rapidly, and 'today world-civilization is no more Latin, but a great part Germanic' – that is, as we should express it, Anglo-Saxon and Germanic.

Whatever the explanation of the world's opinion of the Teuton, Professor Steinhausen admits and even emphasizes that opinion; few of its more notable expressions seem to have escaped him. '*Teutonici, nullius amici*,' was the Latin saying of the thirteenth century transmitted to posterity from England. 'The friend of none!' comments the Professor. 'A sad saying, but very significant. It corresponds to the judgment of many peoples concerning the mediaeval Germans.' The Byzantines were impressed by their gluttony and drunkenness, though the '*furor Teutonicus*' in war was admitted, especially by the Italians. A haughty self-consciousness was noted of them and embodied in fifteenth-century proverbs, as

---

* It must always be remembered that to the Teutonic mind the English, though not 'Deutsch', are 'German'. Hence the resentment felt in Germany at our 'treachery' in turning against a race regarded as being of our own stock. They overlook the fact that 'England', and even 'Deutschland', are really inhabited by races of highly mixed composition, and neither exclusively 'Germanic', even in the widest sense.

was their clownishness. They were not loved by their fellow-crusaders in the Holy Land: '*grossiers et communs*,' wrote the Troubadour Peire Vidal. The Germans, on their part, passed this attitude on, and in their turn have always called the Slavs 'barbarians'. Petrarch continued the tradition, but in his hands it becomes a more refined and discriminating criticism; he admired Cologne, but (like some of the most recent critics of Germany) he could only find signs of material prosperity, none of spiritual exultation. It was, Steinhausen points out, mainly 'the coarse atmosphere of drunkenness and gluttony' which made Germany seem barbarous, so that, in 1471, Giantonio Campano said that it made him sick even to hear the word 'Germany'.

The Germans themselves admitted the truth of the foreigners' charges. 'Alas! I know well,' said Luther, 'that we Germans are, and always will be, beasts and mad brutes, as the peoples around call us, and as we well deserve.' '*Porco tedesco*,' said the Italian proverb; '*Allemands ivrognes*,' the French, though at the same time their prowess was admitted: 'Let him who wants to be hacked in pieces quarrel with the Germans.' Even the English, though they (Steinhausen points out) had the least right of all to make fun of 'other Germans' on these grounds, joined in the general chorus. He quotes the now oft-quoted remark of Shakespeare's Portia on the German, the observations of the judicious Fynes Moryson – whose *Itinerary*, it may be added, was the Baedeker for Europe of the seventeenth century and remains today a more fascinating book than ever – and the epigram of John Owen that if in wine there is truth, certainly it will sooner or later be discovered by the Germans.

In the middle of the eighteenth century there was indeed a sudden fashion of admiration for the German poetry of the time, its sentiment and its naïveté; but this fashion had almost passed by 1790. It was not until Madame de Staël's revelation of the 'German soul' in 1813, in *De l'Allemagne*, that Germany became really a fashion in France. The new industrial development has not made Germany more loved, says Steinhausen, though it has increased respect and admiration. Notwithstanding all the military and industrial and economic activities of Germany, there remains the feeling, he confesses, that the Germans are barbarous, more especially in the developments of Prussian militarism. (It may be noted that Steinhausen, probably because he himself belongs to Prussia, deliberately omits to consider the Prussianization of modern Germany as a factor in the European attitude, and it is an important omission.) 'All Prussians,' says Maurice Barrès, 'are under the operation of beer, which lulls, without changing, their brutal souls,' and René Bazin remarks: 'I do not hate the

Germans – I even admire them – but the more I learn to know them the more I feel that they are different, that I belong to another race, and that I cherish an ideal which they cannot understand.' This feeling of superiority on the part of the Latins, as the judicial Steinhausen observes, is not without justification; it is based on their ancient civilization, and on the possession of a cultivated art of living which, he admits, the Germans, for all their efforts, still lack.

'The Englishman, also, has a definite culture of life, and a civilizational style of living, without which life is unthinkable to him, and which no one denies. He, too, feels himself in consequence to be superior to the noisy and ill-bred Germans, unskilfully stiff, or formlessly jovial, or socially incorrect.' Such feelings it is, Steinhausen concludes, together with hatred of the feudal-military system, regarded as a residuum of mediaeval barbarism, which affect all peoples outside Germany, especially those proud of their 'freedom' (it is the Professor who places that word in inverted commas). So it is that Ferrero in *L'Europa Giovone* calls Bismarck a barbaric genius only fit for Huns.

Behind this exposition one detects a certain sadness. Steinhausen is on the side of that idealistic individualism which he evidently regards as the finest and deepest Germanic trait. 'Today,' he remarks, 'we can only speak of the ideal spirit of Germany in a very restricted sense. Everywhere we see the predominance of a highly external conception of the world, whose purse-proud exponents regard the ideally minded scholar much in the old spirit of Frederick William I of Prussia.' To Germany's other defects is to be added her extreme self-consciousness of superiority, and Steinhausen quotes a Serb as to the Germans 'always crying aloud their own good qualities and running down foreigners whom at the same time they are ridiculously imitating.' This attitude has accompanied Germany's sudden rise to prosperity, which again arouses, especially among the English, 'envy and jealousy' – that oft-repeated German charge which touches most of us so little, and is, indeed, incompatible with the attitude of superiority which is also charged against us. In the end Steinhausen consoles himself with the thought that other nations, at all events, are beginning to regard Germany as a model. The Russians are in science and in economics the pupils of the Germans. So also are the Balkan peoples, especially the Roumanians. Germany's friends are growing in Italy. The French are beginning to be just to Germany. The Belgian Maeterlinck has declared that 'Germany is the moral conscience of the world.' The Americans recognize the blessings which Germany has brought. The Japanese appreciate and imitate Germany. 'So we Germans need not take tragically the world's lack of love for us. Politically it may today be dangerous. But against that danger our might will protect us.'

Doubtless there are some who will smile gleefully to observe how even that place of refuge which Professor Steinhausen imagines that Germany holds in the world's heart has today fallen down at every single point like a house of cards.

But it is matter for tragedy more than comedy. Whatever the might of Germany may prove to be worth, it remains a tragedy for itself and all mankind that one of the youngest and most vigorous of great nations – eagerly striving to snatch at that culture which is the mature growth of centuries – should seek to thrust its gifts on the world by brute force, while yet dimly realizing that one of the greatest of national assets is love.

14 November 1914

Robert Lynd wrote for the New Statesman *from the beginning, first anonymously, then under his own name, finally, and for nearly quarter of a century, over the initials 'Y.Y.' If all the new statesmanly essays he wrote were published in a set of volumes they would constitute the most sustained plea for sweet nature, decent civilized conduct and tolerance, ever made.*

Ruthlessness   Robert Lynd

Germany seems to be the only country in Europe at present in which the soldiers are as ferocious as the journalists. Perhaps this is because in Germany so many of the soldiers are journalists. So far as one can gather from the descriptions of the Christmas truce on the battlefield, the common German soldier is, like the soldier of other nations, a human being who is much more inclined by nature to friendliness than to hatred. But the scribbling German soldier, or the scribbling German sailor – who is almost always a general or an admiral – why, he is as excitably ferocious as anything you could find in Fleet Street. He is almost on the level of the Nonconformist journalist who recently spoke with withering scorn of those of his fellow-Christians who still believed in praying for their enemies. This is, of course, the ancient logic of fighting. The pagan in each of us wishes to give our enemies hell, not only in this world, but in the next. When the tipsy Orangeman shouts 'To hell with the Pope!' he probably expresses with perfect accuracy his opinion of the punishment which he thinks the Pope deserves; and we have heard a devout Catholic, at mention of the name of Tom Paine, say with grim satisfaction: 'He's sizzling in Hell now.' If we can wish our enemies torture that will last through eternity, it seems rather absurd that we should be squeamish about causing them all the pain and misery we can during the brief interval of their habitation of the earth.

Our ancestors certainly did not shrink from the logic of punishment as regards either this world or the next. The history of penal methods, whether in England, France, Spain or China, is a history of ruthlessness which is at times so horrible as to seem almost ludicrous. Ruthlessness, it was usually assumed, was the only safe way of protecting society against its enemies. Ruthlessness, the Count von Reventlows seem to assume at the present moment, is the only safe way of protecting Germany against its enemies. It is not apparently a matter of revenge so much as of policy. They defend the burning of Louvain, the shooting of hostages, the bombardment of undefended towns, and (in a recent instance) the proposal to torpedo merchant ships and send their crews to the bottom, not as glorious acts of national hatred, but as the only means of terrorizing the Allies into submission. One would imagine that, if ruthlessness has been found ineffective as a means of suppressing badly armed and badly equipped criminals, it must be found still more ineffective as a means of suppressing well-armed and well-equipped nations. And, when the history of the present war comes to be written, we shall be surprised if we do not find even the German historians admitting that every act of inhumanity of which their army was guilty only resulted in adding to the numbers and strength of their enemy. There are Germans who point to the comparative peace and quiet which at present reign in Belgium as a proof of the wisdom of German policy. But no one will deny that a people may for a time be intimidated into silence by ruthlessness. What we do deny is that Germany is a step nearer victory as a result of her ruthlessness. The ruthlessness of Germany, we may be sure, did much to strengthen King Albert and his government and forces in their determination to hold out to the last minute in Antwerp and to allow neither themselves nor their stores, neither their docks nor their shipping, to fall into the hands of their pitiless enemies. Germany, indeed, by her conduct in Belgium raised not only Belgium, but half the world against her. There are thousands of Englishmen, Scotsmen, and Irishmen now being trained to fight against Germany who would probably be still sitting at home reading the newspapers if Germany had not forced herself on their imaginations as a big bully torturing a people smaller than herself.

Whether bullying ever pays or not is a question which it is not easy to answer. Clearly, there has always been a great deal of bullying in the relations between strong and weak peoples, as there has been in the relations between strong and weak men. The big Empire has not won its way to its present position by what is called brotherly love any more than the big landlord or the big manufacturer has. On the other hand, there is all the difference in the world between bullying within limits and bullying without mercy. The Roman Republic bullied its provinces without mercy; the Roman Empire by comparison bullied them within limits. The merciless sort of bullying has usually been done either in the name of religion or in the name of culture. Nearly all the great acts of mercilessness which stain the pages of history were interpreted in terms of some lofty purpose like that with which the German apologists justify their creed of ruthlessness today. Alva felt no pang of remorse for his cruelties in the Low Countries. On the contrary, he boasted that, apart from all the thousands he had slain in battle and massacred afterwards, he had delivered over 18,000 people to the executioner. Almost certainly, at the time, he had no doubt that he was establishing Spanish and Catholic culture in the Low Countries for ever. But what remains of Spain and her conquering hosts in those parts now? Nothing but a memory and a reviling. It would be straining language a little, however, to describe Alva's 'Court of Blood' as a crime of culture. We find a much better example of the ruthlessness of culture in the scarcely less famous massacre of Glencoe. Here was a crime plotted by a statesman as civilized as the most civilized of Germans. The Master of Stair, as Macaulay says, was 'one of the first men of his time, a jurist, a statesman, a fine scholar, an eloquent orator.' He was good-natured, not disposed to cruelty, had 'no personal reason to wish the Glencoe men any ill', and 'there is not the slightest reason to believe that he gained a single pound Scots by the act which has covered his name with infamy.' His aim in planning the most treacherous of crimes was neither personal greed nor personal glory. 'His object,' in the words of Macaulay, 'was no less than a complete dissolution and reconstruction of society in the Highlands. . . . This explanation may startle those who have not considered how large a proportion of the blackest crimes recorded in history is to be ascribed to ill-regulated public spirit. We daily see men do for their party, for their sect, for their country, for their favourite schemes of political and social reform, what they would not do to enrich or to avenge themselves. At a temptation directly addressed to our private cupidity or to our private animosity, whatever virtue we have takes alarm. But virtue itself may contribute to the fall of him who imagines that it is in his power,

16

by violating some general rule of morality, to confer an important benefit on a Church, or a commonwealth, or mankind. He silences the remonstrances of conscience, and hardens his heart against the most touching spectacles of misery, by repeating to himself that his intentions are pure, that his objects are noble, that he is doing a little evil for the sake of a great good.'

Public spirit, therefore, is not only one of the most splendid virtues; it may also be one of the most dangerous vices. It is a vice on the part of every man who does not realize that it is as easy to disgrace one's country or one's party as it is to disgrace oneself by certain forms of wickedness. The German theory of the State, however, is that it is something which, like the superman, is beyond good and evil. From this point of view, the State can do no wrong. It is capable of but one virtue – power – and of one sin – feebleness. Those who admit this theory of the State obviously need not be disturbed even if one accuses them, in their public capacity, of all the crimes in the Newgate Calendar. As a matter of fact, the Germans are seriously disturbed by some of the accusations that have been made against them. One day they preach ruthlessness, and the next day they spend in proving that they have not been ruthless at all. They are scarcely more bent upon defying the laws of war than upon proving that they have all along scrupulously observed the laws of war. The truth is, their theory of the State is the invention of their heads, not of their consciences, and they find themselves compelled to salute virtue even as they advocate new crimes.

One of the most interesting examples of a government's refusing to adopt a policy of ruthlessness has been resuscitated lately in more than one quarter. This was the refusal of the British Government to adopt Lord Cochrane's 'secret war plan' for the total destruction of the enemy's fleet. The Government Committee which considered the plan reported that it was effective, but recommended its rejection on the ground that it was inhuman. At the time of the Crimean war Cochrane – or, as he then was, Dundonald – revived his proposals, but again they were rejected. One wonders what they were. Were they really effective or a mad eccentricity? One would like to know what were the limits thus officially set to the ruthlessness of war. Certainly this country has never been in want for advocates of ruthlessness. Mr Norman Angell – with whom one may agree or disagree on general grounds – quotes several apt examples from British military writers in his new (or partly new) book, *Prussianism and its Destruction*. Major Stewart Murray in *The Future Peace of the Anglo-Saxons*, which won the praise of Lord Roberts, laughs at 'the sanctity of international law' as fiercely as any Prussian could, and inveighs against 'sickening humanitarianism'. Dr Miller Maguire, again, is quoted as having written in *The Times* during the Boer War:

'The proper stategy consists in the first place in inflicting as terrible blows as possible upon the enemy's army, and then in causing the inhabitants so much suffering that they must long for peace and force their Government to demand it. The people must be left with nothing but their eyes to weep with over the war.'

This last phrase, which we believe is taken from Tilly, has been quoted several times during the present war as Bismarck's, and has been condemned in accents of horror as an example of the atrocious Prussian theory of war.

One knows very well that when Dr Miller Maguire used it he did not mean to justify the horrors of Belgium or a slaughter of unarmed men and women at Scarborough and Whitby. But if we admit that his sentiment is just, how can we logically protest against these outrages? What are the limits of ruthlessness? Where are we to draw the line? For our part, we think the line is a rather vague one. We hold, however, that in waging war every nation must make up its mind to choose between the policy of 'the less ruthlessness the better' and 'the more ruthlessness the better'; and that deliberately to choose the latter is a crime against the human race. Spain of the Inquisition, Turkey of the Armenian atrocities – these are supreme examples of ruthlessness, and they are clear enough proof that ruthlessness does not necessarily lead to national greatness. England in Elizabethan and Georgian Ireland is another instance of ruthlessness, but has not English policy in Ireland been her great failure? Ruthlessness, no doubt, has its victories no less renowned than mercy. But, on the whole, the history of ruthlessness is not a history of triumph, but a history of shame.

9 January 1915

The Webb method of promoting Socialism in the New Statesman *was to argue its advantages in efficiency, coolly and from the facts, without becoming excited. Webb continued to do this during the war, and at the same time he fought a long and steady campaign in the paper for the factory workers whom it had, in the war situation, become easier than ever for the employers to exploit. Here is an example of Sidney Webb's wartime new statesmanship.*

The Ratting of the Capitalist   Sidney Webb

The war is teaching us a good deal of political economy in a somewhat costly fashion, and at the same time is revealing to the ordinary citizen the drawbacks incidental to our system of entrusting to private ownership the capital by which the nation lives. In the first days of convulsion our much-vaunted banking system, out of which a few thousand people draw some thirty millions of profit a year, suddenly broke down, and had to be protected by a continuation of the Bank Holiday and a prolonged moratorium. At the same time the international remittance system completely failed us; and people prepared to pay down cash in New York and Amsterdam found it impossible to buy credit in London. What was at least as serious was that the Government, which had not been permitted to share in the huge annual profit which this business brought to a few score financial firms, found itself compelled to advance to these firms, just when it needed all its resources, no less than a hundred and fifty million pounds, to save them, and with them all 'the City,' from bankruptcy. Most of that large sum has since been repaid, but over thirty millions sterling is still outstanding, and much of that must now be regarded as lost. No one, by the way, seems to have remarked that the total amount yet contributed by the propertied class in additional taxation since the beginning of the war does not much exceed the balance which is thus still owed to the Government by some members of that class.

But when we turn from capital in its intangible financial form to that larger mass which is embodied in commodities, and in what we may call the 'plant' by which our working life is carried on, the position is even more serious. When the Government wanted all the thousand and one commodities with which war is now made, it found all the stocks of these commodities and nearly all the means of manufacturing them in the hands of private capitalists – patriotic, no doubt, and anxious that this country should be victorious, but equally convinced, as the saying goes, that 'no price is too high – for the War Office to pay – when honour and freedom are at stake.' No price was too high, either, for the enemy to pay; and no one without access to confidential Government enquiries can form an adequate idea of the amount of 'trading with the enemy' that went on in this country, from the respectable Scottish firm convicted of an altogether undue eagerness to dispose of its cargoes of iron to the Germans up to the whole swarm of honest traders supplying just what the Germans most needed, ostensibly to customers in Holland, Denmark, and Sweden, but plainly intended for a further destination. Then again there was the corner in drugs. The happy owners of the world's available stock of a few indispensable drugs naturally – for such are the laws of the Gospel of Greed – did not refrain from making, not only the various Governments, but also all the sick people of the world, pay double, and even tenfold, prices for what was essential to relieve pain and save life. What fortunes were thus made we shall probably never know, any more than we shall know the tale of the men and women and children who suffered and died because of their inability to pay, not the cost of production of what would have saved them, but the unnecessarily enhanced price that the chances of the market enabled the owners to exact.

But, after all, it is only sentimentality that makes us think a corner in drugs more wicked than any other enhancement in the price of that on which the world lives. When the Admiralty summarily annexed the privately owned shipping that was indispensable to us as a nation, on terms which were enormously in excess of peace rates, great was the rush of shipowners who still had vessels under their control to make the most of the situation. It was perhaps only to be expected that freights, even for foodstuffs, should rise sky high – so excellent a chance of bringing all the world to be taxed was not to be resisted – but we realize more vividly all that it means to leave the capital of the nation in private ownership when we learn that literally hundreds of British ships have since the outbreak of war been sold to foreigners and transferred to foreign registers. More than a hundred steamships have, it appears, been thus transferred to Norway alone, many to the United States, some in the first months of the war to Italy, when profit could be made out of Italian neutrality, others to Greece, Denmark, etc. Those who accepted the high prices offered by neutrals are honestly astonished that anyone can criticize their transactions – on the profits of which, by the way, they pay no taxes. They blandly ignore the fact – let us hope that those Britons who retain a hidden share in the ownership under a neutral flag also ignore it – that one of the very objects of the transfer to a neutral register is that the ships may embark in the specially profitable trade of conveying supplies to the enemy. Those ship-owners who resisted the temptation to sell their ships at three or four times their normal value sometimes thought it quite patriotic to warn their tramp steamers away from British territory, letting them run at high freights between neutral ports, in order to keep them out of the clutches of the Admiralty, until the Admiralty's need should grow more desperate, and until it should stretch out its hands, as it eventually did, to bring them within its grasp.

But the culminating point in this story of capitalist patriotism is reached when we learn that the Government is now quite exercised in its mind about the deliberate 'ratting' of certain native-born British capitalists, not entirely unconnected with politics, who control a very large merchant business, yielding an annual income that runs into six figures, and who have sold up their houses and other property in England, abandoned their English domicile, transferred their head office to New York, reduced their London representation to a mere agency making no profits, and, casting from off their feet the dust of the land which has made them wealthy, fled in person (duly provided with Foreign Office passports) by one of the great passenger liners that left Liverpool a fortnight ago. They go to avoid paying war taxes, the high Income Tax, and the Excess Profits Tax. They do not see why they should yield up to the Exchequer one-half of the great additional income they have been making out of the war! They see their way to carry on their business from New York nearly as well as from London; they feel themselves, we may suppose, at least as much at home in Fifth Avenue as in Park Lane; and by all the principles of the business code in which they have been bred it is their right – it is almost their duty – to take every legal advantage that will permit them to double their incomes. This is a true story. How many others are harbouring similar designs we cannot tell. There may be some significant relevance in the hint just given by the Government to *The Times*, to the effect that capitalists may be assured that no further taxation is in contemplation. But it is a feature of capitalism, unlike Democratic Government on the one hand and Trade Unionism on the other, that it works silently and secretly. The departure of a few Irish emigrants for America – a mere remnant of the swarm that, prior to the war, left each year – is published throughout the whole world as a discreditable evasion of national duty. The stokers of the Liverpool liner could not strike on learning that the capitalists were fleeing from England, because their presence on board was unsuspected.

We do not want to suggest that the owners of capital, or 'business men,' are as a class necessarily less patriotic than other classes. It is the very system to which they are brought up, the standard of professional success by which they judge one another, the faith by which (in business hours) they live, that – always within the limits of legality and of the 'customs of the trade' – they should so use their capital as to make as much profit as possible. Reputable economists – chaplains to the pirate ship – have been rash enough in the past to assure them that by such seeking of the largest legal individual profit the public advantage is served. Economists have long since learned better; and the war is making the ordinary citizen realize that private gain is, to say the least, very often public loss. We are quick enough to exclaim when the wage-earners seek to take advantage of any national need to extort for themselves a 10 or 20 per cent increase in wages; though, in fact, the earnings of three-fourths of all the wage-earners are so insufficient for continued health and the adequate discharge of the duties of parenthood and citizenship that even a gradual doubling of wages would be to the national advantage. On the other hand, we pass as a matter of course the enormously enhanced gains of the capitalists in like case, though the excess is of next to no national advantage.

The owners of capital in its more mobile forms have so much power over the world's social and industrial life, and are, in nearly all cases, so completely unconscious of having any other duty than that of using that power to amass wealth, that it is quite natural to find them oblivious of the harm they are actually doing to the community to which they owe all their prosperity. The very anonymity of their capital, the transient forms into which it passes, and its characteristic mobility make the merchants and financiers essentially cosmopolitan in sympathy, and, we fear we must add, systematically 'non-moral' in their business conduct. The aristocracy of a country, the owners of its land, the administrators of its railways, even those responsible for its chief manufacturing industries, are, like its manual workers, necessarily less detached. Happily, the merchant and the financier account only for a small part of our national wealth. Nine-tenths of the capital of the country cannot, fortunately, be taken away, either in the cabin of an ocean liner or by telegraphic transfer. But the war is making it more and more impossible to resist the dictum of the Socialist that if we want to achieve any national end whatsoever – not victory in war only, but even the healthy subsistence of the whole community in peace – we cannot afford to leave the nation's land, its mines, its railways, its ships, or its factories, any more than its roads, its currency, or its schools, to be directed according to the motives of private profit-making.

11 December 1915

The early work of almost every poet to make a name since 1913 appeared in the New Statesman. *The Literary Editors, from J. C. Squire and Desmond MacCarthy to Karl Miller, have made a deliberate policy of seeking out young talent while never neglecting the old.*

To My Thoughts   W. H. Davies

Stay home and hear the birds and bees,
    And see the blossoms grow;
And mock them both – when Echo mocks
    The bird that cries 'cuckoo';
For Love, alas – now understood –
Has many a feather stained with blood.

Though you are my own children born,
    I cannot keep you home;
For though I lock my body up
    Inside an iron room,
You thoughts can still pass through the walls,
To follow her, who never calls.

                                        9 June 1917

The Picture Book   Robert Graves

When I was not quite five years old
    I first saw the blue picture book,
    And Fraulein Spitzenburger told
Stories that sent me hot and cold;
    I loathed it, yet I had to look:
    It was a German Book.

I smiled at first, for she'd begun
    With a back-garden broad and green
And rabbits nibbling there: page one
Turned; and the gardener fired his gun
    From the low hedge: he lay unseen
    Behind: oh, it was mean!

Wounded, they couldn't run, and so
    He stuffed them heads down in a sack
Not quite dead, wriggling in a row,
And Fraulein laughed, 'Ho, ho! Ho, ho!'
    And gave my middle a heavy smack –
    I wish that I'd hit back.

Then when I cried she laughed again;
    On the next page was a dead boy
Murdered by robbers in a lane;
His clothes were red with a big stain
    Of blood, he held a broken toy,
    The poor, poor little boy!

I had to look: there was a town
    Burning where everyone got caught,
Then a fish pulled a nigger down
Into the lake and made him drown,
    And a man killed his friend; they fought
    For money, Fraulein thought.

Old Fraulein laughed, a horrid noise.
    'Ho, ho!' Then she explained it all,
How robbers kill the little boys
And torture them and break their toys.
    Robbers are always big and tall:
    I cried: I was so small.

How a man often kills his wife,
    How everyone dies in the end
By fire or water or a knife.
If you're not careful in this life,
    Even if you can trust your friend,
    You won't have long to spend.

I hated it – old Fraulein picked
    Her teeth, slowly explaining it.
I had to listen, Fraulein licked
Her finger several times and flicked
    The pages over; in a fit
    Of rage I spat at it. . . .

And lying in my bed that night
    Hungry, tired out with sobs, I found
A stretch of barren years in sight
Where right is wrong, but strength is right,
    Where weak things must creep underground,
And I could not sleep sound.

15 June 1918

Idyll   Siegfried Sassoon

In the grey summer garden I shall find you
With day-break and the morning hills behind you.
There will be rain-wet roses; stir of wings;
And down the wood a thrush that wakes and sings.
Not from the past you'll come, but from that deep
Where beauty murmurs to the soul asleep:
And I shall know the sense of life re-born
From dreams into the mystery of morn
Where gloom and brightness meet. And standing there
Till that calm song is done, at last we'll share
The league-spread, quiring symphonies that are
Joy in the world, and peace, and dawn's one star.

29 June 1918

New statesmanship entailed keeping a watchful eye on social trends as well as on everything else. The eye might be serious, laughing or satirical. Desmond MacCarthy's was usually laughing when literature, the thing he took seriously, was not in question.

The Art of Advertisement   Desmond MacCarthy

At the risk of engaging in a subject too great for a small essay, I propose to deliver myself of some reflections upon the Art of Advertisement and its future; an art I believe to be in its infancy, a future I believe to be immense.

Recently progress has been made, especially in the branch of signed testimonials. Shrewd men of commerce have discovered that what weighs with the public is not any statement in favour of their wares or nostrums, however laudatory, but the name of the person who makes it; and we may now regard as old-fashioned those documents in which 'a widow', or 'a post-office assistant', yielding to an impulse of unflinching introspection, describes her symptoms. The handsome, but too anonymous-looking young man, whose portrait is wont to appear under some such pathetic heading as 'I was covered with Pimples', is soon destined to vanish from the pages of the Press. In the future his place will be taken by the familiar faces of our most distinguished statesmen, generals, admirals and men of letters; even the portraits of those who occupy smaller niches, whether on account of their family and traditions or because they have carried themselves with some dignity through life, will not be often absent from those columns. Indeed, the trend of modern taste runs so strongly in this direction that, in a few years' time, never to figure in such contexts will be construed by all as a 'sign' of failure in a public man, or stamp him more fatally as one of those queasy, unaccountable characters, who cannot be trusted 'to get on with' – the war, if it happens still to be raging, or the business of the country, if it has again begun. But I will waste no space in commenting on this branch of the Art of Advertisement, for the lines on which it must advance are clear. It is to the possibility of more delicate developments that I wish to draw attention.

The other day my friend Eagle could not restrain a start of surprise at the commingling of pills and poetry in the advertisement he quoted. There the reader was urged to re-inforce the exhilaration, which certain noble lines of verse might not unnaturally have produced in him, by swallowing in convenient form an inexpensive but stimulating medicine. My criticism of that advertisement is that in it the collocation of ideas was forced and naïve. In method it was as artless as the practice of the inveterate raconteur who drags his stories into company chained one to the other like a row of galley-slaves.

It is true that mere juxtaposition of statements may in time produce the desired impression. I should not go as far as to say that such summaries of the day's news as: 'Progress on three fronts: British Heroism: Mr Lloyd George Recovering', have been without effect. But I do assert that ideas which have been associated by propinquity, without any other link between them, are apt soon after to come apart. It would be only too easy to re-read Keats' fine sonnet the advertiser quoted which closes with the line: 'Silent upon a peak in Darien' without immediately thinking of Pink Rhomboids. We may be certain that this type of advertisement also will soon become old-fashioned. It is merely a step – a hesitating step – in the right direction. The next one is easy to foresee. Firms of any enterprise will publish editions of literary masterpieces with here and there a passage altered (preserving, of course, the original rhythm) to draw attention to their goods. The alterations will be very few, while the edition will be characterized by that expensive simplicity which appeals to the refined. The book will be sold at a nominal price. The purchase of the most beautiful printing founts would be a trifling matter to a large firm, and the cost of hiring a literary man of real talent to give the text an occasional ply in the right direction practically negligible. At first this device may rouse protests; but such a prospect should only intensify eagerness to be first in the field. One anticipates the controversy, the letters pro and con. Some will talk of profanation and vandalism; others whose minds keep abreast with the times will point out that for the first time really covetable editions worthy of what they contain have been put within reach of the masses. Everybody recognized that the publication of masterpieces in a cheap form was a benefit; how then can they object to this further advance? Besides, the alterations, say, in the odes of Keats or the Sonnets of Shakespeare would be so trifling that they could be neatly corrected with a pen by any reader more sensitive to the beauty of words than the beauty of a page. At first sight this possibility might seem to detract from the merits of the scheme; but if the original alterations had been intelligently made, if they really followed, that is to say, the lines of psychological association, the advertiser would have nothing to fear. In spite of subsequent deletion an aroma of his wares would still cling about the poem in question. He would have ensured for them a kind of immortality by associating them with the words which men will not willingly allow to die.

It must make an enterprising young advertiser tear his hair to see the opportunities which custom has forced him to neglect. Take our burial service for example. What do the words 'dust to dust' suggest but a vacuum cleaner? The slight revulsion which such a collocation of ideas produces in sensitive minds is precisely the effect which the advertiser wishes to produce. Nothing makes a deeper impression than an idea which is accompanied by a shock to our sense of reverence. What vistas this opens! How delicately and insinuatingly might not the advertiser play upon this law of human nature! Landscape advertisers who plaster the sides of mountains and waterfalls and caves with notices and pictures of their goods have had an inkling of its resources, but they are only pioneers. Imagine St Paul's crowded to hear some famous preacher or Church dignitary who, not for personal motives of course, but for the sake of some cause which stood in need of financial aid, had consented to introduce into his discourse upon Conscience the phrase, 'His master's voice'. Delicately yet ambiguously, italicized by a first-rate elocutionist, these words might be worth miles of posters, especially as the doubt whether the preacher had indeed intended the congregation to follow for a second a secular train of association could never be satisfactorily cleared up. But even if it had been clumsily done, and no doubt was possible on that head, still the subsequent controversy – how far it is legitimate to go in the cause of charity – would be itself a scoop.

Take again our Divorce Court and Breach of Promise proceedings, which are as assiduously attended and better reported. Is it not astonishing that they have only been used for the purposes of personal advertisement, and never for commercial ends? Imagine a charming respondent in the witness-box being interrogated by her counsel: 'When did your intimacy with the co-respondent begin?'

Witness: On October 16th.

Counsel: Are you sure?

Witness: Yes, I am perfectly sure; because I remember I wore for the first time my new evening dress from Quasimodo's.

These simple words would be worth a large sum of money which would go a long way towards meeting the heavy expenses which are the principal drawback to figuring in those courts.

In M. Courteline's last novel there is a Monsieur Hamiet, who throws out ideas of this kind with the disinterestedness of a grand seigneur who can afford to chuck money out of the window. He has his counterparts in real life. He produces ideas as naturally as a fruit-tree grows apples or cherries. One of the things which struck him as an advertising agent was the absurd way in which advertisements are relegated to special columns of a paper, instead of being literally surrounded by what the public wants to read as completely as a pill is coated with sugar. A man buys a paper for the sake of its views and if he chooses, he need not even glance at its advertisements! Yet nothing is easier to prevent. It is as easy as forcing a card in a card trick.

A CRUCIAL QUESTION

The question whether Germany is to recover her lost colonies at the Peace is not one to be answered by Great Britain alone. Although nothing is certain, we believe it can be confidently asserted that there is no commoner malady, or one more likely to affect the whole system, than sluggish kidneys. Germany's past record shows convincingly that she has not the aptitudes and qualities which make for success in the administration of tropical dependencies. It is the cause of not only numerous small discomforts, such as a bad taste in the mouth, pain in the back, lack of energy or breathlessness while mounting stairs, but of far greater evils. The German is deficient in sympathy and adaptability in the lighter and more attractive qualities which qualify for her happy dealings with dependent races. No people, whatever hue their skins, like to be ground under an iron-shod heel, as were the subjects of Germany in her tropical colonies. The kidneys are the most important filter in the body; upon them depends the purity of the blood. So that there is another factor to be considered: the desire of the human beings who inhabit the provinces in question. Is your blood perfectly pure? We stand, or will soon stand, at a cross road. One path leads, etc., etc.

I need not continue. You see Hamiet's idea. The only objection to it is that if a single paper adopted it, its circulation might suffer and fall to a point at which not even a great increase in advertisement revenue would be a sufficient recompense. But in this country, where so many papers are in the hands of one man, this objection does not arise. The method would be adopted simultaneously in all the Harmsworth papers, and the rest would be obliged to follow suit.

Men of imagination underrate the scope for fantasy and invention which the art of advertisement offers. I remember as a boy hearing of an appeal in some local paper for 'Twelve bald-headed men who would not mind having "So and so's Honey" painted in blue paint on the crowns of their heads.' But what meagre inventiveness this device shows compared with such a suggestion as Hamiet throws out casually while talking across a café table. To make his conception more vivid to English readers I will merely transfer the scene from Paris to London.

It is five o'clock; the end of a fine autumn day. Suddenly, a Rolls-Royce stops opposite the Marble Arch; and from it, like an arrow from the bow, darts a man; a man with wild eyes, wild hair, wild hands. From his mouth, wide open like a charging Hussar's, issues the cry 'Stop! stop! stop!' He flies down Park Lane, the crowd scatters before him, then closes in pursuit. What is it? What is the matter? Nobody knows. A thief? A murderer? He swerves down Piccadilly; the wildest rumours are afloat – an uninterned alien has been sighted! 'Stop! stop!' he shouts, dashing between parti-coloured 'buses and reeling taxis, heedless of the oaths of drivers and the staggering of horses, pursued by an ever-increasing multitude, who, prudence now thrown to the winds and borne forward by an overmastering curiosity, thunder at his heels. Down St James's Street, along the stately street of clubs, impelled by his mysterious mission, on, on towards his unknown goal he flies like a madman. He has reached Trafalgar Square. Look! he has climbed the plinth of Nelson's column, and shading his eyes with his hand as he gazes towards the towers of Westminster, he shouts once more 'Stop! In Heaven's name stop!' 'Stop what?' roars back the crowd in unison. He, then, 'What? – *Your hair falling off!*' And with these words, now grown strangely calm, he dives in his pockets and scatters hundreds of leaflets, which flutter like white doves above the ignorant heads of the mob: 'Gentlemen, the moment for jesting has passed; the wonderful remedy to which I wish to draw your attention, etc. . . .'

Though Hamiet is a character in fiction, and his ideas have not yet been put in practice, he has many counterparts in life. If I seem to have only touched the fringe of my subject it is from an instinct of prudence; for some ideas on this subject are too precious to be given away in an article.

5 October 1918

Editors found the problem of keeping their readers abreast of scientific progress, and of 'criticizing' science, a difficult one. It was solved by publishing a regular contribution from a scientific journalist – 'Lens' (Dr Saleeby) was the first – and by publishing special contributions from leading scientists when they could be persuaded to write comprehensibly. When a scientific investigation revealed a truth which was distasteful to progressives, the New Statesman *did not attempt to obscure it. Here, for example, is 'Lens' throwing scientific cold water on some favourite new statesmanly ideas.*

Nature's Verdict   'Lens'

Let us look on this picture and on that, finding the most ironic contrast the master paradox, and the key to racial destiny in Nature's Verdict thereon.

This picture is the city of Bradford, which presents the most remarkable and poignant vital statistics in England today. It offers its newcomers what would appear to be every possible advantage. The city has long been prosperous, both before the war (which has merely accentuated the lines of the vital-mortal picture) and since 1914. Owing to the importance of wool, Bradford has latterly become more prosperous than ever, and recent figures show that, in such matters as subscriptions to war-charities and so forth, this city takes the lead. In proportion to its numbers, about 300,000, it is perhaps the wealthiest community in the United Kingdom. Further, it is extremely generous – second to none in this also. The citizens give freely to all manner of good causes, and the municipality is as generous as the citizens. It spends some £20,000 a year on infancy alone, and this sum is duplicated by the Local Government Board, so that the few babies of Bradford, born into a community of extremely high general prosperity, also have £40,000 a year spent on their special interests – this working out at the highest rate of expenditure on infancy of any part of these islands.

Given these two large facts we must ascertain only a third in this part of the picture. Is the money so generously spent also spent wisely? The answer again is superlative. All things considered, it is probable that Bradford spends its money on infancy more skilfully, with more foresight, science and co-ordination than any other municipality in this country. It had until recently the services of three spendid servants and students of infancy, Councillor E. J. Smith, Chairman of the Health Committee, whose book on 'Racial Regeneration,' with a particularly valuable account of Bradford's system of municipal milk supply, was published by Messrs P. S. King last year; Dr John Buchan, the Medical Officer of Health; and Dr Helen Campbell, the Director of the Infant Welfare Department. Mr Smith was told by his doctor, some years ago, that he must choose between his business and his public health work. He chose what he loved, and devoted himself to it – nine o'clock every morning at the Town Hall. He regularly travelled to and from London in one day to attend the National Birthrate Commission. Only too suddenly his heart failed, and he died without seeing the fruit of his devoted, exhausting and wholly unrewarded labours. He lost his only son in the war, and gave his own life in the noblest campaign of peace. I honour him as the very type of the men who have made our country great.

Let us note how these three devoted workers proceed. They have, for instance, the finest system of municipal midwifery in the country – so good that visitors from the United States and the Continent used to be sent to study it when they asked the highest authority at the Local Government Board what was really worth seeing. There is also what should perhaps logically have been named first, a splendid system of free feeding for expectant mothers. The mothers, however, are so prosperous – note this well – that they do not patronize their feeding centre, which has been converted into a national kitchen. The Infant Department is a model of its kind. (The reader will understand that I have seen and lived with all these details myself and am not offering him anything merely from reports. I visit Bradford frequently, never without learning from the three students I have named, and I am writing in Bradford now.) No municipality or private person should attempt to set up such a place without making a careful and prolonged study of Bradford's truly admirable Infant Department in all its details of method and equipment. I hope to study such things in New York and other Transatlantic cities in a few weeks, but at the moment I do not see how Bradford could be surpassed in this respect, and I certainly shall be surprised if I find anything as good in either the United States or Canada.

Until the last few years there were two points which perhaps were open to question and which one always raised. One was the lack of any system of ante-natal care comparable to the rest of the machinery. (And pray where was such a system to be found?) The other was that, under the influence of exaggerated teaching about the injury done to milk by sterilizing it, the milk used for the infants was always raw, though the municipality was not able to control the conditions of its production. Both these points have been met. Bradford now has a fine ante-natal equipment, and it has adopted, from the United States, the system of milk grading and certification which the Ministry of Food and Mr Wilfred Buckley, the Director of Milk Supplies, rightly desire to introduce throughout this country. What they hope for, Bradford has already done. Further, there is a large use of the invaluable dried milk which has been a boon to infancy in so many places and which is incomparably superior to any milk the production of which has not been controlled by scientific cleanliness.

And now, you ask, what are the results? Well, the answer is a blow in the face – very nearly but not quite a knock-out blow. What I have described has been running for many years now, with steady improvement in principle and detail. Further, those who work for the babies have had what is almost universally proclaimed to be the immense advantage of a very low birth-rate, which has fallen from year to year, so that their task of saving the few babies that were born should have been easier each year than the year before. The upshot is an infant mortality which now stands at about 135, with no notable improvement for many years, and against a birth-rate which was only 13·06 in 1917 and probably less, according to a provisional estimate, last year. The general death-rates for those two years were, 1917, 14·6, 1918 (provisional), 18·0. The influenza was a large factor of last year's death-rate and the war affected all the figures of the last two years, but when the most liberal discount is made for these exceptional factors, the conclusion remains that wealthy, generous, scientific Bradford is dying out and that these wonderful and admirable efforts to save it seem futile. The explanation that the stock is inherently defective is immediately negatived by the quality of many of the living and by the record in the war of Bradford's splendid soldiers (whose deaths are not included, observe, in the dreadful figures foregoing).

Before we attempt to interpret what seems an absurdity, and to show that it is really a paradox (which is a seeming absurdity), let us help ourselves by looking at the second picture, which I have chosen because of the extreme contrast which it offers to Bradford in every particular I have named – and, above all, in the one particular which I have designedly refrained from naming. (Have you already asked yourself, 'Yes, yes, but what about — ?')

Let us go almost where you will in the West of Ireland or, for choice, since the figures are in my head, to County Roscommon, in Connaught. Instead of wealth here is poverty, as extreme as Bradford's prosperity. Instead of Bradford's applied science here is ignorance – nay, the people's heads are largely crammed with active superstition. In many particulars we see Ignorance in Action, which Goethe called the most dangerous thing in the world. The public and explicit provision for infancy is really best left undescribed. No one would visit or send others to visit Roscommon in order to admire its medical, nursing, ante-natal, obstetric, housing, municipal or voluntary resources. The birth-rate, when standardized to correspond to the number of women of reproductive age, is extremely high. The figure is about 45 or more. In other words, the families are enormous. Now, in very many cases, the birth-rate and death-rate, especially the infant death-rate, go together. Where many babies are born, their death-rate is high; and conversely. This high positive correlation between birth- and death-rate is exploited by the Neo-Malthusians who, begging the question, assume, and base all their Anti-Socialist teaching, all their propaganda against poverty, on the assumption that correlation is causation, that the way to lower a death-rate is to lower the birth-rate. Bradford and Roscommon prove instantaneously that the Neo-Malthusians are guilty of the commonest of all fallacies – to confound correlation with causation. In this, as in hosts of cases in every domain of being, results which are causally independent may and will vary together – show a positive correlation – if, for instance, they be both due to the same cause or set of causes. I do not assert that there is never any causal relation between birth-rates and death-rates; but I do assert that the cases I have cited dispose of the fundamental Malthusian contention, which is clearly an example, supremely dangerous, of the common fallacy.

What, then, is the infant mortality of Roscommon, with its very high birth-rate and its plentiful lack of all those good things which Bradford provides so abundantly? Well, about 35, as compared with Bradford's 135. It is the most significant and astonishing contrast in all the vital statistics that I have ever seen. Omitting 1918, because of the influenza, let me give approximate figures for a typical year in juxtaposition:

		Birth-rate	Infant Death-rate
Bradford	..	13	135
Roscommon	..	45	35

It may be said that this is the contrast between town and country. But that is not so; there are country places – not in Ireland – with figures of the order of Bradford's, and the figures of Huddersfield, for instance, which has the influence of Mr Benjamin Broadbent, our great practical pioneer, are very different to Bradford's with the expenditure of very much less money. Further, as few know, even among real students, the infant mortality of Germany and Holland is higher in the country than in the town. As for the palpable nonsense which has been written about urban smoke, I have disposed of that elsewhere, and so may anyone else who compares, for instance, the respective mortalities of Jewish, Irish and English babies in Whitechapel. That smoke theory ends where it began.

The world-famous student who was until recently our highest official on this subject told me that, with all my praise of Bradford, I had forgotten one omission – that there is 'not enough domiciliary visitation' in Bradford. I am not an official, and will simply call that home-visiting, for the shorter word is the key to all. But why is there not enough home-visiting?

Because there are no homes – or very few. In all the foregoing I have not so much as hinted at the one thing that supremely matters – the mother, the natural saviour of the baby. I have written, in the modern style, as if we were not mammals. I have ignored the fundamental sin of Bradford and our civilization against the laws of life. I do not use the word in a theological sense, for I am not a theologian; here it suffices to be a biologist and a mammal.

In Bradford the mothers are incomplete. Some 90 per cent of them go out to work. The home disappears. 'Humanized' milk, which was cows' milk before 'humanization' and is cows' milk still – the only way to humanize milk being to pass it through a human mother – feeds young Bradford and young Bradford dies. The modern fashion in skirts has permitted me, this afternoon, in walking three hundred yards in Bradford, to see more bow-legs – that is, rickets – than I would see in a lifetime in the West of Ireland. Our Continental friends and enemies call rickets the English disease, as they may; and the Irish may call it so, too, if they will.

Here industry flourishes, and when the mills close we see the procession of mothers rushing to the hovels where they left their babies in the morning, as Mr J. H. Thomas has lately said. Production – of everything but producers – is maintained, wealth aggregated, by the accursed industrial system which breaks up the home, tempts the mother or the possible mother to worship the Calf of Gold in place of the Child of Life, to prevent conception, to procure abortion, or to desert her child if, despite all her efforts, she has one. So Money is to blame after all, despite the splendid generosity of the municipality. It is the worship of the false god called Mammon, which is idolatry; and the wages of sin is racial death.

In Roscommon the mothers are mammals still. The home may not be visited, but it is a home. The housing is poor enough, but the homing is the real thing. The baby is in its poor, ignorant, ignored mother's arms, its lips are at her nipple, and it lives and thrives. If we could add what Bradford has to what Roscommon has, infant mortality and infant damage would practically disappear. (This for Mr Chesterton, who would seem to infer a condemnation of infant welfare work from a recent comment on these figures. Does he know what Mr Broadbent's admirable visitors have achieved in Huddersfield, where many homes still remain, or how welcome they naturally are in the homes they help?) I assume, of course, that the mother can safely be a mother – for syphilis is almost unknown in rural Ireland; whilst I need hardly say that it is rife and increasing in Bradford, as the latest dreadful figures from the Infant Department show. In a word, infant mortality and racial survival are social problems of motherhood. If the social problem of motherhood be solved, the doctor and the student and the visitor are nearly superfluous; if it be not solved, they are nearly futile.

In Bradford, as elsewhere, the manufacturers and the mothers, backed by public departments such as the Ministry of Munitions, are in favour of maintaining the system of prostituting motherhood to machinery which the war of necessity aggravated. I raise this protest against these powerful forces, to which many aggressive brands of anti-female feminism may be added. Those old figures from Birmingham, which show the scarcely astonishing fact that a baby starving to death through poverty is more likely to live if its mother goes out and earns money for food, will be cited against me but will evidently leave my withers unwrung. Survey the range of life, insect, fish, reptile, bird, mammal from monotreme and marsupial – duckmole and kangaroo – up to the tiny grey squirrel I saw in Kensington Gardens on Easter Monday, chased by a horde of horrible boys, carrying its baby in its mouth, running up a tree, jumping from a slender oscillating branch to that of the next tree, which held its nest where it left its young in high safety; and so on to cat and dog and monkey and ape and man, and you cannot but be assured that Bradford expresses, like the illegitimate death-rate anywhere, the consequences of the fundamental social crime, which is to divorce mothers and children, whilst Roscommon, like the sub-human races I have named, expresses the verdict of wisdom – Whom Nature hath joined together let not man put asunder.

24 May 1919

35

Hilaire Belloc thought like a new statesman but feft like the opponents of new statesmanship. He wrote often for the paper in the Twenties and was in due course to write the 'Books in General' feature regularly for half a year.

On Convincing People   Hilaire Belloc

I have just been working at the *Provincials* of Pascal. They are full of lies, and full of errors. They would not convince the stupidest of readers who should seriously compare them with the original documents which Pascal attacked. But no reader save Maynard and Derome has ever done so. My object in reading the book was to expose it, and therefore my object on a small stage was to do what Pascal did on a large one, that is, to convince people: with this only difference. Pascal had only to convince those who agreed with him of something that was not true, but I shall try to convince of something that is true those who heartily wish I would not.

This amiable exercise has set me thinking about the art of convincing people; and I say 'of convincing' and not 'of persuading', for I think that the two arts stand for two different processes. You can persuade a man to do a thing though he still disapproves, and you can lead him into feeling a certain mood. You can also get him into such and such a mood without even persuading him. But conviction is something higher.

It is an appeal to the intelligence. It relies upon the production of proof, and very interested am I in ferreting out the process whereby the thing is done, and in discovering why it will succeed when it is done in one way, and fail when it is done in another.

I must make clearer my distinction between the mere production of a mood, persuading, and conviction.

The mere production of a mood is effected (according to the weakness of your subject) by some form of suggestion. The modern popular Press works that way. Its chief weapon with the completely base is mere iteration: with the run of people less base the thing is done by some seductive art, rhetoric, or flattery, or even music. At any rate, the end of the process is not a certitude of the intelligence, and your intended victim may be jerked out of his mood by any shock – especially if it be a shock of reality.

There is between the mere production of a mood and conviction an intermediate thing and very common. It is advocacy: the advancing of selected arguments towards a certain selected end.

The victim knows he is being played upon, yet he often succumbs. A man does not want to visit a particular place. The method of suggestion would be merely to repeat the name of the place over and over again, and the command to go there. Such are those advertisements which you see upon the walls of great cities in flaming letters commanding you to eat and drink various poisons. Advocacy would put before the man all the real advantages of the place it wanted him to visit and hide all the real disadvantages. It would incline through the intelligence, but also by cheating the intelligence.

Now, conviction is in a different world. When you convince a person you make him really certain. It does not follow that you make him certain of a truth, but you make him certain through the intelligence and not through a mere mood. Nor do you put him, as advocacy does, between two issues, one of which he chooses. You make him wholly at one with the doctrine you give. You implant certitude to the exclusion of every alternative. When you have done that you have done something much more solid and permanent, you have achieved a much greater thing than any advocacy or suggestion can.

I know that in saying this I am going flat against the opinion of my time, for in these days we revere much more the man who can get a mob to think the moon is made of green cheese and then, tomorrow, that it is made of Sapolio, than we do of the man who can convince. And the reason we revere the baser method is that for the moment there is more money in it. For the amount of money that may be got by a trick is our measure of excellence in the mind that plays the trick. Nevertheless I will maintain that to convince is even in practical affairs much the bigger business. For though you convince but a few in a certain time, yet what you do is to plant something durable, and something filled with the power of propagating itself. Conviction breeds.

When it comes to the methods of conviction, however, I hesitate. The great rules (which Pascal himself so admirably followed) are fairly well known: to present the argument fed with concrete example and yet to interest or amuse – not to fatigue.

If you combine those two you should, according to the rules, succeed. The only point about not fatiguing is that however perfect your reasoning, however strong your illustration, both are useless if the mind to which they are addressed cannot receive them. Fatigue interrupts reception. The two points about concrete example are, first, that a concrete example alone is vivid (even in mathematics you must have visible symbols); the next, that in the application of any idea concrete example is the only test of value to man. You will never convince a man, for instance, that protection necessarily impoverishes a nation if he has before his eyes the example of nations becoming suddenly very rich after adopting high tariffs.

It is quite clear that the citation of admirable examples, and even their citation without boredom, is not sufficient. There is something else, some trick of presentation, which lies, I fancy, in the sense of proportion, and which achieves success. It is in this that Pascal had genius. A wag of his

Hilaire Belloc by Low [*17 April 1926*]

own time rewrote one or two of the *Provincials*, substituting another opponent and other quotations, and thereby showing that they made just as good reading and were just as convincing in attacking friends as enemies.

Pascal had the art – which is most important in this matter – of leaving his readers under the impression that they had heard the whole case. It

38

can be done honestly by actually stating the opposite case before giving the counter arguments. But it is more often done dishonestly (as Pascal did it) by making your reader think that he has heard all there is to hear, although he has, as a fact, heard hardly anything, or nothing, of the other side. Pascal was, of course, working on very favourable ground. He attacked what was at once powerful and unpopular, and what was not only powerful and unpopular, but sincere and therefore incapable of using poisoned weapons against himself. There is nothing more interesting in literature than to see how the honest men he attacked blundered in trying to refute him. They blundered because they were too honest. They saw that he was lying, and they took it for granted he was telling simple lies of a childish sort. They accused him of inaccuracies and misquotations, which was not the way to set to work at all.

Pascal's method was in part what may be called the suppressed alternative. It is a method which you often see used by demagogues also, and by any one of those who ridicule a superior to an inferior. Thus, on one occasion Pascal finds an author saying: 'The obligation of a Christian to give alms out of his superfluity hardly ever arises.' The man who wrote this used the technical theological word 'obligation', but Pascal quotes him as though he used it in the loosest conversational sense. The man who wrote it decided (with obvious common-sense) that there were very few cases in which you could say that a Christian had done grievous wrong by not giving alms on a particular occasion. Pascal presented the matter so that his reader thought that the writer he was attacking dis-countenanced giving alms at all.

You very often see the same sort of thing done by people who ridicule the definitions of law. There is nothing easier. The law says, for instance, that a minor, a young giant of twenty years, can avoid payment by pleading 'infancy'.

It is quite easy to make that appear nonsense. It is not nonsense, but it could be made to appear nonsense by using the word 'infancy' in two senses. In the same way one could say by strict definition that the law does not forbid you to murder your grandmother. What the law does is to hang you if you murder your grandmother, which is, in strict definition, quite another proposition. And great play one could make before someone who had never heard of courts of justice, by saying: 'Just think! The law in this country actually allows one to murder one's grandmother!' leaving discreetly aside the legal consequences of the act.

There are those who tell you that not only Pascal and a hundred others but everyone who has ever convinced has used these dishonest methods, and that no one ever convinced by solid proof alone. There are those who will tell you that the admission of opposing arguments and their honest analysis would be either so dull or so damaging, or both, that those who adopted this, the only sincere method, necessarily failed.

I do not agree. Things have been done in that way; and I notice that when they have been so done, they have been done once and for all. People who are too weak to follow out a close chain of reasoning are at first not affected.

But the quality of the achievement is that it is final: it is never reversed. It is done once and for all. The few who follow are fixed and have, henceforward, authority. This is a very great achievement indeed. It is the making of the public mind. It is the ultimate direction of the State.

But it is exceedingly rare. In matters where men have interest against truth, conviction is so rare as to work at first almost imperceptibly. An insignificant body receive. Often they are dispersed. In a century there is a multitude. Soon, the world.

17 April 1920

It often happened that the paper published a man's work long before he had made his name. Thus contributions sometimes reveal aspects of an author's career and mind which are not familiar.

Black Gods

Llewelyn Powys

Free at last after five years of sheep-farming, I, an ex-manager, have time to try to understand something of the secret of Africa.

In the dust and turmoil and fret of work it was impossible to understand. It is not given to managers of sheep-farms to comprehend the Universe; the sheep-counts, the labour-books, the mixing of Cooper's dip, are matters far too engrossing, far too important, to allow their minds to escape.

For a whole month now I have been free, and day after day I have fled away by myself to the shore of Lake Elmenteita. The cool, clear freshness of the early morning has found me there, and I have not gone away until the hour towards evening when the hippopotami yawn and protrude their great heads out of the water. Surely, I have said, if only I can remain still enough, I shall be able to hear the great troubled heart of this strange continent beating out its secret. Sitting motionless under a dead thorn-tree, not far from the edge of the lake, I would forget myself, obliterate myself, and remain merely a being receptive to every sound and sight present upon these sunlit and far removed waters.

The sounds of Africa, how bitter they are! how fantastical! No singing of thrush or blackbird tremulous with the beauty of morning and evening; only, far off, behind in the forest, the monotonous metallic note of the bell-bird, and away over the rushes the petulant crying of some water-fowl sharp as its own quaint bill.

The notes of all the birds in Africa are primitive and crude, just as the colours of all the flowers are primitive and crude: the discordant, tuneless screams of the African birds agree with the flaming crimson orange tints of the African flowers.

And look at these hippopotami – how elementary is their appearance, their presence! Think of them, consider them, tossing and floundering and snorting here from the earliest ages: antique monsters older than Italy and Greece, than Babylon and Carthage – for how many thousands of ages have their vast unforgettable forms come up from the water, night after night, to chew and spit out the fine forest grass!

Before ever the instinctive happiness of this sundrenched, moonlit planet was distracted by the subtle wit of that escaped brain-mad animal, man, these enormous creatures were midnight frequenters of these glades. Two days ago a bull hippopotamus was shot; it required no fewer than twelve oxen to haul its great hulk out of the water.

Take notice too of the pythons, with their manifold coils, moving across the face of the lake: how suggestive they are of prehistoric days – the very water upon which they move not as yet properly brewed – surrounded by jagged volcanoes, and so poisonous that the drinking of it is deadly to all but serpents and hippopotami.

The gods of the hippopotami of Lake Elmenteita, what have they to say as they sit, century after century, with the salt tang of these evilly tasting waters in their nostrils? What expression is in their eyes as they cast their look over these rippling, lapping stretches and along these bleached margins?

The hippopotami splash, the jackals yelp; in the bushes at the water's edge the startled buck rustle and crash, and away behind in the rough country the lions send misgiving into the hearts of all listening midnight creatures. The gods hear and are unmoved.

In the bright sunshine of the African day the impala come down to the water's edge; the wart-hogs also stand feeding, or with tails suddenly erect hurry off; the flamingoes wait in a long line with hooked heads bowed down, or they suddenly rise up all together, and float away in well designed curves of an amazing rose-red. The gods see and are unmoved.

A traveller returns from Egypt by way of the Nile and tells me of the Sphinx. 'Every day,' he says, 'for three thousand years this sandstone monster has watched the sun rise out of the desert.' 'And with what emotion,' I ask, 'does it witness this daily event?' 'Its eye is the eye of an ox,' says he, 'and it has the look of patient indifference which belongs to an ox.'

What kind of an eye, then, have these god-idols by this lake in Central Africa? An expressionless eye; an eye that can remain unmoved while, year after year, generation after generation, the graceful and beautiful bodies of men are given over to the jowls of ill-smelling hyenas. To these old black idol-gods of the lake, to these gods of the hippopotami, to these gods of Africa, nothing matters. Little do they resemble that other One, that lovely tragic being who was so haunted by the world's unhappiness that He laid down His life; thinking in His heroic manner that by doing so He would take away all sorrow from the world. Between the Lake of Galilee and the Lake of Elmenteita flow many rivers, and there are many grassy plains and many deserts, and there is a wide difference – but where is truth to be found?

These gods of Lake Elmenteita are at home and at ease in Africa, but not so the gods of Asia and Europe. In this heartless and terrible land the living, beautiful gods of our world can never be anything but aliens. Even though in Europe their altars remain cold and unlit, Pan and Apollo should never wander this way; the sharp bark of the zebra would deafen them, and the calling of the red-winged lorri would be dreadful in their ears. If Christ Himself, long ages ago, forsaking the well-trodden roads of Samaria and the fields and lanes of Galilee, had come to Africa, do you think He could have reasoned with these Kafferondos, or put purity into the heart of one single Masai?

Under the spell of this merciless sun the country, yes, the whole Universe, seems damned, and throttled by the inevitable sequence of destiny, and all man's fondly cherished beliefs are impalpable and unreal as the mirages by Lake Obolosat. Africa, like one of her own black-maned lions, laps up the life blood of all the delicate illusions that have for so long danced before the eyes of men and made them happy. Truth alone is left alive. What was suspected in Europe is made plain here: at the bottom of the well of Life there is no hope. Under Scorpio, under the Southern Cross and in the clear light of this passionless tropical sunshine, the hollow

42

emptiness of the world's soul is made certain: the surface is everything, below there is nothing. It is an open secret that all can understand. It has even penetrated the thick skulls of these black men: the Masai, following their hump-backed cattle, know of it, and the Kikuyu, bending over their cultivated plots, cannot gainsay it.

Missionaries bravely repeat to these black heads their wonderful and pathetic tales: they are not believed. Indians bring with them their far-fetched spiritual teachings, but under the direct rays of this blazing sun all their oriental mysticism is brought to naught.

The natives of Africa have heard what they have heard, and seen what they have seen, and perhaps by a strange irony it has been given to them more than to any other people to come to the heart of the matter. Their vision of the world had never been influenced by the vague 'immortal longings' engendered in great deserts, neither have their minds been betrayed by the world-deep whisperings of a European countryside. Around them they are aware only of the primitive urge of life, the vast innumerable manifestations of inscrutable Nature; they see the strange ordering of chance and accident, and the irrevocability of each single happening. 'All is foredoomed. Beyond our understanding is an unalterable destiny. Matter alone rules. Alarum! we are betrayed.'

Witness their apparent indifference at the time of sickness – the issue completely out of their hands – they standing aside, as it were, to watch the event, be it fortunate or the reverse. Observe their instinctive recoil from a dead man – the stiff, dark-skinned corpse an ugly reminder of their own doom. In the presence of a dead mortal no Catholic or mystical sentiment obscures their natural reaction: any conception of a glorified body, of a physical resurrection, strikes them as childish and impossible. The man's allotted days are over; let us avoid him lest we be too awfully reminded that our days under the sun have also a fixed end. And so in Africa it comes that wherever a man dies, be it in his house, in his garden, in the forest, there is he left – food for the vultures, for the hyenas, for the maggots. I some-times think that no wisdom of ours has exceeded or can exceed the wisdom of these natives with regard to ultimate things; just as no folly exceeds his folly in all else. His mind is not cloyed or hampered in searching for explanations of the meaning of a life which in his sight requires no explana-tion at all. Man and beast, fish and fowl, grass and trees, have been called to live for a short space at the capricious will of Nature – of the Sun: death awaits each one and, in due course, the very planet itself.

In our cities, in our country places, we have created a sweet and wistful atmosphere heavy with intimations of immortality: the radiant morning sunshine in our woods and meadowlands is redolent of religion: in Africa the sun scorches all this up and leaves the bare naked bones of the earth to tell us her story.

To look for a meaning, a purpose in life, out here in Africa, appears as foolish as to look for meaning in the creation and death of the extinct ichthyosauria whose meaningless existence has already reached its appointed end.

The sun sinks once more towards the bare, formidable outlines of the Mau mountains: I get up at last from where I have sat all this long tropical day. I leave the frothy edge of this sulphuric lake and, moving through the tall reeds and under the huge cedar-like mimosa trees, I pass close by the place where the bull hippopotamus was shot two days ago. This time it is a mass of blackened putrescent matter; the hide, all that is left of it, has a liquid look; its body is one moving surface of innumerable maggots quivering one on top of the other and now and again falling to the ground, which is already thick and blackened with others that have fallen there before.

Upon their thrones the gods of Lake Elmenteita remain silent. They are not deluded: they are not mocked.

10 July 1920

Clifford Sharp, first New Statesman *Editor, was an anti-feminist, but his anti-feminism was confined to political agitation; he never denied or tried to cry down the intellectual equality of the sexes. The following, from Virginia Woolf, took the form of a letter, protesting against an article by Desmond MacCarthy.*

The Intellectual Status of Women   Virginia Woolf

To begin with Sappho. We do not, as in the hypothetical case of Burns suggested by 'Affable Hawk'*, judge her merely by her fragments. We supplement our judgement by the opinions of those to whom her works were known in their entirety. It is true that she was born 2,500 years ago. According to 'Affable Hawk' the fact that no poetess of her genius has appeared from 600 B.C. to the eighteenth century proves that during that time there were no poetesses of potential genius. It follows that the

* Pen-name used by Desmond MacCarthy in writing book notes.

44

absence of poetesses of moderate merit during that period proves that there were no women writers of potential mediocrity. There was no Sappho; but also, until the seventeenth or eighteenth century, there was no Marie Corelli and no Mrs Barclay.

To account for the complete lack not only of good woman writers but also of bad women writers I can conceive no reason unless it be that there was some external restraint upon their powers. For 'Affable Hawk' admits that there have always been women of second or third rate ability. Why, unless they were forcibly prohibited, did they not express these gifts in writing, music, or painting? The case of Sappho, though so remote, throws, I think, a little light upon the problem. I quote J. A. Symonds.

'Several circumstances contributed to aid the development of lyric poetry in Lesbos. The customs of the Aeolians permitted more social and domestic freedom than was common in Greece. Aeolian women were not confined to the harem like Ionians, or subjected to the rigorous discipline of the Spartans. While mixing freely with male society, they were highly educated and accustomed to express their sentiments to an extent unknown elsewhere in history – until, indeed, the present time.'

And now to skip from Sappho to Ethel Smyth.

'There was nothing else [but intellectual inferiority] to prevent down the ages, so far as I can see, women who always played, sang and studied music, producing as many musicians from among their number as men have done', says 'Affable Hawk'. Was there nothing to prevent Ethel Smyth from going to Munich?

Was there no opposition from her father? Did she find that the playing, singing and study of music which well-to-do families provided for their daughters were such as to fit them to become musicians? Yet Ethel Smyth was born in the nineteenth century. There are no great women painters, says 'Affable Hawk', though painting is now within their reach. It is within their reach – if that is to say there is sufficient money after the sons have been educated to permit of paints and studios for the daughters and no family reason requiring their presence at home. Otherwise they must make a dash for it and disregard a species of torture more exquisitely painful, I believe, than any that man can imagine. And this is in the twentieth century. But, 'Affable Hawk' argues, a great creative mind would triumph over obstacles such as these. Can he point to a single one of the great geniuses of history who has sprung from a people stinted of education and held in subjection, as for example the Irish or the Jews? It seems to me indisputable that the conditions which make it possible for a Shakespeare to exist are that he shall have predecessors in his art, shall make one of a group where art is freely discussed and practised, and shall himself have the utmost freedom of action and experience. Perhaps in Lesbos, but never since, have these conditions been the lot of women. 'Affable Hawk' then names several men who have triumphed over poverty and ignorance. His first example is Isaac Newton. Newton was the son of a farmer; he was sent to a grammar school; he objected to working on the farm; an uncle, a clergyman, advised that he should be exempted and prepared for college; and at the age of nineteen he was sent to Trinity College, Cambridge. (See *D.N.B.*) Newton, that is to say, had to encounter about the same amount of opposition that the daughter of a country solicitor encounters who wishes to go to Newnham in the year 1920. But his discouragement is not increased by the works of Mr Bennett, Mr Orlo Williams and 'Affable Hawk'.

Putting that aside, my point is that you will not get a big Newton until you have produced a considerable number of lesser Newtons. 'Affable Hawk' will, I hope, not accuse me of cowardice if I do not take up your space with an enquiry into the careers of Laplace, Faraday, and Herschell, nor compare the lives and achievements of Aquinas and St Theresa, nor decide whether it was Mill or his friends who was mistaken about Mrs Mill.

The fact, as I think we shall agree, is that women from the earliest times to the present day have brought forth the entire population of the universe. This occupation has taken much time and strength. It has also brought them into subjection to men, and incidentally – if that were to the point – bred in them some of the most lovable and admirable qualities of the race. My difference with 'Affable Hawk' is not that he denies the present intellectual equality of men and women. It is that he, with Mr Bennett, asserts that the mind of woman is not sensibly affected by education and liberty; that it is incapable of the highest achievements; and that it must remain for ever in the condition in which it now is. I must repeat that the fact that women have improved (which 'Affable Hawk' now seems to admit), shows that they may still improve; for I cannot see why a limit should be set to their improvement in the nineteenth century rather than in the one hundred and nineteenth. But it is not education only that is needed. It is that women should have liberty of experience; that they should differ from men without fear and express their differences openly (for I do not agree with 'Affable Hawk' that men and women are alike); that all activity of the mind should be so encouraged that there will always be in existence a nucleus of women who think, invent, imagine, and create as freely as men do, and with as little fear of ridicule and condescension. These conditions, in my view of great importance, are impeded by such statements as those of 'Affable Hawk' and Mr Bennett, for a man has still much greater facilities than a woman for making his views known and respected. Certainly I cannot doubt that if such opinions prevail in the future we shall remain in a condition of half-civilized barbarism. At least that is how I define an eternity of dominion on the one hand and of servility on the other. For the degradation of being a slave is only equalled by the degradation of being a master.

16 October 1920

'If'

H. E. C.

With Apologies to Rudyard Kipling

If you could keep your seat when those about you
    Were losing theirs – the men whom once you knew;
If you can keep your job when all men doubt you,
    And know there's reason in their doubting, too;
If you can wait, and not be tired of waiting
    And they, while you 'twixt hopes and fears are torn
Shall judge your merits, carefully estimating
    The price for which your conscience went in pawn;
If you can turn your back on him that taught you,
    If you can think, but not make thought the test,
And say when sounds the voice of him that brought you:
    'Whatever seemeth good to him is best';
If you can hear the truths you used to cherish
    Twisted by knaves to make a trap for fools,
Or see the things you gave your life to, perish,
    And play the game, but not observe the rules;
If you can bear to hear the words you utter
    Branded as lies, and know the charge is true;
If you can trail your manhood in the gutter,
    And swear that black is white, and red is blue;
If you can bring your heart, and mind, and honour,
    And lay them on the altar of your gain,

And woo the fickle jade, and fawn upon her,
  Nor count the sacrifice you make as vain;
If neither foes nor loving friends can hurt you,
  But all men count with you for what they bring;
If you can talk to hungry crowds by virtue,
  Of readiness to promise anything;
If you can spend each unforgiving minute
  In graft and scheming, heeding not the slime,
The Coalition welcomes you within it,
  And, what is more – you'll get a job – in time!

20 November 1920

Robert Graves' poems appeared in the New Statesman *from its earliest days to the Sixties.*

'*A Vehicle, to wit, a Bicycle*'   Robert Graves

'My front-lamp, constable? Why, man, the moon! My rear-lamp?
Shining there ten yards behind me,
  Warm parlour lamplight of the Dish and Spoon!'
But for all my fancy talk, they would have fined me
  Had I not set a rather sly half-crown
Winking under the rays of my front lamp:
  Goodwill-towards-men disturbed the official frown.
My rear-light beckoned through the evening's damp.

16 July 1921

G. D. H. Cole wrote for the New Statesman *for over thirty years. It was especially in economic and social crises that his work was valuable to the paper. The following contribution is interesting for two reasons: it deals with the most important social crisis of the Twenties; and it is a specimen of collaboration between a specialist contributor and the Editor; no prizes are offered for spotting where Cole's work ends and Sharp's begins. Among other things the article demonstrates Sharp's success in creating a new statesmanly style which to some extent absorbed the personal styles of contributors.*

Some Lessons of the Late General Strike

G. D. H. Cole & Clifford Sharp*

We are now, perhaps, far enough removed from the events of the so-called General Strike to form at least some provisional estimate of its significance. Many obscurities indeed remain; the inwardness of the negotiations between Sir Herbert Samuel and the Trade Union leaders is still by no means clear; the exact relations between the General Council and the Miners' Federation have not yet been explained, nor are likely to be until the coal dispute is ended. But, in any judgment on the lessons of the strike, these are points of relatively minor importance. We are concerned rather with the strike itself, than with any particular misunderstandings that arose in the course of it.

Two things, we think, stand out plainly as the main lessons of the strike. The first is that the human strength of the Trade Union movement is far greater than was believed by the public, or by the Government, or by either of the conflicting parties. And the second is that, no matter how strong Trade Unionism may be, it cannot, by the use of purely industrial methods, hope to stand up directly to the power of the modern State. A stoppage on a scale sufficient to hold up the vital services of the country will inevitably call into being an energy sufficient to keep those services going long enough for the strike to collapse or melt away. In this sense, however great the working-class loyalty behind it, a 'General Strike' can never be a direct success. Formally at least it will always be the strikers who have to give way.

This, of course, assumes that the strike is conducted as a strike and as nothing more. If behind the strike there existed a revolutionary movement, or if the strike were called as a protest against a war or, as in Germany a few years ago against a Monarchist coup d'état, then quite different forces would come into play, and the result would depend on quite different factors. No one can prophesy in general terms the results of a revolutionary or counter-revolutionary movement. But the late General Strike was at no point revolutionary either in conception or in method. It was an exceptionally orderly industrial stoppage on an unprecedentedly large scale. And the Government, up to the moment when it was called off, had refrained almost as carefully as the strike leaders from provoking acts of violence. The movement must be judged purely as a strike and not as an inchoate and abortive revolution. For nothing is clearer than that neither leaders nor followers at any time conceived the idea of going beyond the

* G. D. H. Cole down to 'propaganda would have done'. Clifford Sharp to end.

49

immediate objective of the stoppage – the sympathetic support of the miners in their stand for a living wage.

This is, indeed, one of the criticisms that are now being hurled at the General Council by extremist critics. The strike, say the Communists, was doomed to failure from the first, just because it was a mere strike and not a revolutionary movement, and because it was run by leaders who had no faith in revolution. Whether these critics suppose that a revolutionary movement under present conditions would have stood a better chance of success is not very clear. To any sensible person it was plain before the strike, and plainer still while the strike was in being, that the great mass of British workers, while they were ready enough to stop work on a broad industrial issue, neither wanted a revolution nor had any intention at all of taking part in one.

We judge the strike, then, purely as a sympathetic industrial strike on an unusually large scale – large enough to call into play both the forces of the State and the self-protective instincts of the middle-class section of the public. And we say that it showed how the State, with this backing, will always be strong enough to keep the most vital services going, and so to outlast the strikers' power of combined resistance. For at a pinch, and if the cost is treated as unimportant, these services can be kept in action with the aid of a very small supply of skilled labour; and volunteers, while they inevitably damage machines and work with less efficiency than ordinary workers, do quite well enough to carry on for a considerable time.

This is one lesson of the late strike; and those who concentrate their attention on this aspect of it are disposed to pronounce the whole movement a complete failure. But how does this square with the undoubted satisfaction felt by a large number of Labour supporters? Even many Labour men who are very dissatisfied with the way the strike was managed appear to be pleased with its general results. Nor is this a merely negative satisfaction. They believe that the strike has brought their cause real and positive gains.

On its negative side this attitude can be easily understood. It is not too much to say that the collapse of the Triple Alliance in 1921, on what has ever since been known as 'Black Friday', spread through the Trade Union movement a real feeling of shame. Members of other Unions felt both that the miners had been 'let down', and that Trade Unionism as a whole had made an inglorious showing. 'Never again' became the slogan expressing a strong and widespread sentiment. In July 1925, and again in April 1926, the other Unions felt simply that, whatever might happen, they must not give the miners cause again to say they had been let down. And, when the strike call had come and been obeyed, many Trade Unionists were inclined to say with pride, 'Well, whatever may come, this time we have done it.' In short, like Mr Shaw's Blanco Posnet, the Trade Unionist who came out in support of the miners may have 'cursed himself for a fool; but he lost the rotten feel all the same.'

This is why many people in the Labour movement who have no belief in the General Strike as an effective weapon are glad that this particular strike happened. Without it the Trade Union movement would have 'felt rotten'; but it does not feel at all rotten to-day. Moreover, the satisfaction is positive as well as negative. Already there is a marked upward tendency in Trade Union and Labour Party membership. The workers who struck together have got a new sense of community out of their common action. They will be more disposed for some time to work together in Trade Unions, and to vote together at elections. North Hammersmith was only the first repercussion of the great strike on the electoral prospects of the various parties. Probably the nine days of the strike converted more Conservative and Liberal working men to 'Labour' – temporarily at any rate – than nine years of ordinary propaganda would have done.

It is not, in short, too much to say that there are very few people indeed in the Labour movement today, either on its political or its industrial side, who regret the occurrence of the strike or are in the least ashamed of the part they played in it. The political section have gained not only by the accession of a very large number of new voters, but also by the fact that the General Strike has failed and that they will accordingly be relieved for a long time to come of the ungrateful task of proving on platforms that the industrial cannot be an efficient substitute for the political weapon. The majority of the industrialist leaders also have always distrusted and disliked the General Strike, though for different reasons. They prefer to fight – if fight they must – for definite objects affecting their own trade, and are very loath to see their funds depleted in a general struggle in which in any event they and their members have nothing to gain. So they, too, are glad that the experiment has been tried and failed, and that they are not likely again, for a very long time to come, to be called upon to spend hundreds of thousands of pounds in another such quixotic enterprise. The miners, of course, are dissatisfied with the close and the result of the General Strike, and so are the Communists and the Direct Actionists; but the latter are but a small minority, and there is very little real dissatisfaction elsewhere.

In general, therefore, it may be said that the General Strike bubble has been pricked and that there is no likelihood of any attempt to employ this double-edged weapon again, in the same way, for a generation to come at least. It by no means follows, however, that the weapon will be altogether laid aside. It failed last month, but it did not break. On the contrary, the solidarity with which the men obeyed orders showed it to be even stronger than had been supposed. On a political issue on which the rest of the community was divided – for example, an unpopular war or an attempt by the Die-hards to restore to the House of Lords all its ancient powers – its strength might easily prove to be decisive. The assumption, of course, here is that of a Government attempting to defy the real wishes of the majority of the nation: and this assumption may be regarded as extremely improbable. The fact remains, however, that the weapon of the General Strike may be, and certainly in many quarters will be, still regarded as one of the ultimate safeguards of democracy – and even of the Constitution!

There is one other way in which the General Strike might conceivably be used with good effect, and that is as a simple, though gigantic, demonstration of working-class opinion. For such a purpose it would, of course, have to be employed for a strictly limited period announced beforehand. There are many people in the Labour movement who think that this would have been the wisest course for the TUC to have taken last month. They felt obliged to do something to show their sympathy with the miners. If they had simply announced that every Trade Unionist in the country would cease work for, say, seven days or four days or even one day as a demonstration, it would have been impossible for the Government either to arouse the enthusiasm of the volunteers or to drag in the Constitutional red-herring; for the real nature of the strike would have been obvious and insusceptible of misrepresentation, and the miners' cause would probably have been much more effectively advertised and assisted.

Our general conclusion, therefore, is that while the General Strike is a weapon which may again be used, in conceivable circumstances, it is most unlikely again to be abused or to be employed on occasions when the odds are against its success. It may be employed, in short, where public opinion is substantially in favour of its purposes. Then and then only can it succeed. 'But', it may be asked, 'would even success justify the use of so "unconstitutional" a weapon?' To that question we should be inclined to give the pragmatic answer, for all sound political philosophy is necessarily pragmatic. If the General Strike, as recent events seem to have shown, can be successfully employed only when national opinion is opposed to that of the Government, then we see no reason why its use should be unconditionally condemned by anyone but a Constitutional pedant. If, for example, Mr Baldwin and one or two others of his saner colleagues were accidentally to be removed, and the Die-hard section of the Government were thereupon to attempt to use the fortuitous Tory majority to restore the veto of the hereditary House, we should certainly not only support but most strongly advocate the use of the General Strike to force an election and thus preserve the balance of the Constitution. These are mere hypotheses, of course, but hypotheses which are perhaps worth pondering.

19 June 1926

As a very young man, long before he became a best-selling novelist, H. E. Bates made his name as the writer of some of the most exquisite short stories in our language. Some of his earliest work appeared in the New Statesman.

Never   H. E. Bates

It was afternoon: great clouds stumbled across the sky. In the drowsy, half-dark room the young girl sat in a heap near the window, scarcely moving herself, as if she expected a certain timed happening, such as a visit, sunset, a command. . . . Slowly she would draw the fingers of one hand across the back of the other, in the little hollows between the guides, and move her lips in the same sad, vexed way in which her brows came together. And like that too, her eyes would shift about, from the near, shadowed fields, to the west hills, where the sun had dropped a strip of light, and to the woods between, looking like black scars one minute, and like friendly sanctuaries the next. It was all confused. . . . There was the room, too. . . . The white keys of the piano would now and then exercise a fascination over her which would keep her whole body perfectly still for perhaps a minute. But when that passed, full of hesitation, her fingers would recommence the slow exploration of her hands, and the restlessness took her again.

Yes: it was all confused. She was going away: already she had said a hundred times during the afternoon, 'I am going away . . . I am going away. I can't stand it any longer.' But she had made no attempt to go. In this same position, hour after hour had passed her and all she could think was . . . 'Today I'm going away. I'm tired here. I never do anything. It's dead, rotten . . . I'm going away.'

She said, or thought, it all without the slightest trace of exultation and was sometimes even methodical when she began . . . 'What shall I take ? . . . The blue dress with the rosette ? . . . Yes . . . what else ? what else !' And then it would all begin again: 'Today I'm going away. I never do anything . . .'

It was true: she never did anything . . . anything different. In the mornings she got up late, was slow over her breakfast, slow over everything – her mending, her eating, her playing the piano, cards in the evening, going to bed. It was all slow – purposely done, to fill up the day. And it was true, day succeeded day and she never did anything different.

But today something was about to happen; no more cards in the evening, every evening the same, her father declaring: 'I never have a decent hand' . . . 'I thought the ace of trumps had gone!' . . . 'It's too bad!!' and no more; 'Nellie, it's ten o'clock . . . Bed!' and the slow unimaginative climb of the stairs. Today she was going away; no one knew, but it was so. She was catching the evening train to London, was about to run away, to live by herself after all these years of imprisonment!

'I'm going away. I'm going away. What shall I take ? . . . The blue dress with the rosette ? What else ?'

She crept upstairs with difficulty, her body stiff after sitting. The years she must have sat, figuratively speaking, and grown stiff! And as if in order to secure some violent reaction against it all she threw herself into the packing of her things with a nervous vigour, throwing in the blue dress first and after it a score of things she had just remembered. She fastened her bag; it was not heavy. She counted her money a dozen times . . . It was all right! It was all right. She was going away.

She descended into the now dark room for the last time. In the dining-room someone was rattling tea-cups, an unbearable, horribly domestic sound! She wasn't hungry; she would be in London by eight – eating now meant making her sick. It was easy to wait. . . . The train went at 6.18 . . . She looked it up again: 'Elden 6.13. Olde 6.18. London 7.53.'

She began to play a waltz. 'Elden 6.13 . . . Olde 6.18. It was a slow, dreamy time . . . laa-di-da-di-daa . . . la-a-a . . . di . . . the notes slipped out in mournful, sentimental succession. The room was quite dark, she could scarcely see the keys, and into the tune itself kept insinuating: 'Elden 6.13 . . . Olde 6.18,' impossible to mistake or forget.

'I'm going away. I'm going away.'

As she played on she thought: 'I'll never play this waltz again. It has the atmosphere of this room. . . . The last time!' . . . And the waltz slid dreamily to an end; for a minute she sat in utter silence, the room dark and mysterious, the air of the waltz quite dead, then the tea-cups rattled again and the thought came back to her: 'I'm going away. I'm going away.'

She rose and went out quietly. The grass on the roadside moved under the evening wind, sounding like many pairs of hands rubbed softly together. But there was no other sound, her feet were light, no one heard her, and as she went down the road she told herself: 'I'm going away! It's come at last!'

'Elden 6.13 . . . Olde 6.18.'

Should she go to Elden or Olde? At the cross-roads she stood to consider, thinking that if she went to Elden no one would know her. But at Olde someone would doubtless find himself intrigued enough by her going to prattle about it. To Elden, then . . . not that it mattered . . . nothing mattered now. She was going, was as good as gone!

Her breast, tremulously warm, began to rise and fall as her excitement increased. She tried to run over the things in her bag and could remember only 'the blue dress with the rosette,' which she had thrown in first and had since covered over. But it didn't matter. Her money was safe, everything was safe, and with that thought she dropped into a strange quietness, deepening as she went on, in which she had a hundred emotions and convictions. She was never going to strum that waltz again, she had played cards for the last, horrible time, the loneliness, the slowness, the oppression were ended, all ended.

'I'm going away. I'm going away.'

She was warm, her body tingled with a light delicious thrill that was like the caress of a soft night-wind. There were no fears now. A certain indignation, approaching fury even, sprang up instead, as she thought: 'No one will believe I've gone. I'm considered too meek for anything extraordinary to happen to me. . . . I've never even been to London. But now – I'm going now. It's happened at last.'

Her bag grew heavy. Setting it down in the grass she sat on it for a brief while, in something like her attitude in the dark room during the afternoon, and indeed actually began to rub her gloved fingers over the backs of her hands. A phrase or two of the waltz came back to her. The silly old piano! . . . Its bottom G was flat, had always been flat; silly ridiculous thing! She tried to conjure up some sort of vision of London, but it was difficult and in the end she gave way again to the old cry: 'I'm going away,' and she was pleased more than ever deeply. . . .

On the station only one lamp burned, radiating a fitful yellowness that only increased the gloom. And worse, she saw no one and in the cold emptiness traced and retraced her footsteps without the friendly assurance of another sound. In the black distance all the signals showed hard circles of red, looking as if they could never change. . . . But she nevertheless told herself over and over again: 'I'm going away. I'm going away.' And later: 'I hate everyone. I've changed until I hardly know myself.'

Impatiently she looked for the train. It was strange. For the first time it

occurred to her to know the hour and she pulled back the sleeve of her coat.
. . . Nearly six-thirty! She felt cold. Up the line every signal displayed its
red ring, mocking her. 'Six-thirty. . . . Of course, of course,' . . . she tried
to be careless. . . . 'Of course, it's late, the train is late,' but the coldness, in
reality her fear, increased rapidly, until she could no longer believe those
words.

Great clouds, lower and more than ever depressing, floated above her
head as she walked back. The wind had a deep note that was sad too. These
things had not troubled her before, now they, also, spoke failure and fore-
told misery and dejection. She had no spirit . . . it was cold . . . she was too
tired to shudder.

In the absolutely dark, drowsy room she sat down, telling herself: 'This
isn't the only day. Some day I shall go . . . Some day, some day. . . .'

She was silent. In the next room they were playing cards, her father had
just moaned: 'I thought the ace had gone.' Somebody laughed. Her
father's voice came again. 'I never have a decent hand. I never have a
decent hand . . . Never!'

It was too horrible! She couldn't stand it! She must do something to stop
it! . . . it was too much. . . . She began to play the waltz again and the
dreamy, sentimental arrangement made her cry, warm and comforted.

'This isn't the only day,' she reassured herself. 'I shall go. Some day!
Some day!'

And again and again she played her sentimental tune, she would tell
herself that same thing:

'Some day! . . . Some day!'

26 June 1926

Sir Lewis Namier wrote for the New Statesman, *contributing original articles
and book reviews, from the last years of the First World War. Here he is on
Zionism. He could not, of course, foresee Hitler's 'final solution' to the problems
he poses.*

Zionism   Lewis Namier

Eighteen hundred years we Jews have waited for the Messianic miracle and
the return to our own land. It was that hope which imparted a peculiar
meaning to our communal life and survival. We passed the endless

centuries of vigil, fundamentally indifferent to the world around us, indifferent even to our own sufferings, in a state of suspended animation, with survival for our only aim. We believed that, on the day of the return, even the dead whom we buried in the Exile would rise from their graves and wander their last way to Palestine. We tried to found no permanent existence anywhere, we did not even plan our return, but waited for a miracle, conceived as miracles were in previous ages. This faith is now dying fast, and Israel has to face the practical problem of its existence and of its uncertain future – a stupendous process of re-orientation in the oldest and most tenacious of races. Some of us find the solution in dissolution; others are determined actively to work for the 'miracle' for which we have hitherto waited. Orthodox Jewry is a melting glacier and Zionism is the river which springs from it; evaporation and the river result from the same process, and are both its necessary results.

In Jewish orthodoxy, religion and nationality were identical; the loss of the Messianic hope logically leads to separation between them. Tradition still gives a national colouring to our religion and a religious colouring to our nationalism; but a Jewish religion has become possible which is merely a creed, and a Jewish nationalism which is purely political; whilst hundreds of thousands, and by no means the worst among us, taking no interest in theology and ritual and having lost touch with our national tradition, leave the Jewish community altogether and merge in the surrounding nations. Provided they do so without the self-abasement and the insult inherent in a denial of their origin, we have no reason to blame them; if community with us has no meaning for them, why should they remain with us ? The lot of the Jew is such that without a powerful idea it cannot be borne with honour. In a 'testudo' there is no room for anyone who will not hold up a shield.

In fact, dissolution and ultimate disappearance seem the inevitable future of the Jewries of Western and Central Europe; however much pleasure or anxiety the so-called Jewish question may provide even in these parts to obsessed anti-Semites, and however much wonder or discomfort their obsession may cause to us, there is here no real Jewish question, and without further immigration from Eastern Europe, there would be, and there soon will be, no Jews. The orthodox Jews of Eastern Europe multiply quickly, not because their birth-rate is higher than that of their neighbours – it is invariably lower – but because of a lower infantile mortality. But once the religious bar to birth control has disappeared, the same care for the children produces with the Jews a limitation of families far stricter even than it is with the French; and whilst there is no excess of births over deaths among educated Jews, baptisms and inter-marriages dissolve the stock – in Hamburg and Berlin, there is about one mixed marriage to every two Jewish marriages. We have no religious statistics in this country, but anyone can gain a picture of this process of dissolution by considering the Jews (and half-Jews) of his own acquaintance. Still, the Jews of Western and Central Europe form only about two millions out of fifteen – these are the fringes of the glacier from which no river can spring and by which one must not judge the nature and future of the glacier itself.

The two numerically important bodies in Jewry are the seven million, mostly Yiddish-speaking, Jews of Eastern Europe (almost three millions in Poland, over two and a half in Russia, one in Roumania, the rest in Lithuania, Latvia and Carpatho-Russia), and the three and a half million Jews in the United States, the majority of them immigrants from Eastern Europe or children of such immigrants – about 2,400,000 Jews entered the USA between 1881 and 1924. This sudden mass immigration is now abruptly cut off, and it is difficult as yet to form a judgment about the future of the Jews in America. So much, however, is certain, that those settled over there will remain in the country, that they are rising in wealth and education, and that the phenomena known among the Jews of Western and Central Europe – a low birth-rate, inter-marriages and baptisms – have already set in and will in time make appreciable inroads on the stock. Another effect of this migration deserves attention. Before the war the million Jews inhabiting Germany and Western Austria formed the most important body of educated, wealthy Jews in the world, and consequently with them lay the intellectual and financial leadership in Jewry. This is now passing to the American Jews, whilst the Palestine Mandate has fixed in London the political leadership of Jewish nationalism. In other words, the centre of gravity in Jewry has moved from the German- to the English-speaking countries. The main body of Jews, whose existence forms the real Jewish question, remains in Eastern Europe; the Jews primarily called upon to deal with the problem live in America and in England.

In Eastern Europe the nature of the problem is not the same in different countries. In Russia it is now primarily economic; Bolshevism, whilst destroying the livelihood of the Jewish masses in the so-called 'Pale' – small traders and artisans – has disorganized Russia's economic system, which could otherwise easily absorb its Jews in a productive manner. Still, supremely bad as the position is at present, there is room for these people and there are possibilities – witness the effective work of colonization which American Jews are now conducting and financing in Southern Russia. In Roumania the problem is primarily political; its Jews could live and prosper were they allowed to. In Poland, it is both political and economic, which renders the position of its Jews desperate. The country is over-populated; the Jews form a distinct type and a separate community; their numbers are such that, even were there the wish (which there is now on neither side), they could not possibly be assimilated to the Poles in the way common among the nations of Western and Central Europe. Before the war, Poles and Jews alike emigrated in hundreds of thousands; the outlets are now stopped; the possibilities of livelihood are narrowed down; the Poles, to put it mildly, do not like the Jews. It does not worry them if the Jews go to the wall, and as economic life is coming more and more under control, they have hundreds of means in their country to drive the Jews that way. Some find pleasure in it, others do so because they require the place of the Jews for themselves. Where will this end if no outlet is found in time for a new Jewish emigration?

With the loss of the Messianic hope the passivity of orthodox Jewry breaks down. We have to find our own place on earth and live as other people do. Where the Jews live in dense masses, speak their own language, and form a distinct community, they have their own 'nationality', whether they profess it or not; anyhow, they are treated as strangers by their neighbours. It is not true that it is the rise of a conscious Jewish nationality which raises a bar between them; the bar exists anyhow and a national consciousness merely gives the Jews a backbone and relieves them of the feeling of moral inferiority which some of their neighbours like to inflict on them, however much they may loathe its natural consequences – aggressive cringing and pushing. Zionism, whatever possibilities it may open up in future, cannot alone within measurable time solve the economic problems of East European Jewry which cry out for solution; but it can even now help to create an atmosphere in which other remedies will become more effective. A consciousness of nationality, of national purpose and respon-sibility, of the duty to work for a common future and the duty to become normal after eighteen centuries of abnormal life, are in themselves of imponderable value, for along the whole line, in matters economic, national or communal, an end must be made to that nondescript character which the endless, detached waiting has produced in great masses of our people.

Possibly a majority of national Jews will have to remain for ever in the Diaspora, but even so, there must be somewhere a National Home to give them normality – every nation must somewhere have its own territorial centre. There are many more Irishmen scattered throughout the world than inhabiting the Irish Free State, and yet its existence, though they may never see it, is of supreme importance to them; it gives them a standing among other nations. Our very survival was inherently bound up with the hope of a return to Palestine. The passive hope has now changed into an active will; those of us who still adhere to the idea which for eighteen hundred years stood in the centre of our thinking, have to work for that which we no longer expect to come to us in another way. No one who looks with an unbiased eye at the road which the Jewish people has covered, at the sufferings which it has patiently borne, at the spiritual strength it has shown, and lastly at the desperate position in which a large part of it is now placed, can doubt the driving force which there is behind the Zionist movement.

It is now ten years since the Balfour Declaration opened the gate which hitherto had been practically closed to us; the mandate has given a definite international status to our work. We have started upon it. Since 1922 the Jewish population of Palestine has doubled and now amounts to almost 160,000; we have founded a number of agricultural settlements and have started new industries; tens of thousands of Jews, who in Eastern Europe would now be beggars without profession, have learnt to work. But so far we have not been altogether successful. In 1925, when America finally closed up against immigration and the economic crisis became acute in Poland, there was an inrush with which we proved unable to cope; we have suffered a setback and had to take stock of means and methods. The way to increase the possibilities for immigration will be found; under modern conditions the possibilities of each country are what men make them – did Middlesex or Manhattan Island inherently and unmistakably show the possibilities for settlement which we now see in them? If Palestine is to be our national home – and we now can see no other on the globe nor in all our history – we must not even ask what will be the price at which we can achieve it.

Other nations, when their existence or perhaps only their interests were threatened, spent thousands of millions of pounds on war. The wealth of the Jewish community, with half the East European Jewry downright paupers, is *per capita* less than that of England, France, or America, and we bear at least a proportionate share in the burdens of other nations. Still, at this time, when a crisis of unequalled seriousness has supervened after the eighteen centuries of suspended animation, we must not inquire into the size of the sacrifice which we may be called upon to make. Lord Balfour, when defending in the House of Lords the Palestinian policy of the Government, expressed the hope that their Lordships would never sink to 'that unimaginative depth' which excludes experiment or adventure. We Jews certainly must not do so; for should the enterprise in which the

British Empire and the Jewish nation are partners fail, to our friends in Great Britain, perhaps the best we have had since Cyrus and Alexander (we can use quaint comparison, as our memory is long), this would be a disappointment, for ourselves a catastrophe of truly immeasurable consequence. And perhaps even the outside world would then find that a spiritual catastrophe in Jewry cannot remain a matter of indifference to other nations.

5 November 1927

As a young writer William Plomer contributed both poetry and prose.

The Death of a Zulu   William Plomer

The weather is mild
At the house of one of the dead.
There is fruit in the hands of his child
With flowers on his head.

Smoke rises up from the floor,
And the hands of a ghost
(No shadow darkens the door)
Caress the door-post.

Inside sits the wife, frantic, forsaken,
Too wild to weep;
Food lies uncooked at her feet, and is taken
By venturing fowls:
Outside, the dogs were asleep,
But they waken,
And one of them howls;
And Echo replies.

At last, with a sudden fear shaken,
The little child cries.

26 November 1927

Arnold Bennett became a shareholder in the New Statesman *in 1915. He contributed a regular column for some time, and also stories and articles. He became a director of the* New Statesman *and one of the most active, taking a considerable part in the appointment of Kingsley Martin as Editor in succession to Clifford Sharp.*

Leading to Marriage — Arnold Bennett

This is the story of the episode which led to Mr Capstain's second marriage.

The illustrious Mr Capstain sat down at his desk in his vast house, Belgrave Square, London. He was a man of business, a director of the biggest manufactory of its kind in the world. No manufactory could have been directed with less friction. Never a strike there! The delegates of trade unions never troubled there! Mr Capstain was not only the director, but the working staff, the everything of the manufactory. He happened to be a novelist, playwright, and journalist. He knew that he was not a genius, but he also knew that he was the most popular, the most efficient, and the most prolific literary performer of his time. He made more money and spent more than any other author on earth.

The hour was midnight.

At midnight his day's labour began. He toiled till 7 a.m., with an interval at 4 a.m. for light refreshment. He breakfasted at 7 a.m., went to bed, slept six hours, arose at 1 p.m., lunched at 2 p.m., and had then a glorious stretch of ten hours in which to see the world. This wonderful plan of existence he had taken from the life of Balzac. Herein was his sole resemblance to Balzac.

In the blaze of the electric light he passed his hand over some notebooks. He looked at his fingers. Dust. He rang the bell.

A butler entered.

Mr Capstain was reputed to be the only man in London who employed two butlers. This one was the night-butler, necessary because of Mr Capstain's nocturnal refreshment and early breakfast.

'Crowther,' he asked blandly, 'who dusts this room nowadays?'

'The new head-housemaid, sir.'

'What's her name?'

'Maisie, sir.'

'Her surname?'

'I don't know, sir. She's only been here ten days.'

'Has she gone to bed yet?'

'Oh no, sir.'

'Send her to me.'

Mr Capstain had spoken blandly, for the reason that he never allowed himself to be other than bland. He believed in harmony, as the best aid to industry. He never had the slightest dissension even with his two widowed sisters, who lived with him and on him. They adored him, though he was a plump fellow of forty-five, with a bald head, a manner exasperatingly imperturbable, and an ironic tongue.

The new head-housemaid came in. A young lady of pleasant but serious features, very neat.

'Yes, sir.' A rather cultivated voice for a housemaid, even for a head-housemaid.

'Maisie,' said Mr Capstain at his blandest. 'By the way, what is your surname?'

'Dyton, sir.'

'Well, Maisie, I told Crowther yesterday about the inefficient dusting of this room. Did you get the message?'

'Yes, sir.'

'See here, then.' Mr Capstain passed his hand again over the notebooks, and showed dusty fingers.

'I'm sorry, sir.' 45

'You possibly don't realise that this room is the most important in the whole house. Everything comes out of it, including your wages.'

'I'm sorry, sir. I had to go out. I was detained, and there wasn't time....'

'Excuse me, Maisie,' Mr Capstain blandly stopped her. 'Your affairs are not mine. You've been here ten days. You and I are at liberty to cease business relations at the end of the first fortnight.' Mr Capstain knew this interesting fact about the conditions of British domestic service because part of his equipment as a novelist was to know everything. He continued: 'At the end of your fortnight you will have the goodness to leave. One of my rules here is never to give an order twice.'

'Yes, sir.'

Maisie turned to leave. Mr Capstain scribbled, 'New Housemaid' on a note-pad. At the door Maisie turned back and remarked:

'I suppose you wouldn't like me to suggest a plot to you, sir?'

'A plot?' repeated Mr Capstain, alert.

'Yes, sir.'

'If it suits me, I'll pay you five pounds for it,' said Mr Capstain, unperturbed.

'Well, sir. There was a girl who had to earn her living, or part of it. She had literary leanings, and tried to be an author. She wrote two novels. One she couldn't sell. The other was published, but it failed completely. She had a son, a young boy. She couldn't be a secretary, because that wouldn't have suited her temperament. So she decided . . .'

At this point Crowther re-entered, apologetic.

'Crowther,' said his master, 'you well know that you have no right to come in unless I ring.'

'The house is on fire, sir.'

Mr Capstain showed no emotion; neither did Maisie.

'Oh, is it?' said the master. 'Which floor?'

'Above this, sir. Back.'

'Serious?'

'Maybe, sir.'

'Then telephone for the fire-brigade.'

'I have, sir.'

'That's good. Get all the servants downstairs before the staircase is alight. Are your mistresses in?'

'Not yet, sir.'

'Very fortunate. Thank you. That will do . . . for the moment.'

Exit Crowther.

'Fires always burn upwards, not downwards. So we're in no danger,' observed Mr Capstain. 'You're not afraid, Maisie?'

'Oh no, sir.'

'But your things upstairs?'

'I sleep in the basement, sir.'

'Good. Now to continue that plot.'

'So as she understood and really liked housework,' Maisie continued calmly, 'she decided to enter domestic service, and she became a house-maid. Her little boy was ill, and she went out one evening to see him – at her sister-in-law's. And that got her into trouble about some dusting. She had to leave. And to find just the right sort of situation was not very easy. Is that a good beginning of a plot, sir?'

'Very,' said Mr Capstain. 'Are you a widow?'

'Yes, sir.'

'What is called a lady?'

'I suppose so, sir.'

'Will you sit down, Mrs Dyton?'

'Thanks.' Mrs Dyton sat.

They talked for some time – indeed until they heard the beating thud-thud-thud of a fire-engine.

Arnold Bennett

Arnold Bennett by Low [30 Jan. 1926]

'Perhaps we ought to be going,' said Mr Capstain, 'Everything's insured, except my manuscripts. I'd better take them.'

He opened a drawer and pulled out a pile of manuscript. Maisie rose to go.

'One moment,' said Mr Capstain. 'Forgive me, but you're rather a wonderful young woman. I should like to ask you one question. Do you intend ever again to write?'

'Nothing would induce me to.'

'Then you're also a very wise young woman, and I'm relieved,' said Mr Capstain.

They went forth through the double-doors to the landing, smelt smoke, discerned the romantic figures of firemen above.

10 May 1930

Clifford Sharp edited the New Statesman *from its first number in 1913. In 1930 he was sent to the United States for a sabbatical year and his contract with the* New Statesman *came to an end. From there he sent his paper an article on a subject he knew well.*

The Moral Collapse of Prohibition   Clifford Sharp

New York: October 31st

The practical failure of Prohibition in America has long been recognized everywhere, but its sudden moral collapse is a matter only of the past few months. This article is being written in advance of the elections, but it is safe to say that the results of the voting will show quite plainly the widespread character of that collapse. There is, of course, no clear-cut challenge to the electors on the subject (except in some places by referenda). Prohibition is not a party issue. Nevertheless, it is certain that there will be an enormous increase in the number of officials and representatives who will be elected under a pledge in favour of the repeal of the Eighteenth Amendment of the Constitution. Both the candidates, for example, for the Governorship of New York State are 'dry' by personal conviction and by personal habit; yet both, as all the world knows, are in favour of repeal. They dispute only as to the fairness of each other's attempts to gain something of the derelict dry vote.

Though the practical failure of Prohibition is so well known, a few lines

66

about present conditions in New York may not be superfluous. There are houses in London in the upper professional and business classes where one may be invited to dinner and offered no wine; and the same thing may happen in New York. The writer's experience is not sufficiently extensive to enable him to offer any reliable statistical comparison, but it may certainly be supposed, though he happens to have encountered no dry private house in New York, that such are more numerous here than in London. On the other hand, the pre-dinner cocktail in private houses would seem to be a more usual indulgence in New York than in London.

Outside private houses, however, the general facts of the situation may be more confidently described. The bell-boy bootlegger – in other words, the hotel attendant who used to offer to get you a bottle of whisky on the sly – has disappeared. He has disappeared partly, no doubt, because the quality of the goods he vended reinforced the ancient maxim of *caveat emptor* with a new penalty of death by poison, but mainly because his always questionable usefulness has now lapsed. As the humblest servant of a great law-breaking conspiracy in which secrecy is no longer observed or necessary – except at the top – he has no further function to perform. Besides, the stranger to New York, whether he come from Manchester or from Kansas City, has been warned of bell-boys, and unless he is totally without friends in the city can hardly stay there for twenty-four hours without having been introduced to at least one or two perfectly reputable speakeasies. Business and professional men of the very highest standing entertaining a visitor will as a quite natural thing invite him to lunch at a speakeasy where alcoholic refreshments of almost all kinds will be served with the meal. Food and drink alike are excellent, and relatively to the price of food a whisky-and-soda or a liqueur brandy costs no more than it would cost in London or Paris.

There are said to be 50,000 speakeasies in New York, good, bad and indifferent. More conservative estimates place the number at about half that figure. They are never interfered with except in case of disorder, which is rare. At any one of them liquor may be consumed on the premises or taken away. Bottles of whisky remain expensive and perhaps still dangerous, but synthetic gin of a purity and flavour high enough to satisfy all but the most fastidious of cocktail shakers can be obtained in unlimited quantities at a price a little lower than is current in England. And naturally there are no closing hours. If a post-midnight cocktail party runs short of supplies it can replenish them in a few minutes.

This practical failure of Prohibition is not, of course, nearly so complete in other American cities. But the chief point to be observed about the moral collapse of the doctrine itself is that it applies all over the country more or less irrespective of local conditions of enforcement. Enforcement is no longer the main issue. What is everywhere being questioned now by men of understanding and goodwill inside and outside the Churches is the moral justification of the Eighteenth Amendment itself. It is characteristic of the change that is now so rapidly taking place amongst the better minds of the nation that the Rt Rev. Paul Mathews, Bishop of New Jersey, speaking the other day (October 28th) to the Congress of the Episcopal Church at Buffalo should have quoted against the Eighteenth Amendment the profound saying of St Paul: 'If there had been a law which could have given life, verily righteousness would have been by the law.' 'Law,' added the Bishop, 'is the manifestation of life. Life is not the product of law. If the framers of the Eighteenth Amendment had realized that fact they might have hesitated to attempt to create morality by legislation.'

Such utterances are plain indications of the great swing of the pendulum which may be said to have begun a few months ago when Mr Dwight W. Morrow, late American Ambassador in Mexico and delegate to the recent Naval Conference in London, declared in favour of repeal in the course of his Senatorial candidature. His action gave rise to a great deal of hard thinking amongst those who had hitherto regarded him as one of the pillars of compulsory total abstinence, and who could not doubt either his sense or his sincerity; and the fruits of that thinking are now becoming apparent. It is not the political empiricists who are thus being affected. They long ago doubted the expediency of Prohibition in practice. It is the great Puritan heart of unsophisticated America that is beginning to doubt; and to doubt not merely the expediency but even the fundamental righteousness of the Eighteenth Amendment.

Between the beginning of such a doubt and its inevitable conclusion there need be but a short interval. The obviously evil effects of Prohibition – the increasing general disrespect for law, the excessive drinking amongst flask-carrying youths and maidens, the enormous financial resources placed by Prohibition in the hands of the lowest and most dangerous section of the community, the bootlegging gunmen and gangsters – all these Puritan America was prepared to face as long as it remained sure that it was fighting for righteousness. But if even about the motive of the great struggle there can be a sincere doubt, if, indeed, law cannot give life, then plainly the fight must stop.

We have already seen the beginning of the end, and the collapse seems likely to become a landslide almost as rapid and complete as the landslide which brought the great experiment into being a dozen years ago. The change will naturally come more slowly in the great rural States of the South-West than in the urbanized industrial Eastern States; but quite soon, it would seem, there will be no solid support left for the continuance of the experiment save amongst the disciples of force on either side. No doubt some fanatical Prohibitionists will continue to urge that if force has not yet succeeded in stamping out the evil of alcoholic liquor, then more force and more must be used. And certainly on the other side the vast bootlegging industry, with its myriad organizations, will fight to the last against repeal and the loss of wealth and power which repeal would mean to it. But it will be a losing fight. The Churches do not really believe in force, and they are swinging over – not, of course, to anything like the old saloon system, but to some rational system of State control and distribution impossible under the Eighteenth Amendment. In any case, the fate of that famous, or infamous, attempt to create righteousness by law is now sealed. Some say repeal will come within twelve months. The writer's knowledge of the practical working of the American Constitution is enough to make him doubt the accuracy of that forecast but insufficient to enable him to offer an alternative forecast of his own. But that during the past summer and autumn the moral pillars of Federal Prohibition have collapsed there can be no doubt at all.

15 November 1930

If Time be a healer it is also the supreme ironist: by the end of the Thirties political events were to throw Winston Churchill and Kingsley Martin, the New Statesman's *young new Editor, almost into each other's arms; but at the beginning of the Thirties Churchill, as in the Twenties, was the arch-enemy of any toleration of the Left, any understanding with Communism, even for the sake of world peace. The man who was to lead the country into alliance with the Soviet Union had to be taken to task for war-mongering against her.*

Russia and Mr Churchill   Kingsley Martin

Mr Winston Churchill, the notorious British agitator (we adopt the phraseology of the *Morning Post* when describing M. Bukharin and other distinguished Russians now in this country), has now decided that disarmament is impossible, because of the menace of Russia. He explained his reasons in the House of Commons on Monday. He prides himself, as his counterparts in Russia do, on 'realism', on cutting through the idealistic cobwebs which so delight the MacDonalds and Hendersons, Noel Bakers, Norman Angells, and other apostles of peace and disarmament. His contemptuous attitude towards idealists, Socialists, radicals and other renegades who try to prevent the 'inevitable struggle' between Capitalism and Communism is very like that of Trotsky ten years ago. His mind, like Trotsky's, is confined in a militaristic mould; as a young man he learned to see everything in terms of war and preparation for war. He can see in Russia nothing but a menace; nothing but a reason for keeping the French Army and the British Navy at full strength. True, he uttered a pious hope that we might yet avoid war, but always on the understanding that we ceaselessly prepared for it.

There is perhaps not much you can do with this kind of mentality. If 1914 did not teach you that war is the result of competitive armaments and partial alliances, neither will you be convinced, though one – or a million slaughtered soldiers – rise from the dead. It is a dreary, old-fashioned and oddly deterministic way of regarding history to think that we must all act again as we did in the past, that we must always fight against any rising power which menaces our world supremacy, that we must use our power to crush out new ideas of organizing society and choke up the new wells of enthusiasm which will, in spite of Mr Churchill, arise among young people in England, in Russia and elsewhere. But Mr Churchill, whom one used to fancy as an exuberant and stimulating person, hates youth and its idealism: he is equally an enemy of the effort to build an international society as of the attempts to reorganize our economic system on a more equitable basis. He lives deep in the Victorian age, with his mind in ancient ruts about competition and Empire and Balances of Power. He is the oldest old woman in Europe.

There may be some who agree with us so far but who may yet wonder whether Mr Churchill is not right in arguing that the Five Year Plan is, in any case, a menace, since its success would mean wholesale dumping while its failure would drive the Russian Government into adopting a military policy in order to distract its citizens from their disappointment. Both these propositions are worth careful consideration. Both seem to us based on misconceptions. Russia, like everyone else, sells at the best price she can get. The difference between Russia and other countries is that Russian trade is controlled by the Government. It seems likely that the future of international trade will be on these lines. Countries will decide what they want and by systems of import and export boards purchase and sell in bulk. This is what the Co-operative Wholesale Society already does and what big private companies do, though their buying and selling is dictated by the profits they can make out of the consumer, while the Russian Government, with a planned economy, is in a position to adjust its trade to a scientific estimate of public need. In this sense Russian economy is a menace to Western capitalism: it enables the resources of a country to be used to supply the needs of its people instead of allowing the maldistribution of wealth to create unemployment and chaos.

In the second place, industrial experts now agree with other observers – we have seen no competent opinion to the contrary – that the Five Year Plan is unlikely to be a failure in the sense considered by Mr Churchill. It is already transforming Russia with immense rapidity from a poor, undeveloped country into a potentially wealthy, industrial one. For the time being, the mass of workers are accepting a low, though an improved, standard of life in order to hasten still more the process of industrialization. But neither town nor agricultural workers will submit to this indefinitely, and the Government, whether it wishes or no, will almost certainly be compelled to use the increased production of the country immensely to improve the standard of life of the mass of the people – which means, as intelligent business men have been saying recently, that Russia is the great new market of the future.

We do not deny that there is a possibility of war with Russia; indeed, if Mr Churchill gets his way there is a probability of it. But it is, we believe, quite unnecessary and, if we are sensible, easily avoidable. The view that the Russian Government intends war is founded on ignorance of Russian policy. The whole attitude of the Soviet Government towards the West has changed since the exile of Trotsky and the adoption of the Five Year Plan. It was Trotsky's view that no Communist State could exist side by side with capitalist States. According to strict Bolshevik doctrine, they had all to go through a bloody revolution like that of Russia. Relics of that view still persist in Russia and are encouraged by all the Churchills outside Russia. The Soviets still believe or affect to believe – and they have Mr Churchill's war of 1919 to support their view – that the capitalist West intends an offensive against them. But their own policy to-day is peaceful; they desire to be left alone to carry out their immense economic revolution and they persistently state – and there seems no ground for disbelieving them – that they now hope to be able to trade peacefully (if with disturbing efficiency) with other countries, whatever their form of government. So that at the worst we have some years in which to build up a more sensible relationship, some years in which to organize our economic life so that we may be able to deal with industrial Russia on equal terms. Perhaps this may be only a phase, only a reprieve, but it is one which we can use to make conflict more or less unlikely. It is encouraging to find some public men who are beginning to realize this. Lord Lothian, in a remarkable speech at the London School of Economics, has just been advising us to learn from Russia instead of abusing her.

Some may object that the Soviet Government is too tyrannous and oppressive for any improvement in our relations with it. We have never defended, nor shall we defend, cruelty in Russia or elsewhere, and we believe that, even from its own point of view, the Russian Government has often been quite unnecessarily repressive. That, one may notice, is the view of Stalin who put an end to the very misguided effort to expropriate the whole kaluk class by terrorism. The actual conflict now proceeding in the villages of Russia does, of course, involve great hardship. Probably the most truthful and objective account yet written of it is to be found in Mr Maurice Hindus's *Red Bread*. Mr Hindus is a Russian by birth, but he has lived mainly in America and is by no means a Communist in outlook. We see in his account of the life today in the village he was born in, a process of change, devastatingly rapid to the older peasantry, exhilarating and glorious to the younger generation. The new co-operative farming, mechanized and efficient, is being superimposed on a traditional village system; we see the older peasants gradually forced into the system, partly by direct coercion and fear of exile, partly by pressure of public opinion. Russia is over-night abandoning the incredible inefficiency of the old open field system, which we in this country abandoned in the eighteenth century, and adopting the most up-to-date long-scale mechanized farming, which individualism still makes impossible in this country. The change in Russia does not, we venture to assert, now involve a half of the long-drawn-out suffering of our own industrial revolution, when whole generations of men, women and children were ruthlessly sacrificed for the sake of the new profits. The laments of the older peasantry read like the heartrending complaints of our own hand-loom weavers, when they too were deprived of their old method of livelihood by more efficient mechanical means.

The differences are two. First, that in Russia the industrial revolution is being organized deliberately by the State, which must therefore take the blame for mistakes and for suffering which, when caused incidentally by the stimulus of profit, were attributed to unalterable economic laws. Secondly, in Russia, the revolution is being accomplished with the enthusiastic co-operation of the great majority of the younger generation and is being accepted by the mass of the whole population who believe, in spite of present hardship, that the Government, for the first time in history, is their government; they know that those who organize make no profit for

72

themselves, and that their own efforts will be rewarded – as they already are in many cases – by an improvement in their standard of living.

Why then should we not welcome this attempt to break the ice of the ages? We do not hold that the same methods are necessary or desirable here, and there is plenty of room for criticizing the Soviet Government. There have been and still are excesses. But we see in Russia the one country in the world which is doing great things, which is tackling, in the interests of the many, the problem of economic organization which we have so far failed to tackle. It seems an opportunity for learning something, not for indulging in Churchillian bombast.

4 July 1931

There was another way for the New Statesman *to deal with Churchillian reaction.*

The Mouthpiece of Britain   'MacFlecknoe'

Mr Winston Churchill has asked the BBC for an opportunity of 'stating the British side of the cause' with regard to India.

> I saw, in vision, the Congress meet;
> I heard the trampling of countless feet;
> For it seemed to me that the British race
> Had come en masse to the trysting place;
> And I heard them, as with one voice, proclaim
> That the pledges given in Britain's name
> Must be duly honoured; for there they'd stay
> With a resolute will to find a way
> (Tories and Labour for once agreed,
> And those who cling to the Liberal creed),
> Till the obstacles vanished one by one
> And India owned that the work was done.
>
> But through that cry from a million throats
> I heard, though faintly, the harsher notes
> Of a voice that babbled of doubts and fears
> To a tiny handful of backwoods peers;
> Of the treacherous bargains Irwin made;
> Of vested int'rests, and faith betrayed,

Of Gandhi's programme of fire and sword;
Of British blood in a torrent poured;
Of the Empire's doom that was surely written,
Unless men heeded the voice of Britain.
    Yet the British people, I grieve to say,
In their muddle-headed, phlegmatic way,
Just shrugged their shoulders, while Winston still
Expounded (solus) the people's will,
And smiled a little behind their hand;
Then settled down to the work they'd planned.

22 August 1931

The New Statesman *was the only periodical to which James Joyce ever contributed.*

From a Banned Writer to a Banned Singer   James Joyce

In this remarkable document, Mr James Joyce gives his impressions of his friend, Mr Sullivan of the Paris Opera, in several of his leading roles. Many competent critics regard Mr Sullivan as the most extraordinary dramatic tenor that Europe has listened to for the last half century. Mr Joyce complains that Mr Sullivan is 'banned' or at least unknown in England. The reflections written here were sent in a letter to Mr Sullivan by Mr Joyce after an occasion on which the singer was carried shoulder high by his Marseilles admirers after an astonishing performance in Guillaume Tell. *One knows of no other similar documents, no letters in a tone of intense admiration and sardonic banter sent by, say, Manzoni to Rubini, or by Flaubert to Gilbert Duprez, or by Ibsen to the Swedish Nightingale. Lovers of grand opera will recognize the operatic situations and phrases with which the text is studded and detect under the mask of their Christian names the three divi who figure in the final quartette. The document which the singer has kindly placed at our disposal is published with Mr Joyce's permission.*

He strides, booted with anger, along the spurs of Monte Rossini, accompanied solely by Fidelion, his mastiff's voice. They quarrel consonantly about the vocality of the wind, calling each and its other clamant names.

    Just out of kerryosity howlike is a Sullivan? It has the fortefaccia of a Markus Brutas, the wingthud of a spreadeagle, the body uniformed of a metropoliceman with the brass feet of a collared grand. It cresces up in

74

Aquilone but diminuends austrowards. It was last seen and heard of by some macgilliccuddies above a lonely valley of their reeks, duskening the greylight as it flew, its cry echechohoing among the anfractuosities: *pour la dernière fois!* The blackbulled ones, stampeding, drew in their horns, all appailed and much upset, which explaints the guttermilk on their overcoats.

A pugilant gang theirs, per Bantry! Don Philip, Jay Hell, Big O'Barry of the Bornstorms, Arthur, siruraganist who loosed that chor. Damnen. And tramp, tramp, tramp. And T. Deum sullivamus.

Faust of all, of curse, damnation. But given Parigot's Trocadéro for his drawingroom with Ballaclavier in charge at the pianone the voice becomes suburban, sweethearted and subdued. The heat today was really too much of a hot thing and even Impressario is glad to walk his garden in the cool of the evening, fanning his furnaceface with his sweltertails. *Merci, doux crépuscule!*

Who is this that advances in maresblood caftan, like Hiesous in Finisterre, his eyeholes phyllistained, his jewbones of a crossbacked? A little child shall lead him. Why, it's Strongman Simpson, Timothy Nathan, now of Simpson's on the Grill! Say, Tim Nat, bald winepresser, hast not one air left? But yeth he hath. Regard! Auscult! He upbraces for supremacy to the potence of Mosthigh and calls upon his baiters and their templum: You daggones, be flat!

What was in that long long note he just delivered? For the laib of me I cannot tell. More twopenny tosh and luxus languor about I singabob you? No such thing, O son of an envelope. Dr to J.S. Just a pennyplain loafletter from Braun and Brotmann and it will take no rebutter. You may bark Mrs Liebfraumich as long as you love but you must not burk the baker. Pay us disday our daily bread. And oblige.

On his native heath. Speech! Speech! cry the godlets. We are in land of Dan. But their words of Muskerry are harsh after that song of Othello. *Orateur ne peut, charlatan ne daigne, Sullivan est.*

11.59 p.m. *Durch diese hohle Gasse muss er kommen.* Guillaume's shot telled, sure enough. But will that labour member for Melckthal be able to bring off his coo for the odd and twentieth supererogatory time? *Wartemal!* That stagesquall has passed over like water off a Helvetian's back. And there they are, yodelling yokels, none the worse for their ducking and *gewittermassen* as free as you fancy to quit their homeseek *heimat* and leave the ritzprinz of their chyberschwitzerhoofs all over both worlds, cisalpic and transatlantine. And how confederate of gay old Gioacchino to have composed this finale so that Kamerad Wagner might be saved the annoyance

75

of finding flauts for his *Feuerzauber! Pass auf!* Only four bars more! He draws the breathbow: that arrownote's coming. Aim well, Arnold, and mind puur blind Jemmy in the stalls! But, great Scott, whas is thas for a larm! Half a ton of brass in the band, ten thousand throats from Thalwyl: Libertay, libertay lauded over the land. (Tay!) And pap goes the Calville!

Saving is believing but can thus be? Is this our model vicar of Saint Wartburgh's, the reverend Mr Townhouser, Mus. Bac., discovered flagrant in a *montagne de passe*? She is obvious and is on her threelegged sofa in a half yard of casheselks, Madame de la Pierreuse. How duetonically she hands him his harp that once, bitting him, whom caught is willing: do blease to, fickar! She's as only roman as any *puttana madonna* but the trouble is that the reverend T is reformed. She, *simplicissima*, wants her little present from the reverend since she was wirk worklike never so nice with him. But he harps along about Salve Regina Terrace and Liza, mine Liza, and sweet Marie. Till she cries: bilk! And he calls: blak! O.u.t. spells out!

Since we are bound for a change of supper, was that really in faith the reverend Townhouser for he seemed so verdamnably like? *Ecco trovato!* Father Lucullus Ballytheacker, the parish priest of Tarbert. He was a songful soul at the keyboard and could achieve his Château Kirwan with cigar thuriferant, without ministrance from platform or pulpit, chase or church. Nor used he to deny his Mary neither. *Nullo modo.* Up to maughty London came a muftimummed P.P. Censored.

Have you got your knife handy? asks the bellman Saint Andy. Here he is and brandnew, answers Bartholomew. Get ready, get ready, scream the bells of Our Lady. And make sure they're quite killed, adds the gentle Clotilde. Your attention, sirs, please, bawls big Brother Supplice. *Pour la foi! Pour la foi!* booms the great Auxerrois.

Grand spectacular exposition of gorge cutting, mortarfiring and general martyrification, bigleighted up with erst classed instrumental music. *Pardie!* There's more sang in that Sceine than mayer's beer at the Guildhall. Is he a beleaper in Irisk luck? Can he swhipstake his valentine off to Dublin and weave her a frock of true blue poplin to be neat for the time Hugenut Cromwell comes over, gentlest lovejesus as ever slit weasand? Their cause is well sainted and they are centain to won. Still I'll pointe half my crown on Raoul de Nangis, doublet mauve and cuffs of buff. Attagirl! *Ah ah ah ah ah ah viens!* Piffpaff, but he's done it, the bully mastiff again. And woops with him through the window tallyhoed by those friers pecheurs who are self-barked. Dominie's canes. Can you beat that, you papish yelpers? To howl with the pups!

Enrico, Giacomo and Giovanni, three dulcetest of our songsters, in liontamers overcoats, holy communion ties and cliqueclaquehats, are met them at a gaslamp. It is kaputt and throws no light at all on the trio's tussletusculums. Rico is for carousel and Giaco for luring volupy but Nino, the sweetly dulcetest, tuningfork among tenors, for the best of all; after hunger and sex comes dear old *somnium*, brought on by prayer. Their lays, blent of feastings, June roses and ether, link languidly in the unlit air. Arrives a type in readymade, dicky and bowler hat, manufactured by Common Sense and Co. Ltd., carrying a bag of tools. Preludingly he conspews a portugaese into the gutter, recitativing: now then, gents, by your leave! And, to his job. Who is this hardworking guy? No one but Geoge, Geoge who shifts the garbage can, Geoge who stokes in the engine room, Geoge who has something to say to the gas (*tes gueules!*) and mills the wheel go right go round and makes the world grow lighter. *Lux!* The aforesung Henry. James and John stand mouthshut. Wot did I say? Hats off, *primi assoluti!* Send him canorious, long to lung over us, high topseasoarious! Guard safe our Goege!

27 February 1932

From the beginning the New Statesman *published the work of foreign as well as British writers. In 1913 and 1914 it was printing Marinetti, Chekhov and others. In the Twenties and Thirties, Gorky.*

The Old Man and the New   Maxim Gorky

The nineteenth century has been grandly described as 'the age of progress', and the description is appropriate. In that century, reason, scientifically investigating the phenomena of nature and making elemental forces serve economic interests, had reached incredible heights and had created 'the marvels of machinery'. Studying organic life, reason discovered a world of invisible bacteria – a discovery not fully utilized, because of the disgraceful and cynical conservatism of a social system based on classes.

But, along with scientific thought, another line of thought was no less sedulously at work, creating among the bourgeoisie that mood known as *Weltschmerz* – the philosophy and poetry of pessimism. In 1812 Lord Byron published the first Cantos of *Childe Harold*, and soon after Giacomo Leopardi, Count Monaldo, philosopher and poet, began to preach the doctrine that knowledge only reveals the impotence of reason, that everything in the world is 'vanity of vanities' and that only suffering and death are real. The doctrine is not a new one. It has been exquisitely propounded in Ecclesiastes; it was preached by Buddha; it oppressed the mind of Jean-Jacques Rousseau, Chateaubriand, and many other men of intellect and genius. Its revival by Byron and Leopardi is difficult to explain merely on the ground of the unhappiness felt by the representatives of the feudal aristocracy at their defeat by the bourgeoisie, though, of course, when the triumphant bourgeoisie inherited the land of the aristocracy it also inherited certain ideas, and ideas have a pernicious habit of surviving the conditions which created them.

The survival of the idea of pessimism is due to the fact that in essence it is a deeply conservative philosophy; by declaring existence to be senseless it thereby satisfies the inquiries of not very inquisitive minds, and comforts the lovers of tranquillity. Moreover, the circle of consumers of ideas is neither big nor numerous, and there is no abundance of originality and courage in thought.

In the nineteenth century it was Germany which most sedulously supplied Europe with pessimistic thought. Without speaking of the pessimistic philosophy of Schopenhauer and Hartmann, Max Steirner the anarchist showed himself to be a great pessimist in his work *The One and His Property*. This also applied to Nietzsche, the propounder of the 'superman' of bourgeois aspiration, an aspiration which, retrogressing from the illustrious Frederick the Great, came down to Bismarck, to the half-witted Wilhelm II, and, in our own day to the manifestly abnormal Hitler.

In the first twelve years of the nineteenth century, the model of the 'superman' for the bourgeoisie in Europe was *le petit caporal* Bonaparte. The influence of this half-fantastic biography on the thought and feeling of many generations of the bourgeoisie has not yet been sufficiently studied, though it was Bonaparte himself who demonstrated most convincingly the need for the bourgeoisie to back the 'hero' and the inevitability of the 'hero's' fall. We know how beautifully, if somewhat hysterically, the role of the 'hero' as a maker of history was shown by Carlyle. He was believed, but this did not prevent the heroes from shrinking to the dimensions of Clemenceau, Churchill, Woodrow Wilson, Chamberlain and other 'leaders of civilized mankind'.

The 'decline in Europe', that is, the spiritual impoverishment, the exhaustion of genius, the complete lack of organizing ideas, is also common to the two Americas and to the whole world. The bright stars in the firmament of the bourgeoisie are extinguished. The 'Forsytes' in England, the 'Buddenbrooks' in Germany, 'Mr Babbitt' in the United States, are all incapable of producing heroes and are compelled to make them out of small adventurers. In a country where once the hazy placid optimism of Dickens eclipsed the healthy criticism of Thackeray, and where the solemn voice of Thomas Hardy was so recently stilled, such pernicious books, filled with pain and despair, as *Death of a Hero*, by Richard Aldington, are now possible. The literature of twentieth-century France has not even risen to the standard of artistic generalities achieved by Galsworthy, Thomas Mann and Sinclair Lewis. Romain Rolland, the author of that epic *Jean Cristophe*, a man of courage and honesty, is outside national limitations, having been driven out of his own country by the brutal stupidity of the bourgeoisie. This was France's loss, but the world's gain.

Rentier France is in the temper of a boa-constrictor which, having swallowed more food than it can digest, fears at the same time that what it has not managed to devour will be gobbled up by other animals of its type. But, of course, intellectual poverty does not prevent the customary senseless aspiration of the shopkeepers to seize new fertile lands for the enslavement of peoples in the colonies. But the accumulation of this golden fat is pressing more and more monstrously and heavily on the brain of the bourgeoisie. The spectacle of Europe's spiritual impoverishment is amazing, though men are more and more frequently to be met with who are ashamed to live in the cynical conditions created by the shopkeepers, and who realize that the shopkeepers' gamble on the 'hero' individualism is lost.

To the question, 'What did the social culture of Europe achieve in the nineteenth century?' only one answer is possible. It made Europe so monstrously rich that it is self-evident that her riches are the cause of the unprecedented impoverishment of the working class. It dug a pit between the working class and the bourgeoisie so deep that the fall of the bourgeoisie into it had become inevitable.

The process of a cultural revolution is rapidly developing in what was once the old Russia of the Romanov Tsars and half-literate tradesmen who sold the treasures of their land to capitalists of Europe by robbing the peasants and workers and abandoning them to the power of ignorant priests, extinguishers of reason. The pressure of State and Church on the freedom of human reason was heavier and more brutal in Russia than in Western Europe. Lack of opportunity, exile, persecution, even death, were the lot of men of genius in old Russia – and to a degree unheard of in other countries.

I am not one of those blind 'lovers of my country', but I am sure that I know 'the soul of the people'. This big, capacious soul was permeated and

79

poisoned by dark, monstrous superstitions and barbaric prejudices, resulting from the primitive conditions of life. By the way, the knowledge of this soul must be got not through Turgenev, Tolstoy, and Dostoevsky, but through its folk-lore and songs, its tales and proverbs and legends, its customs and church-rites, its sects, its trades, its work in the field of creative craftsmanship. Only this will give a complete idea, and a painful idea, of the deep ignorance of the people, side by side with their wonderful variety of gifts.

In the twentieth century the Russian bourgeoisie had no very attractive picture of a peasant in literature. The moujik in the years 1905–7, having decided to free the land for himself, took to burning and wrecking the estates of the landowners, and, at the same time, treated the workers 'on strike' with hostility and distrust. In the year 1917 he felt the simple right of the working class, and, as we know, stuck his bayonet into the ground and refused to kill the workers and peasants of Germany.

Since then fifteen years have gone by. What has been achieved in the Union of Soviets during those years ? I shall not speak of the great work of industrializing a technically backward country, a country with a primitive economy, which has been finally destroyed by the Imperialist war of capitalists, followed by the war of the working class against the barbarians of their own country and those of Europe – a war in which the working class fought for the right to culture and the intelligentsia for the right of the bourgeoisie to rob.

I shall not refer to the growth of universities and scientific research institutes, the wealth of mineral resources discovered in those years, sufficient to ensure economic and cultural development of the country for centuries to come. All this is known. Only those who are blinded by animal interests and inhuman class prejudices can fail to see these conquests of reason and will. Only those who are too lazy, or those journalists whose masters have forbidden it, can fail to see the truth.

In the Union of Soviets there is one master; that is its fundamental gain and its difference from bourgeois states. This master is the workers' and peasants' organization of the pupils of Lenin. The aim they have set themselves is perfectly clear. It is to create for every unit of the 160 millions of peoples of different races conditions for the free growth of their gifts and genius. In other words, to set in motion this inert mass of potential nerve and brain power, to stir it to creative effort. Is this possible of achievement ?

It is actually being achieved. The mass of people, before whom all roads of culture are opening, have, springing up in their midst, tens of thousands of gifted youths who go into every sphere in which energy can be applied –

science, engineering, art, administration. Inevitably, so far, we live and work not without mistakes. The property instinct, stupidity, laziness, and vices inherited from the centuries cannot be eradicated in a decade and a half. Only a lunatic, or one whose spite amounts to lunacy, will dare to deny this undisputed fact – the distance dividing the young generation of workers in Europe from the manifest achievements of universal human culture is, in the Soviet Union, decreasing at an amazing rate.

Leaning on what is of stable value in the old culture, the people of the Soviet Union are courageously developing their national yet universal human values. Anybody who wants to can see it for himself in the young literature and music of the national minorities in the Union. We must mention the emancipated woman of the Turkish and Turco-Finnish races, and her aspirations and efforts for a new mode of life.

Legislation in the Soviet Union springs from the working masses of the people, from the soil of their practical experience and the changing conditions of their work. The Soviet of Peoples Commissaries merely translates experience into law. They can make no laws that are not in the interests of the working class, because there is no other master in the country.

No one could point to a single decree passed by the Soviet of Peoples Commissaries which had not as its aim the satisfaction of the cultural needs and demands of the working people. Leningrad is to be reconstructed, and participating in the conferences relating to this reconstruction are architects, sanitary specialists, physicians, writers, artists, and, of course, workers representing the factories. As far as I know this is not a practice followed in Europe.

The Soviet Press, with a quarrelsomeness which, to my mind, is excessive and even harmful, because it arouses impossible hopes in the brain of the bourgeoisie, criticizes any mistakes made in the work of construction and shows up the pernicious stupidity of the old life, a thing not permitted to the bourgeois Press, which corrupts the uncultured reader with sadistic details of murders and sensational stories of clever rogues.

For fifteen years the masses of workers and peasants have been sending forth from their midst thousands of inventors, and are still doing so – inventors who save the Union hundreds of millions of roubles and are gradually doing away with needless imports. A worker who feels himself to be master of production naturally develops a sense of responsibility towards the country, and this impels him to greater efforts to improve the quality of his work and to lower the cost of production.

Before the revolution the peasant worked in conditions of the seventeenth century; he was entirely dependent on the caprices of the elements, on his exhausted soil, split up into tiny plots. Now he is rapidly being supplied with tractors, sowers, combines; he makes extensive use of fertilizers, and at his service are twenty-six agrarian research institutes. He had no idea of science, yet experience makes him see the force of it and the power of human thought.

The young fellow from the country who enters the factory, run on the most modern and perfect inventions of technical science, enters a world of phenomena which strikes his imagination and sets him free from the old barbaric superstitions and prejudices. He sees the work of the mind embodied in complex machinery and machine tools, and though he may spoil something or other, the growth of his intelligence compensates for any material loss sustained. He sees that the masters of the factories are workers like himself, that the young engineer is the son of a worker or peasant. He soon comes to regard the factory as a school, opening up opportunities for an unrestricted development of his abilities. If he shows promise he is sent to one of the higher educational institutions, though there are works now which have their own higher technical schools. His nerve and brain power, in which the gift of investigation and perception of world phenomena is latent, is vigorously stirred by the many amenities his father had never known. He frequents theatres acknowledged to be the best in Europe, he goes to concerts, he reads the classic literatures of Europe and old Russia, he visits museums, he studies his country, as no one before him had studied it.

The capitalists, in their cynical game, are gambling on the stupidity of the masses, while in the Soviet Union an order is in process of development based on the conscious right of the working class to power. A new man is growing up in the Soviet Union and already one can form an accurate estimate of his quality.

He has faith in the organizing force of reason, a faith lost and spent by the intelligentsia of Europe in sterile endeavours to reconcile the anomalies of class. The new man feels himself to be the creator and master of the new world, and though he still lives under hard conditions he knows that it is his function to establish better; that is his purpose, the business of his rational will. That is why he has no ground to be a pessimist. He is not young biologically only, but historically as well. He is a force which has only just realized its direction and significance in history, and he is going on with his work of cultural construction with all the daring of a young, still unused force, guided by a clear and simple teaching. The groanings and the lamentations of a Spengler, frightened by machinery, amuse him, because he well knows that machinery has never been utilized in the cultural interests of the hundreds of millions of men slavishly employed in manual work. He sees that the bourgeoisie has ignominiously lost in its gamble on individualism; that, on the whole, the bourgeoisie has not helped the development of individuality; that, in self-interest, the bourgeoisie has limited that development by overtly and covertly proclaiming as an 'eternal truth' the right to power over the majority of men. Repudiating bourgeois animal individualism, the new man realizes only too well the high integrity of individuality closely bound up with the collective. He himself is that individuality, freely pouring his energy and inspiration into the whole, into the process of the labour of the whole. Capitalism has brought men to anarchy, with the menace of a great catastrophe hanging over them. Any honest man can see it.

The aim of the old world is to restore, by process of physical and moral violence in the shape of wars in the field and bloodshed in the streets of cities, the old, rotten, inhuman 'order' outside of which Capitalism cannot exist. The aim of the new man is to free the working masses from old superstitions and prejudices of race, nation, class and religion, to create a universal brotherhood, each member of which will work according to his capacity and receive according to his need.

14 May 1932

For the socially significant poets of the Thirties the New Statesman *was at once a medium and a scapegoat; they used it; and abused it. Much early work by their* chef d'école *appeared in its pages.*

Poem   W. H. Auden

      O Love, the interest itself in thoughtless Heaven
      Make simpler daily the beating of man's heart; within
      There in the ring where name and image meet

      Inspire them with such a longing as will make his thought
      Alive like patterns a murmuration of starlings
      Rising in joy over wolds unwittingly weave;

Here too on our little reef display your power
This fortress perched on the edge of the Atlantic scarp
The mole between all Europe and the exile-crowded sea;

And make us as Newton was who in his garden watching
The apple falling towards England became aware
Between himself and her of an eternal tie.

For now that dream which so long has contented our will,
I mean, of uniting the dead into a splendid empire,
Under whose fertilizing flood the Lancashire moss

Sprouted up chimneys and Glamorgan hid a life
Grim as a tidal rock-pool's in its glove-shaped valleys,
Is already retreating into her maternal shadow

W. H. Auden [*9 June 1956*]

84

Leaving the furnaces gasping in the impossible air
The flotsam at which Dumbarton gapes and hungers,
While upon wind-loved Rowley no hammer shakes

The cluster of mounds like a midget golf-course, graves
Of some who created these intelligible dangerous marvels;
Affectionate people, but crude their sense of glory

Far-sighted as falcons, they looked down another future,
For the seed in their loins were hostile, though afraid of
    their pride,
And tall with a shadow now, inertly wait

In bar, in netted chicken-farm, in lighthouse,
Standing on these impoverished constricting acres,
The ladies and gentlemen apart, too much alone

Consider the years of the measured world begun
The barren spiritual marriage of stone and water.
Yet, O, at this very moment of our hopeless sight

When inland they are thinking their thoughts but are watch-
    ing these islands
As children in Chester look to Moel Fammau to decide
On picnics by the clearness or withdrawal of her treeless
    crown

Some dream, say yes, long coiled in the ammonite's slumber
Is uncurling, prepared to lay on our talk and kindness
Its military silence, its surgeon's idea of pain.

And called out of tideless peace by a living sun
As when Merlin, tamer of horses, and his lords to whom
Stonehenge was still a thought, the Pillars passed

And into the undared ocean swung north their prow
Drives through the night and star-concealing dawn
For the virgin roadsteads of our hearts an unwavering keel.
                                        16 July 1932

In 1932 George Orwell was still signing his work for the New Statesman *with his real name, Eric Blair. His connection with the paper extended over many years and was not ended even when Kingsley Martin was forced to take a very difficult decision – to refuse to publish Orwell's articles against the Spanish Government at the height of the Spanish Civil War.*

Common Lodging Houses   Eric Blair

Common lodging houses, of which there are several hundred in London, are night-shelters specially licensed by the LCC. They are intended for people who cannot afford regular lodgings, and in effect they are extremely cheap hotels. It is hard to estimate the lodging-house population, which varies continually, but it always runs into tens of thousands, and in the winter months probably approaches fifty thousand. Considering that they house so many people and that most of them are in an extraordinarily bad state common lodging houses do not get the attention they deserve.

To judge the value of the LCC legislation on this subject, one must realize what life in a common lodging house is like. The average lodging house ('doss house', it used to be called) consists of a number of dormitories, and a kitchen, always subterranean, which also serves as a sitting-room. The conditions in these places, especially in southern quarters such as Southwark or Bermondsey, are disgusting. The dormitories are horrible fetid dens, packed with anything up to a hundred men, and furnished with beds a good deal inferior to those in a London casual ward. Normally these beds are about 5 ft. 6 in. long by 2 ft. 6 in. wide, with a hard convex mattress and a cylindrical pillow like a block of wood; sometimes, in the cheaper houses, not even a pillow. The bed-clothes consist of two raw umber-coloured sheets, supposed to be changed once a week, but actually, in many cases, left on for a month, and a cotton counterpane; in winter there may be blankets, but never enough. As often as not the beds are verminous, and the kitchens invariably swarm with cockroaches or black beetles. There are no baths, of course, and no room where any privacy is attainable. These are the normal and accepted conditions in all ordinary lodging houses. The charges paid for this kind of accommodation vary between 7*d.* and 1*s.* 1*d.* a night. It should be added that, low as these charges sound, the average common lodging house brings in something like £40 net profit a week to its owner.

Besides the ordinary dirty lodging houses, there are a few score, such as the Rowton Houses and the Salvation Army hostels, that are clean and decent. Unfortunately, all of these places set off their advantages by a discipline so rigid and tiresome that to stay in them is rather like being in jail. In London (curiously enough it is better in some other towns) the common lodging house where one gets both liberty and a decent bed does not exist.

The curious thing about the squalor and discomfort of the ordinary lodging house is that these exist in places subject to constant inspection by the LCC. When one first sees the murky, troglodytic cave of a common lodging house kitchen, one takes it for a corner of the early nineteenth century which has somehow been missed by the reformers; it is a surprise to find that common lodging houses are governed by a set of minute and (in intention) exceedingly tyrannical rules. According to the LCC regulations, practically everything is against the law in a common lodging house. Gambling, drunkenness, or even the introduction of liquor, swearing, spitting on the floor, keeping tame animals, fighting – in short, the whole social life of these places – are all forbidden. Of course, the law is habitually broken, but some of the rules are enforceable, and they illustrate the dismal uselessness of this kind of legislation. To take an instance: some time ago the LCC became concerned about the closeness together of beds in common lodging houses, and enacted that these must be at least 3 ft apart. This is the kind of law that is enforceable, and the beds were duly moved. Now, to a lodger in an already overcrowded dormitory it hardly matters whether the beds are 3 ft. apart or 1 ft.; but it does matter to the proprietor, whose income depends upon his floor space. The sole real result of this law, therefore, was a general rise in the price of beds. Please notice that though the space between the beds is strictly regulated, nothing is said about the beds themselves – nothing, for instance, about their being fit to sleep in. The lodging-house keepers can, and do, charge 1s. for a bed less restful than a heap of straw, and there is no law to prevent them.

Another example of LCC regulations. From nearly all common lodging houses women are strictly excluded; there are a few houses specially for women, and a very small number – too small to affect the general question – to which both men and women are admitted. It follows that any homeless man who lives regularly in a lodging house is entirely cut off from female society – indeed, cases even happen of man and wife being separated owing to the impossibility of getting accommodation in the same house. Again, some of the cheaper lodging houses are habitually raided by slumming parties, who march into the kitchen uninvited and hold lengthy religious services. The lodgers dislike these slumming parties intensely, but they have no power to eject them. Can anyone imagine such things being tolerated in a hotel? And yet a common lodging house is only a hotel at which one pays 8*d*. a night instead of 10*s*. 6*d*. This kind of petty tyranny can, in fact, only be defended on the theory that a man poor enough to live in a common lodging house thereby forfeits some of his rights as a citizen.

One cannot help feeling that this theory lies behind the LCC rules for common lodging houses. All these rules are in the nature of interference-legislation – that is, they interfere, but not for the benefit of the lodgers. Their emphasis is on hygiene and morals, and the question of comfort is left to the lodging house proprietor, who, of course, either shirks it or solves it in the spirit of organized charity. It is worth pointing out the improvements that could actually be made in common lodging houses by legislation. As to cleanliness, no law will ever enforce that, and in any case it is a minor point. But the sleeping accommodation, which is the important thing, could easily be brought up to a decent standard. Common lodging houses are places in which one pays to sleep, and most of them fail in their essential purpose, for no one can sleep well in a rackety dormitory on a bed as hard as bricks. The LCC would be doing an immense service if they compelled lodging-house keepers to divide their dormitories into cubicles and, above all, to provide comfortable beds; for instance, beds as good as those in the London casual wards. And there seems no sense in the principle of licensing all houses for 'men only' or 'women only', as though men and women were sodium and water and must be kept apart for fear of an explosion; the houses should be licensed for both sexes alike, as they are in some provincial towns. And the lodgers should be protected by law against various swindles which the proprietors and managers are now able to practise on them. Given these conditions, common lodging houses would serve their purpose, which is an important one, far better than they do now. After all, tens of thousands of unemployed and partially employed men have literally no other place in which they can live. It is absurd that they should be compelled to choose, as they are at present, between an easy-going pigsty and a hygienic prison.

3 September 1932

Nearly all the most considerable novelists of the century wrote from time to time for the New Statesman. *E. M. Forster deals here with the Grundys and Nosey Parkers with their mania for interfering with private lives.* New

Statesman policy under Kingsley Martin called for more control of public business by the State; but it campaigned just as consistently and steadily for social freedom and non-interference by the State with private morals.

Mrs Grundy at the Parkers' E. M. Forster

When Mrs Grundy called at the Parkers', she was informed by the maid that they were 'Not at home.'

'Do you mean that your mistress is out or is not out?' she asked. Doris collapsed, and said that Mrs Parker was in, but had rather a headache, and so was resting.

'Then have the goodness to tell her I am here, without further prevarication,' said Mrs Grundy, and seated herself in the austere drawing-room – such a contrast to her own cosy parlour. The Parkers enjoyed making themselves as well as other people uncomfortable, which she had never been able to understand.

'Ah, Amelia,' said her friend, coming in. 'Quite a voice from the past!'

'Edith, I called about something or other, but Doris's untruthfulness has put it clean out of my head. Why did she say you were not at home when you are?'

'Well, it is only a form of words; a modern convention. One has to keep pace with the times if one is to guide them and they sorely need our guidance.'

'And have you the headache or have you not?' Mrs Grundy persisted.

'I have. Still I am glad you forced your way in, for I want to talk about our methods of work. You don't interfere with people in quite the right way, you know. You are too desultory and impetuous. That was all right in the nineteenth century, when life was slow, and one could point out one impropriety after another with one's umbrella as they crossed the street – but today! Why, you'll get knocked down. You'll be run over by a motor bicycle, and before you can see whether it was a girl on the pillion she will have disappeared. Today one must select and one must plan; civilization is so complicated. Think of our triumph the other month – that man who was arrested for bathing at Worthing.'

'Ah, don't talk to me about bathing. I often wish there was no such place in these islands as the sea-shore.'

'That is shallow of you. If there was no sea-shore, how could we catch people on it? Besides, I approve of bathing, provided it is so regulated that no one can enjoy it. We are working towards that. You were a great pioneer, but you made the mistake of trying to suppress people's pleasure.

I try to spoil their pleasure. It's much more effective. I don't say, "You shan't bathe." I say, "You shall bathe in an atmosphere of self-consciousness and fear," and I think I am succeeding. I certainly have at Worthing.'

'I expect I read about Worthing, but where everything is so shameless one gets bewildered.'

'Why, the case of the visitor who bathed properly clad, and then returned to his bathing machine to dry. Thinking no one could see him, since the machine faced the ocean, he left its door open. He had reckoned without my foresight. I had arranged that a policewoman should be swimming out at sea. As soon as she observed him, she signalled to a policeman on shore, who went to the machine and arrested him. Now, Amelia, would you have ever thought of that?'

'I certainly shouldn't have. I don't like the idea of women policemen at all. A woman's proper place is in her home.'

'But surely there can't be too many women anywhere.'

'I don't know. Anyhow, I am glad the visitor was arrested. It will stop him and others going to English seaside resorts, which is a step in the right direction, and I hope the magistrate convicted.'

'Oh, yes. Magistrates nearly always convict. They are afraid of being thought to condone immorality. As my husband points out, that is one of our strong cards. In his private capacity the magistrate was probably not shocked. The average man simply doesn't mind, you see. He doesn't mind about bathing costumes or their absence, or bad language, or indecent literature, or even about sex.'

At this point she rang the bell. 'Doris, bring the smelling salts,' she said, for Mrs Grundy had fainted. When consciousness had been restored, she continued: 'No, nor even about sex, and we social workers of the twentieth century cannot ignore sex; what we can do is to make it a burden. And we are faced with the difficulty that the average man, if left to himself, does not brood, and forgets to persecute. He has habits instead of ideals. Isn't that too dreadful! He says in effect, "I go my way about sex or whatever it is, and I let others go theirs, even if I think it queer. It isn't my funeral." But it is going to be his funeral – at least I hope so.'

'And what is the average woman?'

'She is a little more satisfactory, a little more apt to be scared. Though I have known sad cases of women saying, "Pore thing, we don't take no notice although she did 'ave a little Unwanted, we treats her like one of ourselves." You see what we are up against – tolerance, good-temper, and unsuspiciousness. It has been no easy matter to cover England with regulations from end to end.'

Mrs Grundy sighed. 'I admit you manage to interfere more than I did,' she said. 'I expect it is as you say, and I was too impulsive. I hurried too much from vice to vice when I was young. I stood outside the music halls, to stop people going in, and then I heard profanity in the cab-shelter, and went to silence that, and while I was doing so the music hall filled up. I went to Africa to make the cannibals monogamous, and during my absence the Deceased Wife's Sister's Bill became law in England. When it's daylight I can see people, which is scandalous, and at night-time I can't see them, which is worse. I simply don't know where to turn, and while I am insisting on ulsters for sunbathing the Deceased Husband's Brother's Bill will probably become law, too. You have a sounder method, Edith. You have brought in education, of which I never dreamt, and I am not surprised that your wonderful work gives you the headache.'

'My headache, to which you now refer, has nothing to do with my work,' replied her hostess. 'It has been caused by a piece of bad news which has just arrived from the Continent. Even my husband is upset by it.'

'If I had my way there never would have been any Continent,' cried Mrs Grundy, and proceeded to ask a series of agitated questions, such as had the bad news to do with chocolates being allowed in theatres, were sweepstakes to be legalized, was Sunday cricket spreading, had the King been seen patting a race-horse, and so on.

'No, you are quite off the lines. It has to do with something inside us.'

'And pray, what can the Continent have to do with my inside?'

'Amelia, you must make an effort to understand. It concerns you as much as myself. It is a sort of discovery that has been made by a kind of doctor. Just as our work was prospering and we were making people stodgy and self-conscious under the pretence of building better citizens, just as we had bullied the lay authorities and coaxed the clerical into supporting us, just as interference was about to be launched on a colossal scale. . . . But I despair of explaining what it is. Perhaps my husband will be able to.' And she called out, 'Nosey!'

Mr Nosey Parker, who now joined the ladies, was scarcely their equal as a field worker. Where he excelled was on committees. Without being obtrusive, he managed to generate that official uneasiness upon which all their work depended. Let me explain. Each member of any committee has, of course, broken the law at some time or other, and desires to prove to his colleagues that he hasn't; he can do this best by being timid in discussion, and by voting for any measure that deprives the public of enjoyment. Furthermore, each member either has a daughter or feels that he ought to have one, and dares not oppose any censorship of art or literature in consequence. Mr Parker realized all this. He had only to say 'We must think of our daughters' and every one thought of their skins. He had only to say 'I am not narrow-minded, but . . .' and broadness became impossible. He raised the banner of respectability and called it idealism. *Sauve qui peut* was embroidered in brown on its folds. And under it the municipal councillors or the board of magistrates or the jurymen gathered, all afraid of being found out, and when their duties concluded they had not done at all what they intended (which was, generally speaking, to let their fellow creatures alone), but had stopped one man from doing this and another from doing that, and had sent a third man to prison.

'Nosey, do explain what has happened,' his wife said.

'Nothing has happened. It is only an idea.'

'Ideas have never troubled me, especially from abroad,' said Mrs Grundy.

'You are fortunate. I own myself worried by this one. The idea is that we, who have helped others, ought now to be helped, and it is proposed to help us by pulling us to pieces.' He shuddered. 'To you that means little. But I have always had doubts of my own solidity. How can I bring it home to you? They desire to examine your intimate fabric, Mrs Grundy: they suspect it of being diseased. My wife's and my own they assert to be even fouler than yours. They believe that we all three try to improve people because we envy their happiness and had bad luck ourselves when we were young. What so alarms me is that there is no bitterness in the new attack. We are actually objects of pity.'

'And, pray, is that all?' said Mrs Grundy, with her dry little laugh. 'You may have given Edith a headache over this, but you have no such effect on me. I am quite accustomed to pity. I got a lot as a girl. It is merely a term of abuse, and I shall castigate it in due season. Good-bye, my dear sir, and take an old woman's advice: keep away from foreign newspapers in the future.' And, gathering up her skirts, she left their house – perhaps for her doom.

'Poor thing, she doesn't know the danger,' said Mrs Parker, looking after their friend anxiously, and observing how she first scowled at Doris and then lectured some navvies for using a word which had been devitalized twenty years previously by Mr Bernard Shaw. 'She is brave because she is out of date. But we – oh Nosey, Nosey! Fancy, if it gets known that interference is a disease which ought to be interfered with. Men and women will live as they like, they will be natural and decent about one another, and we shall boss and nag at them no more.'

'Too true, too true,' said her husband, 'and yet I see a ray of hope. Our enemies cannot interfere with us unless they organize. As individuals they are helpless. They will have to form Freedom Leagues, or Anti-Fuss Societies or sign Beach Pyjama Covenants, and they cannot do so without constituting themselves into committees. And as soon as they meet on committees . . . yes, I think we shall survive after all.'

Will they survive? Only Doris, who is the future, can tell.

10 September 1932

'Timothy's got some very bad habits.'

Famous novelists were not the only artists to find a medium for their opinions and experiences in the New Statesman.

The Waterfall   Ethel Smyth

An Autobiographical Incident

The following adventure, easily the most vivid of many childish recollections, does not figure in my autobiography *Impressions That Remained*, because the author-friend on whom I inflicted the early chapters of the MS inquired if I really imagined any publisher would print such an anecdote?

The scene was Paris, 1917; and as this victim of budding author's ruthlessness was on three days' leave from the front, at first I believed he must be suffering from shell shock; and so did two intelligent and literary women of our acquaintance: 'Comment!' they cried, 'vous voulez qu'elle supprime cette histoire délicieuse! . . . si essentiellement anglaise, si drole, si innocente! et puis si jolie!!'

But the face of the Englishman (his name was M----ce B----g) assumed a mulish expression well known to his friends, and he went on quietly repeating 'It must be cut out.' And cut out it was.

Last summer I told the story to a group of dashing, up-to-date, equally literary but *English* experts. All scoffed at the idea of its shocking anyone nowadays; such prudery was a thing of the past, they said.

I thought to myself at the time '*I wonder?*' And today more than ever do I wonder, remembering the recent case of a Polish Count who gave rein to an apparently irresistible passion for certain monosyllabic words: good strong Anglo-Saxon words which, however, are seldom met with in polite letters. The publisher not only returned his poems with horror, but thought well to communicate with the police; and presently these judges of literature were escorting the poet to prison.

We of Puritan extraction are careful to lock up in our bosoms any hair-raising monosyllables that come our way. Yet at this moment the thought of that guileless foreigner haunts and daunts me a little; so does a picture by Gillray – or is it H.B.? – showing a female of unprepossessing appearance seated in the stocks, so ran the legend, for having used language ill becoming a lady. And I do so want to attend a 'Court' disguised as a Doctor of Music. The robes are gorgeous and ritually quite correct according to the Lord Chamberlain's Office. . . .

It's no use; I simply cannot keep this thing to myself! Risk or no risk, consequences or no consequences, here's the story.

Like most little girls I envied boys on many counts, but chiefly for a costume which does away with difficulties and dangers that embitter the lives of their athletic sisters. How blessed to climb trees without risk of finding yourself suspended in mid air by your sash; to jump wheelbarrows and not catch your toe in a hem; to crawl through hedges and never get stuck half way because of your petticoats; to fall head over heels without the added humiliation of what our French governesses called making an exposition of yourself! Altogether, how wonderful must be a life in which hooks and eyes, strings and pins play no part: a life solidly based on buttons!

At this point one thought of various matters; of occasions when, nature being nature, things have to be done secretly and swiftly; O how simple merely to . . .

Stop; that's not a safe road to travel. Better make a fresh start.

In my memoirs I spoke of our passion for dressing up; also of our box of grandeurs (pronounced grandjers), consisting of old ball dresses, wreaths, and spangles of my mother's, military oddments of my father's – false beards, feathers, and so on. Well; one cold autumn day, in the holidays, looking as like Fenimore Cooper's Indians as these rather sophisticated 'properties' allowed, out we rushed, war-whooping, into the garden.

Now the fancy dress on which I had set my heart was one of my brother's suits. He was twelve, I only eight, and the idea was unfavourably received as derogatory to the dignity of a male wardrobe. But eventually, tricked out with a gold-braided Horse Artillery forage cap and a crimson sash, I was graciously permitted to be a Bush Policeman and told to look alive.

My duties were turn about to hide in the shrubbery and dash out in pursuit of Indians; but all too soon came the moment when nice-minded little girls explain they have left their pocket-handkerchief up at the house and will be back directly. Not so this Bush Policeman. Here at last was a chance of testing the greatest of all advantages conferred by male attire; had I not often seen my brother disappear behind a tree . . . to emerge almost immediately, gazing aloft as though looking for birds' nests? . . . The Red Indian game seemed slacking off . . . there was no time to be lost . . . I nipped into the shrubbery. . . .

O horror! Midway in a devastating experience that proved the difference between dreams and realities, came shouts of 'Ethel! quick, quick! collect wood! We're going to build a wigwam,' and simultaneously the tramp of approaching feet! . . . All but caught in a shocking situation, too flustered to invent an excuse for bolting up to the house, condemned to stand in misery for the rest of that icy afternoon handing boughs to my elders, I think the severest moralist will allow that, far from fitting the crime, the punishment was several sizes too large for it.

The deed was never discovered; in such cases the ingenuity of the young is limitless. But, incredible as it seems in a country-bred child, not till some years later did I grasp why this gallant experiment was foredoomed to failure! Children can be very unobservant, and such was the case with me.

How dark it has got! Is that you, Polish Count, in the corner? . . . and that odd-looking object near the fire, is it the stocks, or only one of those T-shaped foot-rests beloved of the gouty ? . . . And you, dim but resplendent vision in knee-breeches, a queer-shaped peaky hat tucked under your arm ? . . . Mercy on us! You must be, you are, the Lord Chamberlain! . . .

Avaunt phantoms, or rather come out into the open, Polish Count, Lord Chamberlain, and gouty foot-rest! I defy the lot of you. Of course, people can read anything they choose into words, but unless you tamper with mine I defy you to make clear to the jury what, exactly, happened that day in the garden at Sidcup Place, Foots Cray, Kent. And to avoid possible misapprehensions I will only add what perhaps should have been said sooner, that the spot chosen for our wigwam was just where a little stream runs into the pond. And that is the reason – the sole reason – why this story is called 'The Waterfall'.

8 October 1932

Cyril Connolly wrote for the New Statesman *for many years. He sent some of the best despatches which the paper had from the front during the Spanish Civil War. Above all, it was in the* New Statesman *that he established himself as a critic with his novel reviews which set a new high standard for that branch of journalism. Here he is in Greece.*

Spring Revolution   Cyril Connolly

The boredom of travel! There is an acute condition which develops in enforced lulls before the wholesome drudgery of getting from place to place makes a brute of one again. If you knew how bored we were in Athens! Stagnation and self-disgust engender a low fever that wastes the curiosity and resolution that might have cured them. The weather was too bad to go anywhere and the nearest sun was in Egypt. Sleeping late to shorten the day, one went to the window and found the Acropolis and the Parthenon blocking the horizon. A thing of beauty, that is a joy once or twice, and a standing reproach afterwards. Downstairs it would be nearly lunch time. In the bar, which was an embottled corridor smelling of gin and Gold Flake, the Greek business men jollied each other up in cinema American and Trocadero English. The sombre dining-room was like the Dickensian coffee-room of a Midland hotel. The French dishes all tasted the same, like food on a liner; the Greek joints seemed made of sweetened gelatine.

Coffee was served in the lounge amid the engineering papers, and snatches of conversations.

'I hope you are never troubled by the green-eyed monster.'

'Pliss, Mr Ansull?'

'Why, you know what the green-eyed monster is! Jealousy!'

'O yais, Mr Ansull. Pliss?'

A walk in the afternoon. Tram-lines, blocks of yellow houses, demolition, everywhere the metamorphosis of a tenth-rate Turkish market town into a tenth-rate Californian suburb. A pause in the book-shop where one must choose between expensive art books on the Acropolis and diseases of the stomach, or sixpenny editions of Edgar Wallace and Wilhelm Meister. There were also the newspapers, and glancing at them phrases would enter with a little stab and begin to fester. 'Ruskin, one felt, would have disapproved,' 'wherein promise and achievement touch hands very agreeably,' and 'Bébé is painting a portrait of Baba.' Before the Dragoman's ingenious vulgarities I would gape like a mesmerized chicken.

In the hotel thé dansant would have begun. A hundred bearded ladies have brought their black little daughters. The ballroom reeks with stale flowers and cheap scent. All the tables are taken. The fathers in spats and clean collars try to eradicate from their faces the expression which forty years of Levantine practices have implanted. The mothers employ the vocabulary of the underworld of elegance. 'Très réussi . . . convenable . . . on aura dit . . . ça se remarque.' The daughters fidget. The young men attempt polish. All move in the psychologist's wonderland which is revealed to us when we watch charmless people trying to be charming. The band strikes up 'Come on, uglies, do your stuff!'

At dinner a piano and a violin play evening music, with *Peer Gynt, Rosamund, Chansons sans Paroles, Toselli*, wistful and gallant compositions that empty over one all the slops of capitalist sentiment. Afterwards, there are the cinemas with wooden seats and German films unknown to the Academy, and a few places for supper. In Greek cabarets one is not allowed to sit with a woman unless one has champagne. The sexes are therefore divided on opposite sides of the floor. If a young man dances with a 'hostess' he scurries back at the finish like a male spider trying to escape from the nuptial embrace before he is eaten. The girls are sulky, the whisky bad. Back in the room there are mosquitoes in February and the *Continental Daily Mail*, four days old, with an article saying that our greatest living stylist is Mr Somerset Maugham. This day, repeated ten times, was typical of Athens. As boredom gathered momentum one felt all the ingredients of personality gurgling away like the last inch of bathwater. One became a carcase of nonentity and indecision, a reflection to be avoided in mirrors. Why go abroad ? Why travel ? Why exchange the regard of a clique for the stare of a concierge ?

On the day of the elections the sun was shining. It was one of those Sundays in early spring when there is an air of displacement. A sensation of keels lifting from the mud, of new skin, and of new acquaintances. We motored to Kephissia for lunch. The butter was good. Refugees paraded about in their hideous best, and gramophones played in Tatoi. At Hagios Mercurios we looked down over the plain to the blue lake of the Aegean, Chalcis, Eretria, and the snows and forests of Euboea. In the wet weather we could not conceive a reason for being here, in a moment it became impossible to imagine being anywhere else.

Everybody had voted when we got back to Athens. The bars and cinemas were closed, and in the restaurant wine was served from tea-pots and drunk in cups as in an old-fashioned speakeasy. Crowds cheered. Venizelos was sweeping the polls. 'The best thing for the country.' As in all companies where politics are discussed, to compensate the dullness of the subject, one began to feel an illusion of far-sightedness and worldly wisdom.

Next morning the town was quiet. I was particularly annoyed to find an antique shop closed and tried to get the concierge to rout up the missing proprietor. Down the empty street moved a kind of grey Noah's Ark on wheels. At the English tailor's we heard the news. Venizelos had lost the election. Tsaldaris, the head of the Royalist-Popular party, was in, but he and all his colleagues had been put in prison. There had been a revolution in Macedonia. The shops were closing and the proprietors of travel agencies stood in the doors with the keys in their hands. Lorries of mud-coloured soldiers passed down the street distributing handbills. Martial law was proclaimed, newspapers suppressed, groups of people shot at sight, by order of the Chief of the revolution, Plastiras. By lunch-time it was accepted that we were under a dictatorship. All the plats du jour were 'off' and we bawled out the head waiter. An aeroplane flew over, dropping pamphlets in which Plastiras described the collapse of parliamentary government. Rumours collected. Plastiras was a Venizelist. He was going to cancel the elections and keep Venizelos in office. He was not a Venizelist and was going to govern by himself. I walked down the University boulevard. It was warm and sunny. A straggling crowd that was moving about suddenly thickened and made way for two archaic fire engines, whose hoses were playing over them. The smell of wet earth followed their path through the sunshine. Everybody laughed and teased the soldiers on the engines, who laughed back at them. One could not tell if they were

98

shouting Tsaldaris or Plastiras. In the hotel we received more explanations. Plastiras was in prison. 'It had all been done very quietly.' Venizelos and Tsaldaris had arranged it with the President of the Republic. The soldiers had fraternized. The dictatorship was a wash-out. General Condylis had flown last night to Athens from Salonica. Plastiras had taken him prisoner, but he had escaped and was marching with his army from Thebes on Athens. Tonight there would be a big battle as Condylis wished to avenge Plastiras's execution of the Cabinet in 1922.

We went out again. 'Tsaldaris' was being shouted everywhere. There were still crowds in the boulevard, but suddenly down a side street we saw a ragged collection of men marching with staves in their hands. On many of these the olive leaves still remained. Some only carried small untrimmed branches. They looked like a woodcut of Jack Cade's rebellion in a child's history book. It was at this moment that we heard the rattle of machine-guns. Everyone ran giggling into doorways. 'They're only blank, of course,' was said knowingly. Turning into Stadium Street some soldiers rushed up to us pointing down and crying 'Kato, Kato!' The machine-guns began again.

The street, in normal times so straight and dull, became an enormous affair of shadows and relief, of embrasures and exposed spaces. The kiosk at the corner seemed as far away as it would to a baby who could just walk, or a very lame old man. As we ran round the corner volleys seemed to come from every direction. People threw themselves flat on the ground and hid behind trees. The Noah's Ark passed down the end of the street with the snouts of machine-guns thrusting from the wooden windows. We came to a little restaurant where we had dined the day before. The crowd surged on the steps and the doors were barricaded, but when they recognized us we were let in. From the balcony more men with staves could be seen in the falling night. A small cannon boomed at intervals and shook the windows. A man was helped by with a bleeding arm. While one-half of my brain dealt in realities – revolution, street fighting, baptism of fire – the other continued to function as if nothing had happened, and remembering that someone was coming for a cocktail, I insisted on trying to telephone to the hotel that we should be a little late. The wires were cut, but if we went back directly we should still be in time for them. Back on the balcony we saw a crowd collecting at the foot of the University. A man ran up the steps waving something. A machine-gun rattled, the crowd fell apart, and revealed him lying in a growing pool of blood and brains. An ambulance bell sounded and a man with a woman in a mink coat walked down the middle of the street from the other side. We slipped out and made our way round by alleys and crossed the Place de la Constitution in the yellow dusk. We reached the side entrance to the Grande Bretagne. It was heavily barricaded. We knocked and rang, when another crowd of people surged round the corner and up the steps. There was a feeling of real hopelessness and panic. After them, turning elaborately, slid the armoured car. What had seemed comic and antediluvian was now implacable and fatal. The machine-guns pointed straight at us; a fat woman tried to turn us out from behind a pillar where we were, but we shoved her quickly away. The car passed without firing and we got round to the other entrance. Inside all was cheerfulness and commotion; everyone felt important and with a reason for living. We dined in a large party, including several people whom we had avoided for two weeks, and retired upstairs with a gramophone and a bottle of whisky. A business man explained everything. Plastiras was master of the situation. He was a patriot. He would force a coalition between Venizelos and Tsaldaris. The latter's victory was illegal because he had promised the refugees bonuses which he hadn't got. 'Plastiras does not play. He knows his head is at stake. If he fails he will shoot himself. He had eight officers shot who tried to arrest him. General Condylis was locked up. He sent him a telegram signed "Tsaldaris" telling him to fly to Athens. When he landed he took him prisoner. There would be no battle.' It was the best thing that could happen for Greece. The army was with him. The night was dark and cold. Outside a few small tanks patrolled the streets. Machine-guns looked down from the balcony of the palace. The armoured car in previous volleys had chipped bits off the masonry along the front of the hotel. It was quiet and with the cessation of firing people began to feel the anti-climax and grow irritable. One wondered why one was cooped up with the tiresome business man; with the young Frenchman and his crisp platitudes; the clergyman's daughter chorus girl of dubious status, who was explaining why she would never have a lady-dog in the house. Everyone separated, secretly hoping for the roar of Condylis's artillery.

Next morning we were woken by the noise of trams. There were no guns on the palace. Newspapers arrived. The shops were open and nothing remained of the day before but the pool of wet blood by the University, surrounded by gaping students. At a time when Plastiras was supposed to be master of the situation, he had surrendered to the eight generals who commanded the rest of the army for Venizelos.

The dictatorship was over, and had been over since eight o'clock the night before. Plastiras had seized the government with only one regiment; his party had repudiated him. Whether a patriot or a power-grabber he was ridiculous. He had wounded thirty-three people, and killed one and cured two or three discontented pleasure seekers of the curious stoppage of the sensibilities to which they had fallen victims. They, while secretly admitting the futility of the eye-witness, the meaninglessness and stupidity of all that had happened, knew also that they had tasted the intoxication, and the prestige of action, and were soon rearranging the events of the day on a scale, and in an order, more worthy of the emotions which had been generated by them.

18 March 1933

During the Thirties many of Stephen Spender's poems appeared in the New Statesman.

The Bird   Stephen Spender

Passing, men are sorry for the birds in cages
And for constricted nature hedged and lined;
But what do they say to your pleasant bird
Physical delight, since years tamed?

Behind centuries, behind the continual hill,
The wood you felled, your clothes, the slums you built,
Only love knows where that bird dips his head;
Only the sun, soaked in memory, flashes on his neck.

Dance, will you? And sing? Yet pray he is dead.
Invent politics to hide him and lawsuits and suits:
Now he's impossible and quite destroyed like grass
Where the fields are covered with your more living houses.

I never hear you are happy but I wonder
Whether it was at a shiny bazaar,
At a brittle dance or a party, that you could create
Procrastination of nature, for your talk and laughter are
Only a glass that flashes back the light
And that covers only hate.

Will you not forgive him? I have signed his release,
Alarming and gentle like the blood's throb,
And his fountain of joy wakes the solitary stag
From his cherished sleep.

But if you still bar your pretty bird, remember
Revenge and despair are prisoned in your bowels.
Life cannot pardon the ideal without scruple,
The enemy of flesh, the angel and destroyer,
Creator of a martyrdom serene, but horrible.

27 May 1933

Short stories were printed, not very often, simply as works of art, but authors writing with the New Statesman *in mind tended to give their work a social significance which made it new statesmanly. It would, in fact, be easy to collect from its pages a large volume of 'committed' fiction; but Literary Editors did not by any means insist on 'committal' and Kingsley Martin was scrupulous in never interfering with his Literary Editors, so that the front and back halves of the paper seemed sometimes out of step. In spirit they never were.*

The Property of a Lady Sylvia Townsend Warner

Rooms in London require dusting daily if they are to look like the rooms of a lady. And so, every morning, Miss Amy Cruttwell's rooms were dusted from head to foot, first the bedroom and then the sitting-room; for all things belonging to her must look like the property of a lady, it was their doom and hers. Twice a week the silver was carefully polished, and the china, the Dresden figures and the two *millefleur* boots, entirely encrusted with sharp microscopic forget-me-nots, were washed in the handbasin. While the dusting was being performed Miss Cruttwell was energetic, angry, and contented, the natural rancour of a single woman of sixty living on a small pension flowing easily from her like a sweat. But by eleven o'clock, when all was over, and the brooms and brushes and dusters put away in the ottoman, it was an even hazard whether her pride or her weariness would conquer, whether she would look round with a toss of the head, saying to herself: 'Well, if any one comes, it's ready for them,' or, suddenly prostrated by a longing for a cup of tea, stare at the gas-ring and remember how lonely she was, how old, and how neglected, and how, all her life long, she had kept the lady-standard flying, had been scrupulously clean, scrupulously honest, scrupulously refined, and nothing had come of it save to be old and neglected and lonely.

For though the rooms were so neat, so ready for company, even to having a little bunch of flowers always fresh and daintily arranged, very few people entered them. Sometimes the wife of the clergyman looked in, sometimes the retired matron of the nursing-home where Miss Cruttwell's appendix had been removed, sometimes the widow of the gentleman whose secretary Miss Cruttwell had been. They were all nice people, she had never known any but nice people. They appreciated her delicacy of mind and of person, they admired the tea-set, they said how refreshing it was to see a tree from the window; and sometimes, tactfully, they would leave behind a tin of fancy biscuits or a cardboard box containing grapes.

But they did not come often. And when they came, they went. And when they invited her to their houses and she accepted the invitation (she did not always accept) she, too, had to go away; and the warmth of the white wine would evaporate in the bus, and when she had reached home and put away her gloves and shaken her hat and hung up her coat and put her walking shoes on their trees and lit the gas-fire there was not much left but melancholy.

And so things went on till she was sixty-five. Then, almost simultaneously, she had influenza and was given a portable wireless. The wireless came from the widow of the gentleman and with it came a note, saying: 'Dearest Amy. I am so sorry I have not been to see you for such a long time. I am still terribly rushed, I do not quite know when I shall get to you. But with this wireless and all the delightful things which are now being broadcast, I'm sure you will not miss my stupid conversation. Your ever affly, Muriel.'

Suddenly enraged by the hollowness of the universe and of all human intercourse, Amy Cruttwell sniffed contemptuously at the wireless as a cat sniffs at milk which it knows to be sour, and turned away; but presently she came back, as a starving cat will, and turned it on. Out came, swimmingly, a polite voice announcing football news. Not interrupting it she went and sat in the farthest corner, stiffly upright, clenching her hands together, darting furious glances about the empty room. So that was what it was all worth, their pretence of friendship! That was all the appreciation one might look for, all the sympathy! – great vulgar wirelesses which they had not even the civility to bring themselves. And every now and then an orange.

'Why should I stay alive?' she asked the announcer. Why, indeed, to buy herrings and the cheapest china tea, to mend old nightdresses, take circulars from the letter-box, dust two rooms daily which no one entered but herself. No one noticed her, she glided through the wet streets unscanned. No one would notice if she died, she said to herself, passionately tasting the sweet strong knowledge of what a to-do her death, her suicide, would create, what stabbing surprise, what pangs of conscience, what convicting self-reproaches among her false friends.

The football news had given place to music on the organ. Those sturdy waves bore her onward, buoying her resolve. And with tears coursing down her cheeks she wrote several farewell letters, letters which would be found after her death, and read at the inquest, and published in the papers. But at last, alas! she must descend from her happiness, she must decide how to kill herself.

Not water, not gas. She rejected those two elements. Her rooms were at the top of the house, but she did not want to die in the street, with people treading in her blood. A seemly death, something dignified. (*She looked so wonderfully peaceful, so inscrutable, lying there, with all her wrinkles gone. But Oh! so sad.*) Aspirin! A whole bottle of Aspirin, and she had such. One did not swallow the tablets, one crushed them in water and drank.

'The last time I shall use this teaspoon,' she thought proudly. And the tablets were all crushed, and the drink, chalky white, deadly white, ready in the medicine glass. . . . Like knowing that two and two make four she knew that she had not the courage to drink. Cold with fear, sick with shame she turned off the wireless, and tore up the farewell letters, and emptied the medicine glass into the slop-pail. A whole bottle of Aspirin wasted.

It was dusk, and the muffin-bell had gone ringing down the street, when she came out of her despair as out of a terrible slumber. But one thing came with her, a raging resolve to claw her way into those easy minds which could forget her, a living woman, for weeks and then send her a wireless. If she could not get into the papers by one means she could by another.

So she dressed with her usual exact care, lacing her shoes briskly, smoothing on her gloves; for a lady is always known by her neatness of hand and foot. The drizzle of rain was rather pleasant than otherwise. She felt herself walking lightly and elegantly, comparing well with those other figures bundled in their winter coats, dragging children after them or foolishly pursuing buses. She passed the dairy, and the fish-shop, and the rather vulgar greengrocer with an outside stall where, shopping, she fortified herself with thoughts of Parisian economy. But tonight she had no business with these. She was going to Whiteleys to steal, to be a shoplifter. Grandly the soft full illumination of Whiteleys flowered on the dowdy

Queen's Road. There in the windows were those composition women whose hair never needed cutting, who never felt the cold. In their taper fingers they held silk stockings or dangled silver foxes, and at their feet were scent-sprays and eiderdown quilts and tickets saying neatly, £5 19s. 6d. She would begin by stealing a scent-spray.

Under that floodlit central dome everything was warm and luxurious and orchid-like. The air was sweet, the carpets were soft, the lights, like sharp amorous caresses, pinched little gasps of reflected light from cut-glass bottles and crystal powder bowls and sleek virgin boxes of cosmetics and rich sleepy cakes of soap. Out of this glittering jungle looked the blueish flesh-tints of the woman behind the counter, thinking she knew Miss Cruttwell, nodding good evening to her. 'Can I assist you, madam?' 'No, thank you,' said Miss Cruttwell and lingered ostentatiously, fingering the clasp of that large useful bag which had been a present from the retired matron of the nursing-home. And slowly she walked round, her mind licking the smooth soaps, the flasks of scent, the powder-puffs and the rejuvenating face-creams. This she would have, and that; and when she had finished with that counter she would go on to the adjacent cheap fashionable jewellery, the pearls as large as cherries, the jade earrings; and end up with the gloves.

To one who has led a virtuous life, sin is the easiest thing in the world. No experience of unpleasant consequences grits that smooth sliding fall, no recollection of disillusionment blurs that pure desire. Like a blackbird singing, Amy Cruttwell stole two cakes of soap, a swansdown powder-puff, a scent-spray, and a bottle of golden perfume which swayed voluptuously within its glassy walls; and then, going on to the cheap and fashionable jewellery, she stole a brooch on a velvet pad, an enamelled cigarette case, and a bracelet of weighty false pearls. Theft was in itself such rapture, such calm of paradise, that she forgot that she was stealing for a purpose; it was only at the glove counter, surveying the more serious texture of leather, that she recollected the need to be discovered and arrested and taken to the police and put into the papers. Parading herself, making a slow motion of theft, she took a pair of gloves; but no one noticed. Another pair; and now the bag was full. But it was all right. They never arrested one at the counter because of the unpleasant impression it made upon the other customers. They shadowed one, followed one to the door, struck there. And walking proudly over the dense carpets she reached the swinging doors of glass and metal, and passed into the raw cold outside.

A man came hastily after her, brushed against her, set the bag swinging, and went on.

She waited. She waited. People went in and out, but no one noticed her. Tethered to one of the pillars was a dog, a poodle, whose shaved flanks twitched with cold. It lengthened itself towards her, gave a sniff, sighed disappointedly and turned away again, to sit with patience under the draughty portico on the cold stone. She waited. But no one came, no one noticed her.

At last she began to walk home.

14 October 1933

Cecil Day Lewis was another young poet whose work appeared in the New Statesman.

Sonnet   C. Day Lewis

This man was strong, and like a sea-cape parted
The tides; there were not continents enough
For all his fledged ambitions; the hard-hearted
Mountains were moved by his explosive love:
Was young; yet between island and island
Laid living cable and whispered over seas;
When he sang, our feathery woods fell silent;
His smile put the fidgeting hours at ease.
See him now, a cliff chalk-faced and crumbling,
Eyes like craters of volanoes dead;
A miser with the tarnished minutes fumbling;
A queasy traveller from board to bed:
The voice that charmed spirits grown insane
As the bark of a dog at the end of a dark lane.

26 May 1934

In 1934 H. G. Wells was in Moscow. He had a long talk with Stalin and this was published as a dialogue in the New Statesman: *it is of historical interest and value.*

Stalin - Wells Talk: The Verbatim Record

Wells: I am very much obliged to you, Mr Stalin, for agreeing to see me. I was in the United States recently. I had a long conversation with President Roosevelt and tried to ascertain what his leading ideas were. Now I have come to you to ask you what you are doing to change the world.

Stalin: Not so very much.

Wells: I wander around the world as a common man, and, as a common man, observe what is going on around me.

Stalin: Important public men like yourself are not 'common men'. Of course, history alone can show how important this or that public man has been; at all events you do not look at the world as a 'common man'.

Wells: I am not pretending humility. What I mean is that I try to see the world through the eyes of the common man and not as a party politician or a responsible administrator. My visit to the United States excited my mind. The old financial world there is collapsing; the economic life of the country is being reorganized on new lines. Lenin said: 'We must learn to do business', learn this from the capitalists. Today the capitalists have to learn from you to grasp the spirit of Socialism. It seems to me that what is taking place in the United States is a profound reorganization, the creation of planned, that is, socialist economy. You and Roosevelt begin from two different starting-points. But is there not a relation in ideas, a kinship of ideas and needs, between Washington and Moscow? In Washington I was struck by the same thing that I see going on here; they are building offices, they are creating a number of new State regulation bodies, they are organizing a long-needed civil service. Their need, like yours, is directive ability.

AMERICA AND RUSSIA

Stalin: The United States is pursuing a different aim from that which we are pursuing in the USSR. The aim which the Americans are pursuing arose out of the economic troubles, out of the economic crisis. The Americans want to rid themselves of the crisis on the basis of private capitalist activity without changing the economic basis. They are trying to reduce to a minimum the ruin, the losses caused by the existing economic system. Here, however, as you know, in place of the old destroyed economic basis, an entirely different, a new economic basis has been created. Even if the Americans you mention partly achieve their aim, i.e. reduce these losses to a minimum, they will not destroy the roots of the anarchy which is inherent in the existing capitalist system. They are preserving the economic system which must inevitably lead, and cannot but lead, to anarchy in production. Thus, at best, it will be a matter, not of the reorganization of society, not of abolishing the old social system which gives rise to anarchy and crises, but of restricting certain of its bad features, restricting certain of its excesses. Subjectively, perhaps, these Americans think they are reorganizing society; objectively, however, they are preserving the present basis of society. That is why, objectively, there will be no reorganization of society.

Nor will there be planned economy. What is planned economy, what are some of its attributes? Planned economy tries to abolish unemployment. Let us suppose it is possible, while preserving the capitalist system, to reduce unemployment to a certain minimum. But surely no capitalists would ever agree to the complete abolition of unemployment, to the abolition of the reserve army of unemployed the purpose of which is to bring pressure on the labour market, to ensure a supply of cheap labour. Here you have one of the rents in the 'planned economy' of bourgeois society. Furthermore, planned economy presupposes increased output in those branches of industry which produce goods that the masses of the people need particularly. But you know that the expansion of production under capitalism takes place for entirely different motives, that capital flows into those branches of economy in which the rate of profit is highest. You will never compel a capitalist to incur loss to himself and agree to a lower rate of profit for the sake of satisfying the needs of the people. Without getting rid of the capitalists, without abolishing the principle of private property in the means of production, it is impossible to create planned economy.

Wells: I agree with much of what you have said. But I would like to stress the point that if a country as a whole adopts the principle of planned economy, if the Government gradually, step by step, begins consistently to apply this principle, the financial oligarchy will at last be abolished, and Socialism, in the Anglo-Saxon meaning of the word, will be brought about. The effect of the ideas of Roosevelt's 'new deal' is most powerful, and in my opinion they are socialist ideas. It seems to me that instead of stressing the antagonism between the two worlds, we should, in the present circumstances, strive to establish a common tongue for all the constructive forces.

Stalin: In speaking of the impossibility of realizing the principles of planned economy while preserving the economic basis of capitalism, I do not in the least desire to belittle the outstanding personal qualities of Roosevelt, his initiative, courage, and determination. Undoubtedly Roosevelt stands out as one of the strongest figures among all the captains of the contemporary capitalist world. That is why I would like once again to emphasize the point that my conviction that planned economy is impossible under the conditions of capitalism does not mean that I have any doubts about the personal abilities, talent, and courage of President Roosevelt. But if the circumstances are unfavourable, the most talented captain cannot reach the goal you refer to. Theoretically, of course, the possibility of marching gradually, step by step, under the conditions of capitalism, towards the goal which you call Socialism in the Anglo-Saxon meaning of the word, is not precluded. But what will this 'Socialism' be? At best, bridling to some extent the most unbridled of individual representatives of capitalist profit, some increase in the application of the principle of regulation in national economy. That is all very well. But as soon as Roosevelt, or any other captain in the contemporary bourgeois world, proceeds to undertake something serious against the foundation of capitalism, he will inevitably suffer utter defeat. The banks, the industries, the large enterprises, the large farms, are not in Roosevelt's hands. All these are private property. The railroads, the mercantile fleet, all these belong to private owners. And, finally, the army of skilled workers, the engineers, the technicians – these too are not at Roosevelt's command, they are at the command of the private owners; they all work for the private owners. We must not forget the functions of the State in the bourgeois world. The State is an institution that organizes the defence of the country, organizes the maintenance of 'order'; it is an apparatus for collecting taxes. The capitalist State does not deal much with economy in the strict sense of the word; the latter is not in the hands of the State. On the contrary, the State is in the hands of capitalist economy. That is why I fear that, in spite of all his energy and abilities, Roosevelt will not achieve the goal you mention, if indeed that is his goal. Perhaps, in the course of several generations, it will be possible to approach this goal somewhat; but I personally think that even this is not very probable.

SOCIALISM AND INDIVIDUALISM

Wells: Perhaps I believe more strongly in the economic interpretation of politics than you do. Huge forces striving for better organization, for the better functioning of the community – that is, for Socialism – have been brought into action by invention and modern science. Organization, and the regulation of individual action, have become mechanical necessities, irrespective of social theories. If we begin with the State control of the banks and then follow with the control of the heavy industries, of industry in general, of commerce, etc., such an all-embracing control will be equivalent to the State ownership of all branches of national economy. This will be the process of socialization. Socialism and individualism are not opposites like black and white. There are many intermediate stages between them. There is individualism that borders on brigandage, and there is discipline and organization that are the equivalent of Socialism. The introduction of planned economy depends, to a large degree, upon the organisers of economy, upon the skilled technical intelligentsia who, step by step, can be converted to the socialist principles of organization. And this is the most important thing, because organization comes before Socialism. It is the more important fact. Without organization the socialist idea is a mere idea.

Stalin: There is not, nor should there be, an irreconcilable contrast between the individual and the collective, between the interests of the individual person and the interests of the collective. There should be no such contrast, because collectivism, Socialism, does not deny, but combines individual interests with the interests of the collective. Socialism cannot abstract itself from individual interests. Socialist society alone can most fully satisfy these personal interests. More than that, socialist society alone can firmly safeguard the interests of the individual. In this sense there is no irreconcilable contrast between Individualism and Socialism. But can we deny the contrast between classes, between the propertied class, the capitalist class, and the toiling class, the proletarian class? On the one hand we have the propertied class which owns the banks, the factories, the mines, transport, the plantations in colonies. These people see nothing but their own interests, their striving after profits. They do not submit to the will of the collective; they strive to subordinate every collective to their will. On the other hand, we have the class of the poor, the exploited class, which owns neither factories, nor works, nor banks, which is compelled to live by selling its labour power to the capitalists and which lacks the opportunity to satisfy its most elementary requirements. How can such opposite interests and strivings be reconciled? As far as I know, Roosevelt has not succeeded in finding the path of conciliation between these interests. And it is impossible, as experience has shown. Incidentally, you know the situation in the United States better than I do, as I have never been there and I watch American affairs mainly from literature. But I have some experience in fighting for Socialism, and this experience tells me that if Roosevelt makes a real attempt to satisfy the interests of the proletarian class at the expense of the capitalist class, the latter will put another President in his place. The capitalists will say: Presidents come and Presidents go, but we go on for ever; if this or that President does not protect our interests, we shall find another. What can the President oppose to the will of the capitalist class?

Wells: I object to this simplified classification of mankind into poor and rich. Of course there is a category of people which strives only for profit. But are not these people regarded as nuisances in the West just as much as here? Are there not plenty of people in the West, for whom profit is not an end, who own a certain amount of wealth, who want to invest and obtain an income from this investment, but who do not regard this as their main object? They regard investment as an inconvenient necessity. Are there not plenty of capable and devoted engineers, organizers of economy, whose activities are stimulated by something other than profit? In my opinion there is a numerous class of capable people who admit that the present system is unsatisfactory, and who are destined to play a great role in future capitalist society. During the past few years I have been much engaged in, and have thought of the need for conducting, propaganda in favour of Socialism and cosmopolitanism among wide circles of engineers, airmen, military-technical people, etc. It is useless approaching these circles with two-track class-war propaganda. These people understand the condition of the world. They understand that it is a bloody muddle, but they regard your simple class-war antagonism as nonsense.

THE CLASS WAR

Stalin: You object to the simplified classification of mankind into poor and rich. Of course there is a middle stratum; there is the technical intelligentsia that you have mentioned and among which there are very good and very honest people. Among them there are also dishonest and wicked people, there are all sorts of people among them. But first of all mankind is divided into rich and poor, into property owners and exploited; and to abstract oneself from this fundamental division and from the antagonism between poor and rich means abstracting oneself from the fundamental fact. I do not deny the existence of intermediate, middle strata which either take the side of one or other of these two conflicting classes, or else take up a neutral or semi-neutral position in the struggle. But, I repeat, to abstract oneself from this fundamental division in society and from the fundamental struggle between the two main classes means ignoring facts. This struggle is going on and will continue. The outcome of the struggle will be determined by the proletarian class—the working class.

Wells: But are there not many people who are not poor, but who work and work productively?

Stalin: Of course there are small landowners, artisans, small traders; but it is not these people who decide the fate of a country, but the toiling masses, who produce all the things society requires.

Wells: But there are very different kinds of capitalists. There are capitalists who only think about profits, about getting rich; but there are also those who are prepared to make sacrifices. Take old Morgan, for example. He only thought about profit; he was a parasite on society, simply; he merely accumulated wealth. But take Rockefeller. He is a brilliant organizer; he has set an example of how to organize the delivery of oil that is worthy of emulation. Or take Ford. Of course Ford is selfish. But is he not a passionate organizer of rationalized production from whom you take lessons? I would like to emphasize the fact that recently an important change in opinion towards the USSR has taken place in English-speaking countries. The reason for this, first of all, is the position of Japan, and the events in Germany. But there are other reasons besides those arising from international politics. There is a more profound reason, namely, the recognition by many people of the fact that the system based on private profit is breaking down. In these circumstances, it seems to me, we must not bring to the forefront the antagonism between the two worlds, but should strive to combine all the constructive movements, all the constructive forces in one line as much as possible. It seems to me that I am more to the Left than you, Mr Stalin; I think the old system is nearer to its end than you think.

THE TECHNICIAN CLASS

Stalin: In speaking of the capitalists who strive only for profit, only to get rich, I do not want to say that these are the most worthless people, capable of nothing else. Many of them undoubtedly possess great organizing talent, which I do not dream of denying. We Soviet people learn a great deal from the capitalists. And Morgan, whom you characterize so unfavourably, was undoubtedly a good, capable organizer. But if you mean people who are prepared to reconstruct the world, of course you will not be able to find them in the ranks of those who faithfully serve the cause of profit. We and they stand at opposite poles. You mentioned Ford. Of course he is a capable organizer of production. But don't you know his attitude towards the working class? Don't you know how many workers he throws on the street? The capitalist is riveted to profit, and no power on earth can tear him away from it. Capitalism will be abolished not by 'organizers' of production, not by the technical intelligentsia, but by the working class, because the aforementioned strata do not play an independent role. The engineer, the organizer of production, does not work as he would like to, but as he is ordered, in such a way as to serve the interests of his employers. There are exceptions of course; there are people in this stratum who have awakened from the intoxication of capitalism. The technical intelligentsia can, under certain conditions, perform miracles and greatly benefit mankind. But it can also cause great harm. We Soviet people have not a little experience of the technical intelligentsia. After the October Revolution a certain section of the technical intelligentsia refused to take part in the work of constructing the new society; they opposed this work of construction and sabotaged it. We did all we possibly could to bring the technical intelligentsia into the work of construction; we tried this way and that. Not a little time passed before our trained intelligentsia agreed actively to assist the new system. Today the best section of this technical intelligentsia is in the front ranks of the builders of socialist society. Having this experience, we are far from underestimating the good and the bad sides of the technical intelligentsia, and we know that on the one hand it can do harm, and on the other hand it can perform 'miracles'. Of course, things would be different if it were possible at one stroke spiritually to tear the technical intelligentsia away from the capitalist world. But that is Utopia. Are there many of the technical intelligentsia who would dare break away from the bourgeois world and set to work to reconstruct society? Do you think there are many people of this kind, say, in England or in France? No; there are few who would be willing to break away from their employers and begin reconstructing the world.

ACHIEVEMENT OF POLITICAL POWER

Besides, can we lose sight of the fact that in order to transform the world it is necessary to have *political power*? It seems to me, Mr Wells, that you greatly underestimate the question of political power, that it entirely drops out of your conception. What can those, even with the best intentions in the world, do if they are unable to raise the question of seizing power, and do not possess power? At best they can help the class which takes power, but they cannot change the world themselves. This can only be done by a great class which will take the place of the capitalist class and become the sovereign master as the latter was before. This class is the working class. Of course, the assistance of the technical intelligentsia must be accepted; and the latter, in turn, must be assisted. But it must not be thought that the technical intelligentsia can play an independent historical role. The transformation of the world is a great, complicated, and painful process. For this great task a great class is required. Big ships go on long voyages.

Wells: Yes, but for long voyages a captain and a navigator are required.

Stalin: That is true, but what is first required for a long voyage is a big ship. What is a navigator without a ship? An idle man.

Wells: The big ship is humanity, not a class.

Stalin: You, Mr Wells, evidently start out with the assumption that all men are good. I, however, do not forget that there are many wicked men. I do not believe in the goodness of the bourgeoisie.

Wells: I remember the situation with regard to the technical intelligentsia several decades ago. At that time the technical intelligentsia was numerically small, but there was much to do, and every engineer, technical and intellectual, found his opportunity. That is why the technical intelligentsia was the least revolutionary class. Now, however, there is a superabundance of technical intellectuals, and their mentality has changed very sharply. The skilled man, who would formerly never listen to revolutionary talk, is now greatly interested in it. Recently I was dining with the Royal Society, our great English scientific society. The President's speech was a speech for social planning and scientific control. Today, the man at the head of the Royal Society holds revolutionary views, and insists on the scientific reorganization of human society. Your class-war propaganda has not kept pace with these facts. Mentality changes.

Stalin: Yes, I know this, and it is to be explained by the fact that capitalist society is now in a cul-de-sac. The capitalists are seeking, but cannot find, a way out of this cul-de-sac that would be compatible with the dignity of this class, compatible with the interests of this class. They could, to some extent, crawl out of the crisis on their hands and knees, but they cannot find an exit that would enable them to walk out of it with head raised high, a way out that would not fundamentally disturb the interests of capitalism. This, of course, is realized by wide circles of the technical intelligentsia. A large section of it is beginning to realize the community of its interests with those of the class which is capable of pointing the way out of the cul-de-sac.

Wells: You of all people know something about revolutions, Mr Stalin, from the practical side. Do the masses ever rise? Is it not an established truth that all revolutions are made by a minority?

Stalin: To bring about a revolution a leading revolutionary minority is required; but the most talented, devoted, and energetic minority would be helpless if it did not rely upon the at least passive support of millions.

Wells: At least passive? Perhaps subconscious?

Stalin: Partly also the semi-instinctive and semiconscious, but without the support of millions the best minority is impotent.

THE PLACE OF VIOLENCE

Wells: I watch Communist propaganda in the West, and it seems to me that in modern conditions this propaganda sounds very old-fashioned, because it is insurrectionary propaganda. Propaganda in favour of the violent overthrow of the social system was all very well when it was directed against tyranny. But under modern conditions, when the system is collapsing anyhow, stress should be laid on efficiency, on competence, on productiveness, and not on insurrection. It seems to me that the insurrectionary note is obsolete. The Communist propaganda in the West is a nuisance to constructive-minded people.

Stalin: Of course the old system is breaking down, decaying. That is true. But it is also true that new efforts are being made by other methods, by every means, to protect, to save this dying system. You draw a wrong conclusion from a correct postulate. You rightly state that the old world is breaking down. But you are wrong in thinking that it is breaking down of its own accord. No; the substitution of one social system for another is a complicated and long revolutionary process. It is not simply a spontaneous process, but a struggle; it is a process connected with the clash of classes. Capitalism is decaying, but it must not be compared simply with a tree which has decayed to such an extent that it must fall to the ground of its own accord. No; revolution, the substitution of one social system for another, has always been a struggle, a painful and a cruel struggle, a life-and-death struggle. And every time the people of the new world came into power they had to defend themselves against the attempts of the old world to restore the old order by force; these people of the new world always had to be on the alert, always had to be ready to repel the attacks of the old world upon the new system.

Yes, you are right when you say that the old social system is breaking down; but it is not breaking down of its own accord. Take Fascism for example. Fascism is a reactionary force which is trying to preserve the old world by means of violence. What will you do with the Fascists? Argue with them? Try to convince them? But this will have no effect upon them at all. Communists do not in the least idealize methods of violence. But they, the Communists, do not want to be taken by surprise; they cannot count on the old world voluntarily departing from the stage; they see that the old system is violently defending itself, and that is why the Communists say to the working class: Answer violence with violence; do all you can to prevent the old dying order from crushing you; do not permit it to put manacles on your hands, on the hands with which you will overthrow the old system. As you see, the Communists regard the substitution of one social system for another, not simply as a spontaneous and peaceful process, but as a complicated, long, and violent process. Communists cannot ignore facts.

Wells: But look at what is now going on in the capitalist world. The collapse is not a simple one, it is an outbreak of reactionary violence which is degenerating into gangsterism. And it seems to me that when it comes to a conflict with reactionary and unintelligent violence, Socialists can appeal to the law, and instead of regarding the police as the enemy they should support them in the fight against the reactionaries. I think that it is useless operating with the methods of the old rigid insurrectionary Socialism.

LESSONS OF HISTORY

Stalin: The Communists base themselves on rich historical experience which teaches that obsolete classes do not voluntarily abandon the stage of history. Recall the history of England in the seventeenth century. Did not many say that the old social system had decayed? But did it not, nevertheless, require a Cromwell to crush it by force?

Wells: Cromwell operated on the basis of the constitution and in the name of constitutional order.

Stalin: In the name of the constitution he resorted to violence, beheaded the king, dispersed Parliament, arrested some and beheaded others!

Or take an example from our history. Was it not clear for a long time that the Tsarist system was decaying, was breaking down? But how much blood had to be shed in order to overthrow it?

And what about the October Revolution? Were there not plenty of people who knew that we alone, the Bolsheviks, were indicating the only correct way out? Was it not clear that Russian capitalism had decayed? But you know how great was the resistance, how much blood had to be shed in order to defend the October Revolution from all its enemies, internal and external.

Or take France at the end of the eighteenth century. Long before 1789 it was clear to many how rotten the royal power, the feudal system, was. But a popular insurrection, a clash of classes was not, could not be, avoided. Why? Because the classes which must abandon the stage of history are the last to become convinced that their role is ended. It is impossible to convince them of this. They think that the fissures in the decaying edifice of the old order can be mended, that the tottering edifice of the old order can be repaired and saved. That is why dying classes take to arms and resort to every means to save their existence as a ruling class.

Wells: But were there not a few lawyers at the head of the great French Revolution?

Stalin: I do not deny the role of the intelligentsia in revolutionary movements. Was the great French Revolution a lawyers' revolution and not a popular revolution, which achieved victory by rousing vast masses of the people against feudalism and championed the interests of the Third Estate? And did the lawyers among the leaders of the great French Revolution act in accordance with the laws of the old order? Did they not introduce new, bourgeois-revolutionary law?

The rich experience of history teaches that up to now not a single class has voluntarily made way for another class. There is no such precedent in world history. The Communists have learned this lesson of history. Communists would welcome the voluntary departure of the bourgeoisie. But such a turn of affairs is improbable, that is what experience teaches. That is why the Communists want to be prepared for the worst and call upon the working class to be vigilant, to be prepared for battle. Who wants a captain who lulls the vigilance of his army, a captain who does not understand that the enemy will not surrender, that he must be crushed? To be such a captain means deceiving, betraying the working class. That is why I think that what seems to you to be old-fashioned is in fact a measure of revolutionary expediency for the working class.

HOW TO MAKE A REVOLUTION

Wells: I do not deny that force has to be used, but I think the forms of the struggle should fit as closely as possible to the opportunities presented by the existing laws, which must be defended against reactionary attacks. There is no need to disorganize the old system, because it is disorganizing itself enough as it is. That is why it seems to me insurrection against the old order, against the law, is obsolete, old-fashioned. Incidentally, I deliberately exaggerate in order to bring the truth out more clearly. I can formulate my point of view in the following way: first, I am for order; second, I attack the present system in so far as it cannot assure order;

third, I think that class-war propaganda may detach from Socialism just those educated people whom Socialism needs.

Stalin: In order to achieve a great object, an important social object, there must be a main force, a bulwark, a revolutionary class. Next it is necessary to organize the assistance of an auxiliary force for this main force; in this case this auxiliary force is the party, to which the best forces of the intelligentsia belong. Just now you spoke about 'educated people'. But what educated people did you have in mind? Were there not plenty of educated people on the side of the old order in England in the seventeenth century, in France at the end of the eighteenth century, and in Russia in the epoch of the October Revolution? The old order had in its service many highly educated people who defended the old order, who opposed the new order. Education is a weapon the effect of which is determined by the hands which wield it, by who is to be struck down. Of course, the proletariat, Socialism, needs highly educated people. Clearly, simpletons cannot help the proletariat to fight for Socialism, to build a new society. I do not underestimate the role of the intelligentsia; on the contrary, I emphasize it. The question is, however, which intelligentsia are we discussing? Because there are different kinds of intelligentsia.

Wells: There can be no revolution without a radical change in the educational system. It is sufficient to quote two examples – the example of the German Republic, which did not touch the old educational system, and therefore never became a republic; and the example of the British Labour Party, which lacks the determination to insist on a radical change in the educational system.

Stalin: That is a correct observation.

Permit me now to reply to your three points. First, the main thing for the revolution is the existence of a social bulwark. This bulwark of the revolution is the working class.

Second, an auxiliary force is required, that which the Communists call a party. To the party belong the intelligent workers and those elements of the technical intelligentsia which are closely connected with the working class. The intelligentsia can be strong only if it combines with the working class. If it opposes the working class, it becomes a cipher.

Third, political power is required as a lever for change. The new political power creates the new laws, the new order, which is revolutionary order.

I do not stand for any kind of order. I stand for order that corresponds to the interests of the working class. If, however, any of the laws of the old order can be utilized in the interests of the struggle for the new order, the old laws should be utilized. I cannot object to your postulate that the present system should be attacked in so far as it does not ensure the necessary order for the people.

And finally, you are wrong if you think that the Communists are enamoured of violence. They would be very pleased to drop violent methods if the ruling class agreed to give way to the working class. But the experience of history speaks against such an assumption.

Wells: There was a case in the history of England, however, of a class voluntarily handing over power to another class. In the period between 1830 and 1870, the aristocracy, whose influence was still very considerable at the end of the eighteenth century, voluntarily, without a severe struggle, surrendered power to the bourgeoisie, which served as a sentimental support of the monarchy. Subsequently, this transference of power led to the establishment of the rule of the financial oligarchy.

Stalin: But you have imperceptibly passed from questions of revolution to questions of reform. This is not the same thing. Don't you think that the Chartist movement played a great role in the reforms in England in the nineteenth century?

Wells: The Chartists did little and disappeared without leaving a trace.

THE BOURGEOISIE IN BRITAIN

Stalin: I do not agree with you. The Chartists, and the strike movement which they organized, played a great role; they compelled the ruling classes to make a number of concessions in regard to the franchise, in regard to abolishing the so-called 'rotten boroughs', and in regard to some of the points of the 'Charter'. Chartism played a not unimportant historical role and compelled a section of the ruling classes to make certain concessions, reforms, in order to avert great shocks. Generally speaking, it must be said that of all the ruling classes, the ruling classes of England, both the aristocracy and the bourgeoisie, proved to be the cleverest, most flexible from the point of view of their class interests, from the point of view of maintaining their power. Take an example, say, from modern history – the general strike in England in 1926. The first thing any other bourgeoisie would have done in the face of such an event, when the General Council of Trade Unions called for a strike, would have been to arrest the Trade Union leaders. The British bourgeoisie did not do that, and it acted cleverly from the point of view of its own interests. I cannot conceive of such a flexible strategy being employed by the bourgeoisie of the United States, Germany or France. In order to maintain their rule, the ruling classes of Great Britain have never forsworn small concessions, reforms. But it would be a mistake to think that these reforms were revolutionary.

Wells: You have a higher opinion of the ruling classes of my country than I have. But is there a great difference between a small revolution and a great reform? Is not a reform a small revolution?

Stalin: Owing to pressure from below, the pressure of the masses, the bourgeoisie may sometimes concede certain partial reforms while remaining on the basis of the existing social-economic system. Acting in this way, it calculates that these concessions are necessary in order to preserve its class rule. This is the essence of reform. Revolution, however, means the transference of power from one class to another. That is why it is impossible to describe any reform as revolution. That is why we cannot count on the change of social systems taking place as an imperceptible transition from one system to another by means of reforms, by the ruling class making concessions.

WHAT RUSSIA IS DOING

Wells: I am very grateful to you for this talk, which has meant a great deal to me. In explaining things to me you probably called to mind how you had to explain the fundamentals of Socialism in the illegal circles before the revolution. At the present time there are in the world only two persons to whose opinion, to whose every word, millions are listening – you and Roosevelt. Others may preach as much as they like; what they say will never be printed or heeded. I cannot yet appreciate what has been done in your country; I only arrived yesterday. But I have already seen the happy faces of healthy men and women, and I know that something very considerable is being done here. The contrast with 1920 is astounding.

Stalin: Much more could have been done had we Bolsheviks been cleverer.

Wells: No, if human beings were cleverer. It would be a good thing to invent a Five-Year Plan for the reconstruction of the human brain, which obviously lacks many things needed for a perfect social order. (*Laughter*)

Stalin: Don't you intend to stay for the Congress of the Soviet Writers' Union?

Wells: Unfortunately I have various engagements to fulfil, and I can stay in the USSR only for a week. I came to see you, and I am very satisfied by our talk. But I intend to discuss with such Soviet writers as I can meet the possibility of their affiliating to the PEN Club. This is an international organization of writers founded by Galsworthy; after his death I became president. The organization is still weak, but it has branches in many countries, and what is more important, the speeches of its members are widely reported in the press. It insists upon this, free expression of opinion – even of opposition opinion. I hope to discuss this point with Gorky. I do not know if you are prepared yet for that much freedom. . . .

Stalin: We Bolsheviks call it 'self-criticism'. It is widely used in the USSR. . . .

27 October 1934

Ernst Toller, Maynard Keynes and others made their comments in the New Statesman *on this singular encounter. The best comment in the paper was Bernard Shaw's. It led to a reply from Wells, who was offended, and a counter-reply from Shaw, who was not contrite. Here I can give only Shaw's original comment on the interview.*

Stalin – Wells Talk: Bernard Shaw's Comment

The conversation, or rather collision, between these two extra-ordinary men has not told us anything we did not know as to their respective views; but it is entertaining as a bit of comedy; and I suspect it was not lost as such on Stalin; for he is a man with a keen sense of comedy and a very ready and genial laugh. Here are points to be noted and enjoyed.

Stalin listens attentively and seriously to Wells, taking in his pleadings exactly, and always hitting the nail precisely on the head in his reply. Wells does not listen to Stalin; he only waits with suffering patience to begin again when Stalin stops. He thinks he knows better than Stalin all that Stalin knows. He has not come to be instructed by Stalin, but to instruct him. He is going to save the world by Clissoldism. He does not know that Clissold is only the moralized capitalist of Comte, Comte being a back number because he had no better solution of the class-war difficulty. Rotary Clubs, founded to organize Clissold, almost instantly became luncheon clubs for men who had never heard of Comte or Clissold or even of H. G. Wells. But H. G., who pays no more attention to Rotary Clubs than to Stalin, and never had, as the Fabians had, to argue with Comtists whilst that species still existed, believes Clissoldism to be the latest thing and assures Stalin, *sans* tact, that the class war is nonsense.

Stalin, who knows by experience what Clissolds are worth when it comes to the point, politely attempts to put H. G.'s ideas in Marxian order and proportion for him; but H. G., convinced that Stalin is obsessed with a silly formula about the class war, treats his expositions as irrelevant and tedious interruptions, and, dismissing them with a kindly 'I agree with much of what you have said', resumes his expatiation on the importance of Clissold.

Stalin, with invincible patience, again gives Wells a lucid elementary lesson in post-Marxian political science. It produces less effect on Wells than water on a duck's back. Before pursuing the thread of his own remarks, he puts Stalin in what he conceives to be his place by the gentle warning: 'Perhaps I believe more strongly in the economic interpretation of politics than you do.' He then reproves Stalin for 'approaching these people [the Clissolds] with two-track class-war propaganda', forgetting that Stalin has found it necessary to approach them in two-track form with a job in one hand and a gun in the other. 'These people', H. G. declares, forgetting the days when Clissold's name was Ponderevo, 'understand the condition of the world. They understand that it is a bloody muddle; but they regard your simple class-war antagonism as nonsense.'

Stalin replies, in effect, that this is exactly what is wrong with them, and sorts them out nicely for H. G. But nothing can shake Wells's British conviction that Stalin, being a foreigner, and having never attended a meeting of the Institute of International Affairs in St James's Square nor read *The Round Table*, has no grasp of the possibilities of Clissoldism and has had his mind destroyed by a malicious degenerate named Marx. To drive this home he makes Clissold, late Ponderevo, suddenly jump into the conversation in a new avatar as Morgan-Rockefeller-Ford. These men could organize. Then why not call them in to co-operate with Stalin? The suggestion is clinched by, 'It seems to me that I am more to the Left than you, Mr Stalin.'

Stalin gallantly admits that these Clissolds could organize, but adds that the problem is how to organize *them*, which is precisely the problem that the Soviet has successfully solved, though not on a basis of private property, and not in all cases without a gentle but persistent pressure of a pistol muzzle on the Clissold occiput.

And so it went on. It is not literally true that the interview contains no evidence that our dear H. G. possesses a sense of hearing; but I will venture so far as to say that Robert Owen's famous tactic, 'Never argue: repeat your assertion', has seldom been applied more rigorously than by Wells on this occasion. I enjoy it the more because when I met Stalin the very first thing I noticed about him was that he was a first-rate listener. I never met a man who could talk so well and yet was in less of a hurry to talk than

Bernard Shaw by Low [*27 Feb. 1926*]

Stalin. Wells is a very good talker; but he is the worst listener in the world. This is fortunate; for his vision is so wide and assured that the slightest contradiction throws him into a blind fury of contemptuous and eloquently vituperative impatience. And to this Stalin might not have been so indulgent as H. G.'s more intimate friends at home.

Stalin gave him one opening. He said:

'What can they [the Clissolds] do, even with the best intentions in the world, if they are unable to raise the question of seizing power, and do not themselves possess power? At best they can help the class which takes power; but they cannot change the world themselves. This can be done only by a great class which will take the place of the capitalist class and become the sovereign master as the capitalist class was before. Such a class is the working class. The technical intelligentsia [Clissolds to wit] cannot play an independent historical role. The transformation of the world is a great, complicated, and painful process. For this great task a great class is required.'

This is curiously like Gladstone or Bright making respectful gestures before the altar of that nineteenth-century idol, Public Opinion. H. G. might have reminded Stalin that the Bolsheviks were carried to victory by the great peasant-soldier class, bent to a man on private property in its most extreme form of peasant proprietorship. Ever since, Stalin and his colleagues have been engaged in the great task of exterminating these peasants and replacing them by cultured industrialists. Now it is not a paradox to say that this policy has the enthusiastic support of its more intelligent victims; for there can hardly be an intelligent proletarian in the world who does not heartily agree that the more different his son's lot from his own, the better. But the ordinary workaday Russian, like other workaday folk, has to take what Stalin and his Government think good for him; and the question Wells might have asked is, were not the Bolshevik leaders the Clissolds of Russia, and is not Wells right in looking for social salvation to a conspiracy of Clissolds, self-dedicated and self-elected? And is not Stalin also right in holding that they will be men of irresistible vocation, convinced that Capitalism is an organized robbery of the proletariat, men ruthlessly determined to put it down as other sorts of brigandage are put down, and quite indifferent to their immediate interests in the pursuit of this end? That is a recognizable description of Lenin and Stalin, but not of Clissold or Rockefeller or Ford.

Anyhow, whether our deliverers are to be apostles or energetic parvenus, there is no denying Stalin's proviso that they cannot change the world until they obtain political power. Also that unless they have a communistic ideal for which they care more than for any personal advantage to themselves, they will use their power to rationalize Capitalism instead of to destroy it. Wells has no fear of this, because he thinks that Capitalism is not a system but a chaos. He never made a greater mistake. Capitalism, on paper, is the most systematic and thoroughly reasoned of all the Utopias. It was its completeness and logic as a plan for getting the optimal social result from the institution of private property that reconciled humane thinkers like De Quincey, Austin, Macaulay and the Utilitarians to it in full view of its actual and prospective horrors before Socialism became conceivably political. It is still taught as a standard system in our universities and still threatens the horrible possibility that Wells may study it some day and be lost to Socialism through it as completely as Asquith or Inge. The issue is really between private property with its automatic privileged distribution and public property with deliberately enforced equal distribution. Clissold can be of no use to Socialism as long as he dodges that issue. William Morris is described by Wells as a poet and decorator. That is not the significance of William Morris to us; there are plenty of poets and decorators about. Morris's significant speciality was his freely expressed opinion that idle capitalists are 'damned thieves'. And the word 'damned' was more than mere decoration. One misses that note in Clissold; yet it is the key-note of Socialism.

In this report of the Stalin-Wells collision between an irresistible force and an immovable obstacle we miss Wells's description and opinion of Stalin.* We crave also for Stalin's description and opinion of Wells. Wells has a genius for such descriptions; but Stalin also wields a trenchant pen, and can put controversial opponents 'on the spot' as effectively as Kulaks. Perhaps we shall enjoy both treats some day.

Meanwhile, let us thank Providence that they never came to grips over their differences. Stalin has exiled Trotsky and become the Pontifex Maximus of the new Russo-Catholic Church of Communism on two grounds. First, he is a practical Nationalist statesman recognizing that Russia is a big enough handful for mortal rulers to tackle without taking on the rest of the world as well (Wells will have nothing short of a World State). Second, Stalin, inflexible as to his final aim, is a complete opportunist as to the means. He puts this to Wells in two memorable sentences. 'I do not stand for any kind of order. I stand for order that corresponds to the interests of the working class.' It is evident that Stalin is a man who

* The omission is supplied in the second volume of Wells's fascinating autobiography. In it he does handsome justice to Stalin's straightness and good nature, but is blinded by his Marx phobia to Stalin's strength of mind and realistic grasp of the historic situation. – G.B.S.

will get things done, including, if necessary, the removal of Trotsky and the World Revolution from the business of the day. Wells, with his World State without Revolution, he also strikes out of the agenda for the present.

I think it unfortunate that Wells left Stalin in some doubt as to whether he is a friend or an enemy of the new Russia. On Wednesday of last week Mr Chesterton, broadcasting from Portland Place, dealt an eloquent rebuke to Edmund Burke for the way in which his Liberalism crumpled up when it was put to the test by the French Revolution, and eulogized Fox for standing by his guns. And in the very same sentence Mr Chesterton suddenly collapsed into the arms of the Duchess of Atholl (I write figuratively) like a mountain on the breast of a daisy, by quite gratuitously describing Bolshevism as 'unlimited sweating'.

Now if so fearless a commentator, professing as a Distributist to be on the Left of Communism, can out-Burke Burke thus, whom in England can Stalin trust? I have long been laughed at in Russia as 'a good man fallen among Fabians'; but the two old hyperfabian Fabians, Webb and Shaw, have stuck to their guns like Fox whilst the sentimental Socialists have been bolting in all directions from Stalin, screaming, like St Peter, 'I know not the man.' Stalin is almost *persona grata* at the Foreign Office as our only bulwark against Japanese Imperialism, whilst our professedly Socialist Societies and Parties are blindly helping the rabble of capitalists who are trying to export our too scanty money to secure a share in the exploitation of Manchukuo and China, and to spite Communism. A pretty sort of cricket, this.

Mr Wells, magnificently overlooking the existence of the League of Nations Committee for Intellectual Co-operation, and all the Internationals, first, second, and third, offers Russia the PEN Club as a substitute. The offer has struck Russia speechless. I am a member of that Club; and I feel strongly tempted to test its political enlightenment and unanimity by moving that we invite Stalin to the next Club dinner.

3 November 1934

The New Statesman *never made the mistake of treating Mussolini with indulgence. But it was never quite possible to treat him and his régime as monstrous, like Hitler's, because absurdity kept breaking through. Stephen Potter's was one way of dealing with this; this example of his work is less characteristic than much that appeared in the paper later.*

Even from train windows, it is easy to see real signs of the new, acceler-
ated, martial Italy. Even in the train itself, with its time-table, and the
freedom of its staff from such major tricks as the stealing of luggage, or
such minor tricks, common three years ago, as selling you pillows at one
station, and waking you up at the next to remove them forcibly as 'soiled'
in the hope that you will buy new ones. Inside and outside the railways
are efficient and clean: the foreign coaldust has all been licked up by the
new electric engines. Beyond, the fields really are cultivated to the margins.
Only near Rome does waste grass appear, and one is told of this, that part
is the area recently reclaimed from a three-thousand-year-old dynasty of
swampy malarial mosquitoes, and part has been ceded to the State because
its owners had failed to improve it. On the Appian way, in Rome itself,
no rubbish is allowed to collect in the corners of ancient monuments.
And there are certainly soldiers, and an atmosphere of uniforms. The guard
of this train has a holster at his hip. Not only officers seem able to wear
cloaks with the experienced grace of Shakespearean actors, nor can these
be all of them mountain troops who add 5 per cent to their height by the
tremendous nailiness of their boot-soles. Ranks and uniforms are so
numerous that porters, postmen and black-shirts merge into one overwhelming soldierish majority.

'Soldierish' rather than 'militarist', if there is such a distinction. For once
in Italy, walking about in Rome, it is easy to observe, from these very
soldiers, that there is little alteration in the Italians themselves. That there
is something here which must be absolutely distinguished from the boring,
inhuman, German militarism. Watch them marching. No detachment,
however small, marches without a band. Often it is a band and nothing
else. And there is no correct playing, elbows stiff, of toneless march music,
but a gay comic opera tune, with bugles waving from left to right to
balance the marcher, heads bowing in exaggerated time to the music,
exactly like children playing. It is true that foreign correspondents sometimes give a different picture. I observed on blank walls the sign 'W DUCE',
which they have told us about, and knew that it meant 'Long Live the
Duce'. Or 'W FASCISMO', I saw. And I moralised on the fact that in this
country a 'W RAMSAY' would not live five minutes without some rude addition, whereas in Italy the signs receive no such defacement. But my
respectful interest was suddenly turned to righteous indignation when I
saw next to a 'W DUCE' a 'W GUERRA' – and then a few yards farther on the
same, next to other sinister words which I could not translate.

It was only by chance that I found out that 'GUERRA' did not stand for WAR, but was the name of a champion bicyclist. The Italians are still too gay, and their climate is still too sunny, for them to be fanatical very long, or very exclusively. All the more wonder, that on this unteachable race, least susceptible to logic, whose national characteristic for fifteen hundred years has been an inability to be loyal to anything larger than a town, a race incapable of acting to rule (whether *Thou shalt not kill*, or *Thou shalt use hand signals when driving a car*), should have been imposed a new Italy logical, obedient, and unified.

The world's answer to this problem – 'Mussolini' – needs some elaboration. Mussolini himself, it seems, is the most scientific of men. Critics are misled by his face, an intensification of a well-known Italian type which happens to follow rhetorical, 'strong man', lines. But he is not at all above being amused at himself, and at the fantastic extent of his power. Ministers, ambassadors, etc., are given to understand that Mussolini prefers a good joke to salaams at the end of an interview. His personal life is much more domestic than imperial. He seems to have no thoughts of money, taking a small, unspecified, and variable allowance from the State when he wants it. His working time (as prime minister, foreign minister, war minister, etc.) is beautifully organized down to five hours a day—the Italians sometimes rather unkindly contrast Ramsay MacDonald, semi-Prime Minister only, yet propped up by Lord Horders, King's Throat Specialists, and similar stimulants.

But one of Mussolini's specialities, indeed his most notable gift, is certainly a talent for rhetoric. As an orator, he must not be judged by English standards. Our English speakers of repute are emotional enough, but the emotion played for in this country follows the line *sound old, solid old, England after all . . . no frills . . . man to man*. In Italy, the emotional sequence follows more classical lines. It is a rhetoric of *onward . . . idealism . . . forward ye peoples*. Of this kind of speech, Mussolini is an academic master. However rational he may be as an explainer of policy in speeches when rhetoric is not pertinent, it is by his emotive oratory that he is known. He himself has seen to that. For Mussolini has added another to his many portfolios. He is minister of emotion. The ramifications of this office are wide, and extend far beyond speech making. In Rome, its works are ever present. Towering above all is the Emotion headquarters, the Victor Emmanuel monument, which last week seemed to be in better form than ever, floodlit, and lined with hundreds of flickering lamps for an anniversary. In the Rome beneath, the subordinates of the department are at work. The news placard announces an Italian football

victory over Austria as NEW TRIUMPH FOR FASCIST SPORT. In the movie of
Cleopatra (Cecil B. de Mille), which I had seen in London, it was notice-
able that Caesar's rapid, dictatorish walk was popular with an amused
Roman audience. Would there be any special reaction to the assassination
et tu Brute scene? It was cut out. The department will not allow the
possibility of such an act to be even suggested.

But most obvious in Rome last week were the book-shops. Photographs
of the Duce were obscured by maps, filling half the window. Each map
showed North-East Africa, and on each the Italian possessions were
painted green, looking strangely large against the uncoloured remainder.
Even from the other side of the street one could see, in the Ethiopian
corner, green Italian land bearing down on the pale, colourless Abyssinia,
so that the hand fidgeted to paint out what looked an irritating intrusion,
a sterile island holding apart two waves of fertile civilization.

In this kind of organization, surely, is to be found one explanation of
Mussolini's power. It certainly seems to be the explanation of his mysterious aggressiveness in Abyssinia. Mussolini, so careful to keep his
relations with big powers cordial; Mussolini, whose kind of dictatorship
has begun lately to seem so admirable a contrast to Hitler's, appears to
be about to perform an act of blatantly Nazi bellicosity. Commonsense
reasons for such a war, whatever penetrations of Africa Germany or Japan
may be contemplating, seem such as must appear to the Duce, even if his
Achilles heel is a Roman mania for expansion, negligible. But for a
director of public feeling, such a war would have much to recommend it.
United Italy has never, till now, been united. Difficult as we find it to
imagine a time when its big-gumboot shape was not part of the map, it
is one of Europe's most recent additions. Nor, so far, has Italy ever won a
war, however many times the Italian children are made to recite 'Italy
won the war at the battle of Vittorio Veneto.' More pertinently still, even
the children know that at Adowa, in Abyssinia, the Italians suffered a
disgraceful reverse. Now can Adowa be avenged – indeed the department
have been preparing for this line of thought by maintaining that Adowa
was a disaster, but not a defeat: a setback in the gradual 'civilization' of a
barbaric race now at last about to be completed. One small victory is all
that is required, and in the course of winning it the sending off of troop-
trains, the effective use of beautiful Italian engines in the mechanized
divisions, and the triumphant return of not too badly wounded war heroes,
will bind the bound *fascisti* closer than ever. Mussolini will know how to
build his triumphal arches over the measliest little strip of semi-desert
acquisition. It is all part of his daily round. For it is by giving the governing

to the governors, and emotions to the people, that he has succeeded in setting up the world's least democratic, most scientific rule (bar Russia) in the country least likely to submit to it.

20 April 1935

Osbert Sitwell's shorter works appeared from time to time.

The Next War   Osbert Sitwell

The Long war had ended.
Its miseries had grown faded.
Deaf men became difficult to talk to,
Heroes became bores.

Those alchemists,
Who had converted blood into gold
Had grown elderly.
But they held a meeting,
Saying,
'We think perhaps we ought
To put up tombs
Or erect altars
To those brave lads
Who were so willingly burnt,
Or blinded,
Or maimed,
Who lost all likeness to a living thing,
Or were blown to bleeding patches of flesh
For our sakes.
It would look well.
Or we might even educate the children.'
But the richest of these wizards
Coughed gently;
And he said,
'I have always been to the front
  – In private enterprise –

I yield in public spirit
To no man.
I think yours is a very good idea
– A capital idea –
And not too costly. . . .
But it seems to me
That the cause for which we fought
Is again endangered.
What more fitting memorial for the fallen
Than that their children
Should fall for the same cause?'
Rushing eagerly into the street,
The kindly old gentlemen cried
To the young:
'Will you sacrifice
Through your lethargy
What your fathers died to gain?
The world *must* be made safe for the young!'

*   *   *

And the children
Went. . . .

19 October 1935 (written in 1915)

The policy adopted by both Sharp and Kingsley Martin of keeping readers in touch with foreign talent was followed consistently, although nothing is more difficult for a weekly journal in a country with a large fund of native wit to draw upon.

Geography – A Remedy for Happiness Luigi Pirandello

Wouldn't it be much better for us to consider all our sorrows from the point of view of the stars, and to come to the conclusion that in the end everything becomes almost nothing?

Very well – you will say – but in the meantime if one of my sons died here, on this very earth of ours, what would you do then?

Yes, I know. It would be a serious matter, and it would become even more serious when you begin to get over your sorrow, and in front of those eyes who would like never to see again, you perceive – perhaps – the charming white little flowers blooming at the first rays of the April sun, and a new feeling of life enters your body which your son will never again be able to enjoy.

Well? How could you really expect to be consoled for the death of your son? Is it not better to expect no consolation at all, to look to nothing and to be satisfied with this feeling of 'nothing' which embraces sorrows and happiness alike, the absolute 'nothing' of human events when we compare them with stars like Sirius or the Alpha Centaurus?

I know it's not easy: but did I ever tell you it is easy? Astronomy is a difficult science not merely to study but also to apply to ordinary events of life.

Besides, you are inconsistent. You claim that this planet of ours deserves a certain amount of respect, and that it is not so small when compared with human passion, and yet you shut yourselves in a cocoon and don't even grasp all the life which escapes unnoticed while you labour in some obsessing thought or in some depressing sorrow.

I know: you are going to answer that it is not possible to let your imagination lead you into a new and different life while a passion is blinding your present one, but I don't ask you to imagine yourself elsewhere nor even to figure yourself in a different life from the one which is causing you so much trouble. Yet this is what you usually do when you sigh: 'If only it were so! If only I could have this or that! If only I could be there!' And they are utterly useless wishes, for if your life could be really different from what it is, how different too would be your feelings, your hopes, your desires. So much so that you cannot stand those who are as you would yourself like to be, or those who possess what you would like to possess, or those who live where you would like to live merely because you think that they cannot be as happy as you think you would be if you were in their place. Which – allow me to say – is a ridiculous feeling because you would no longer envy them if – being in their place – you would cease to be your own self, that is if you would no longer wish to be different from what you are.

No, my dear friends, no: my remedy is quite different: not an easy one – I admit – but quite practicable – so much so that I have actually been able to successfully experiment it on myself.

I had a first glimpse of it one night – one of those many terrible nights –

when I had to keep vigil at a long, everlasting agony – when my poor mother lay for months and months almost a living corpse.

To my wife she was the mother-in-law: to my children someone was dying whose son I was. I am saying this because one of them, I hope, will keep vigil in his turn at my deathbed. Do you understand me? On that night it was my mother who was dying and it was my business, not theirs, to keep vigil.

'Yet' – you will say – 'it was their grandmother.' Yes, their grandmother: their dear 'Granny' . . . and besides they might have shown some pity for me instead of keeping me standing all night, chilled through, almost dropping from fatigue after a day of very hard work.

But the truth was that Granny's days, the days of 'dear old Granny' had passed long ago. As for a toy which had gone wrong, the grandchildren had lost all interest in Granny from the day they had seen her after her operation with one small and one large lifeless eye behind the concave lenses of her spectacles! A Granny like that was no longer a pride to them. Besides, she had gradually become stone-deaf, the poor Granny: she was eighty-five and she no longer understood what was going on round her, merely a mass of flesh that gasped and stooped, heavy and needing a lot of nursing which my love for her could alone make me bear.

But even love, my friends, cannot replace sleep: no amount of affection can replace certain necessities of life which must be satisfied even against will.

Try not to sleep for several consecutive nights, after a heavy day's work. The thought of my children who had done no work during the day and yet were now warm and soundly asleep while I was shivering with cold in that room stinking with drugs, was driving me as wild as a bear, and was well near pushing me to rush to them and pull off the bedclothes from their cots and from my wife's bed to see them jump up from their sleep in the cold. But then as I felt in my own body how dreadfully they would shiver and I realized I was envying their places merely to see them shiver instead of me, I stopped revolting against them and turned myself against the cruelty of fate for still keeping alive my mother's body, now almost unrecognizable, groaning and fully unconscious – and I could not help thinking that, please God, she might at last stop panting.

Presently, the panting ceased, there was a terrible silence in the room. Turning my head – I don't know why – I caught sight of myself in the mirror of the wardrobe, bending over my mother's bed, watching her close to see if she were dead.

I looked at my own face with horror.

The same expression of almost joyful terror was still there, as when I was bending over my mother's body closely watching for her release.

A fresh gasping at that very moment gave me such a horror of myself that I hid that awful face of mine into my hands as if I had committed a crime. But soon I began to weep like a child – like the child I had been for that good saintly mother of mine whose pity I still needed to comfort me against cold and fatigue, though I had just been wishing for her death, my dear saintly mother who had spent so many waking nights for me when I was young and ill. . . . Torn with anguish I began to pace up and down the room.

It soon became impossible to look at things round me, for everything in the room – in their anxious immobility – seemed to have become alive: the bright edge of the wardrobe, the brass knob of the bedstead which I had recently pressed with my hand. In despair I threw myself on the chair of the writing desk of my youngest daughter, 'her' little granddaughter who still did her school work in Granny's room. I don't know for how long I sat there. All I know is that it was broad daylight when – after what seemed an enormous lapse of time during which I had entirely forgotten fatigue, cold and despair – I found myself holding in my hands my daughter's geography text book, open at page 75 with heavy smudges on the margins and a large spot of blue ink on the *m* of Jamaica.

I had apparently spent all that time in the Island of Jamaica, where the Blue Mountains are, where the sands seem gently to rise from the north until they reach the easy slopes of the hills. I had seen under the clear waters of the sea the walls of Porto Reale, sunk at the bottom after the terrible earthquake: I had seen the sugar and coffee plantations, the wide fields of Indian corn and millet, the mountain forests: I had rejoiced at inhaling the warm smell of the bedding in the large stables of the cattle-breeders: I had seen all this not merely as a vision, but as if I had really lived there, in those meadows where the sun always shines, where men, women and children carry on their heads the baskets of coffee which they then spread in small heaps in the sun to dry. I had seen all this with the feeling that it was equally true, equally real in that distant country as the sad reality which surrounded me in the room of my dying mother.

I had found the remedy. Geography. Nothing else than this certainty of some real life, far off and entirely different to place against the present oppressing reality. Merely something different, even without any connection to your present life: just something which happens to be as it is and which you cannot prevent being what it is. This is the remedy, my friends, this is the remedy which chance made me discover that night.

134

And so that you need not strain your brain let me advise you to do exactly as I did, allotting to each of my four children and my wife a part of the world, to which I direct my mind the moment they start worrying me.

My wife, for instance, is Lapland. When she asks from me something which I cannot give her, for instance, I immediately place myself in the Gulf of Bothnia and I warn her seriously:

Umea, Lulea, Pitea, Skelleftea. . . .

Are you mad? she asks.

Not at all, my dear – just the rivers of Lapland.

The rivers of Lapland? What have they got to do with me?

Nothing at all, my dear, nothing at all. But they exist, and neither you nor I can deny that at this very moment they are flowing into the gulf of Bothnia. And if you could see, my dear, as I see, the dreariness of some of the willows and of some of the birch trees. . . . Yes, I know, even the willows and the birch trees have nothing to do with you, but they too exist, my dear, and they look so dreary round the frozen lakes of the steppes. 'Lap' or 'Lop' – would you believe it? – is an insult to the Laps. They call themselves the Sami. Dirty little dwarfs, my dear! Just imagine – yes, I know, all this has nothing to do with you – but just imagine that while I prize you so highly they prize conjugal fidelity so little that they offer their wife or daughters to the first strangers whom they meet. Be sure, my dear, I shall never try to do as they do.

But what in God's name are you talking about? Are you mad? I was asking you. . . .

Yes, my dear. You were asking me for something else, I don't say you weren't. . . . But what a dreary country it is – Lapland.

7 December 1935

For twenty years 'Sagittarius' wrote a weekly satirical poem on current affairs in the New Statesman – *over a thousand such poems, constituting a feat unrivalled in the history of journalism if the consistent brilliance of the work be taken into account. Here is her handling of the League of Nations' feebleness in face of the truculent aggressiveness of the Fascist and Nazi dictators.*

135

Benitoland 'Sagittarius'

'Mussolini . . . may announce at any moment that Abyssinia is to be called Benitoland.' — Star

Benitoland, utopian
realm of imperial omen,
where even the Ethiopian
may learn to be a Roman,
there all will be rewarded
who sped Rome's hop to glory,
their aid and trade recorded
in re-named territory –

Monte Laval ascending
majestic in the pluvia,
and Via Flandin wending
athwart the moist alluvia,
while Swiss supporters dump there
snug Alpine hotel chalets,
and oil vendors pump their
concessions in the valleys.

The peace of Rome enfolding
the landscape Abyssinian
may soon be felt re-moulding
the League in its dominion,
till, firmly reinstated,
Geneva yet may be
to Italy mandated
with a German guarantee.

16 May 1936

Among those, apart from the Editor himself, who wrote for the New States-man *on the Spanish Civil War, were Cyril Connolly and Stephen Spender. Unlike George Orwell, Spender's eyes were not opened to the nature of Moscow Communism by what he saw in Spain. Poetry reinforced his prose contributions.*

The Town Shore at Barcelona   Stephen Spender

I walk down to the wind-swept winter shore
Where knifed-off slum blocks like stub teeth
With gaps and cheap enamel, post around
The blank and roaring mouth of sand.
This bony, falling jaw reads ocean's long advertisement
Endless with ozone and salts of disinfectant.

To my right, the cranes, poised birds
Coiled on their iron stilts admire the liner
Whose flamingo funnels and creamed, folded sides
Cliffed above nodding fields of handkerchiefs
Point to excitement of that glossing coast
Beyond me and the gasworks, where the clouds
Flaglike wave over mountain elephant hides.

Fixed in this central sand, bodies are derelict
Spoked wheels dismantled; minds are slag;
To the political eye men stink on scrap-heap;
But being less sensible than rusted machines
To know when they are waste, these cry with calls
Of cormorant, feed like gulls, and turn cartwheels;
Gentlemen lean and look from balustrades.

Paused in that dead town mouth, I note what winds
Have tanned the wrestlers redder than their sands
– Them waves applaud, for them foam thoughtless flowers.
Straddled against the sea, two gods contesting
Are mocked at by their sprawling girl whose breasts
Figure above the wet and dipping light
Like those of Ceres above her corn and horn.

Man passing, hiccups. I rattle trousered coins
And think how money, governmentally outlaid,
Could root these houses out. Imagine a boulevard
With sand-flowers bedded. Let palm-trees flourish
Their summer brocade and trumpet of success.
Race with your eyes the sport car boys and girls
Curvetting passionate tarmac coastal roads.

Ō the lights at night when horizontal syllables
From wave, hushed bush, and chinking cactus, lip;
The gramophones from off-shore insect boats;
Cicadas shrill in grass; red-hot guitars;
Bouquets from nightingales. Again, our lights
Endlessly repeated in electric stars.

But such is not. Rocket me in a lift
Of girdered skeleton towering from the dock
There where the aerial cable railway climbs
Till Barcelona withers to its map.
Drive me in trams down all main avenues.
Launch me as Icarus from this shore, whom winds
Eddy across the ocean in one gust.

What rimmed horizon like a noting sun
Tainted with Europe and the derelict coast
Has seared my path ascendant and melts down
Spirit-exalting wax to falling water?
Relapsed in the town jaws, I am a tongue
That praised the journeys of the mind
Coloured the sight, sang what it heard. All lies,
But the bone prison where I wag and mourn.

11 April 1936

---

*One of the phenomena of the age for which new statesmanship had a distaste
was Buchmanism, even before it developed clearly into an instrument of
reactionary politics. Kingsley Martin deals with one of the Buchmanites'
Albert Hall meetings.*

God-Control   Kingsley Martin

The Albert Hall full to the ceiling. Tonight it is for the Buchmanites, not
long ago it was for Sir Oswald Mosley, tomorrow for the centenary of
Joseph Chamberlain. A vast Union Jack drapes the organ; a smaller
Union Jack is wrapped round the rostrum. The flags of the British
Dominions are under the organ, and to the right and the left of the floodlit

choir are the flags of the many nations where the Oxford Groups have taken their message. A swastika banner stands out in the line of conventional patterns. Only the flag of Soviet Russia is absent. The organ is playing gay and inspiriting tunes, changing quickly from one to another. I enter a box at the extreme back of the hall, facing the organ, to the tune of 'Britons Scorn to Yield'. The setting would need little alteration for tomorrow night's meeting, and the audience will, I take it, be much the same people, predominantly well-dressed, upper middle-class people with rather a high proportion of women. A well-known benevolent employer sits in a box not far from me and next door is a carefully preserved lady with the set smile that is born of many bazaars. I watched a serious young woman listening attentively; she was looking, it seemed to me, in desperate earnestness for some compensation for not having any useful work to do. We stand to sing 'God Save the King'. The conductor and the choir lead us; this is no perfunctory ceremony. So far I might have dropped into any of the three meetings, Fascist, Conservative or Buchmanite. Can it be that the religion of all three will prove to be much the same too?

The leader of the meeting Mr A. S. Loudoun Hamilton, MC, formerly at Christ Church, Oxford, is a more attractive spiritual guide than Mr Frank Buchman, who sits modestly amongst his followers. I first saw Mr Buchman at an Oxford Group meeting in Geneva when I sat next to Kapp while he drew his admirable portrait.

Mr Hamilton is a clean-cut university man with no frills and he wears his old school tie without ostentation. The keynote of the meeting, he tells us, is to be 'national safety', only to be obtained by God-control. (Does God need a big air-force or not?) God must govern England through God-controlled homes, God-controlled schools, God-controlled business, God-controlled professional life and God-controlled international policy. A Brigadier-General, who trains racehorses, next tells us how he enlisted in the Oxford Movement and was changed. He used to swear at his men just as they swore at the horses. Now the men too are changed. No more war. To change society to a God-guided basis is a bigger job than an army command. We have to choose 'between gas-masks and God's tasks'. A lady from Aberdeen describes the change in her home life when her sons came under the influence of the Oxford Movement – 'We have proved in our home that God controlling and guiding each individual is the answer to divorce, strikes, unemployment and war.' A chartered accountant, a DSO and an International Rugby player, tells us how God controls his business and home life, and a journalist, who used to drink too much, looks forward to the time when newspapers will be different because the people who make the news will be changed. (I wish questions were allowed at Buchman meetings: what happens to changed journalists if proprietors and advertising managers do not change too?) Mr Holme, Winchester and New College, was studying for the Foreign Office. Very sensibly he asked how he could hope to solve international conflicts if he could not solve his own. We British played the part of a 'hypocritical schoolmaster' confessing other people's sins instead of our own. We may not like other people's political structures, but they 'may at least learn to work as a unit' and have 'leaders with youth enthusiastically behind them'. In certain countries 'full responsibility for the state of the nation was taken by a few people. They started with their own country. They did what they meant to do . . . England can only take the lead when she has taken the lead from God.' A Government, as one speaker put it, of 'God-controlled experts'. The Labour Lord Mayor of Newcastle spoke long and eloquently, but not into the microphone. He had been 'in the seventh heaven' since his conventional Methodism had been turned to reality by the Groups. God would save Newcastle from unemployment. Five workers from the woollen mills of Yorkshire, who had been changed, had travelled down that afternoon to tell us about it and would be at work again at seven o'clock in the morning. Each had his or her little metaphor or jest prepared; the weaver was now weaving God into his cloth; Marion Clarkson, a 'twister', had been shown by God 'how to twist her life into others and help them to know that even twisters can be straight'. Each of the five told us how they had not always worked honestly and well. One of them used to drink; they slacked off on flat rates and scamped through on piece-work. They had confessed to God and the foreman, and now they worked for God and made everyone happy in the workshop. The lady next to me quivered with pleasure. 'So direct and simple', she said. She put down her lorgnette for a little volley of claps with small, chubby hands.

Then there was a novelty – a sort of recitative by a group of young people helped out by the choir. They told us they had been from the darkest Congo to barren Tibet, from the Arctic to the Antarctic, and they had everywhere found a worn-out and broken-down past. The Statesman planned and organized but the structure tottered; the Rich man could find no satisfaction in his riches; the Poor woman complained that her home was destroyed and asked why 'her heart grew dull with hatred'. Then God sang a solo and each of the characters found salvation. The Statesman found his work enduring:'Confidence spreads from our united work'; the Soldier pressed on in constructive work; and the Church, which had complained that no one listened, raised the cross in victory. The Rich man became a steward of God's property, 'triumphant when God guides me', the Poor woman found friends. 'My troubled mind I have unlocked. God has taken care of all my need and poverty. It is spring-time in my home.' (Had God paid the rent?) A French baroness told

us of strikes in Paris, settled by a member of the Oxford Group. (I wanted to know the terms of the settlement.) Professor Norval of Pretoria, once a champion of Boer rights and a hater of Englishmen, told us how he had been changed, formed a coalition with his adversaries, now loved England and the British Empire and saw God's solution for all the racial problems of Africa. (I badly wanted to know whether God approved of the colour bar and the Pass system for natives.) Another baroness (God does much of his work through people with titles and decorations), 'the daughter of Prince and Princess Lieven of Russia', reported progress from Riga. She had seen real revolution; her property, everything, was lost. She had been bitter, until changed by the Oxford Movement. Her country (no one mentioned Bolshevism) had been too late to accept God's guidance. England was not yet too late. The thin intellectual thread which ran through the meeting had guided us to its predestined conclusion.

I have good friends who are Buchmanites, and I get annoyed with those of my generation who affect to think that religion is unimportant. The technique for obtaining internal peace by surrendering one's life to a movement and a purpose beyond oneself works today as it has always worked. The four tests – absolute love, honesty, unselfishness and purity (which the sophisticated Buchmanite will explain in private as meaning unselfishness and fidelity in sex life) – these tests of conduct have changed people and given quality to life in every generation. There are, I am sure, many homes in England which are sweeter and less contentious places because the Groups Movement has reawakened people to a genuine belief in their nominally accepted morality. Selfish women make peace with their daughters and are kinder to their maids; children are more considerate to their parents; husbands and wives who were estranged honestly discuss their difficulties and rebuild on a firmer foundation. Greedy employers are more considerate to their workmen and their workmen respond. They tell us that Buchmanism is good business. Well, it is no new discovery that honesty pays and that in any branch of life the day is more happy and successful if its prelude is a quiet period of meditation and consecration to serious purpose. It is difficult to believe that life can be well lived or relationships happy without a deliberate use of the ethical tests which are common to all religions.

But the Oxford Movement is not content with individual salvation. It will change human society, it tells us, through individual change. I recall the history of many religious revivals. They have made the same claim. The stream of history has run on and the current of the age has swept them along with it. Wesley, who began a greater and more genuine revival, had no notion when he shook to its foundations a negligent Church and called the individual sinner back to Christ, that the historian a hundred years later would say that the social effects of Methodism were to sanctify ugliness and canonize those virtues of obedience, thrift and industry which were essential if the new industrialism was to prosper. He did not know that we should agree today that his great religious revival served above all to persuade the starving workers of that period that they would be well fed in the next world; and that his hymns, that certainly comforted the dying and helped men to forget the misery of the slums, were a potent factor in inducing people to accept a slum life and a slum death. As I listened to the testimonies in the Albert Hall tonight, I asked myself whether this new

Salvationism was really so very different. The shape has changed; doctrine is unfashionable; Heaven and Hell are gone. This is religion without tears. Today, with the world tumbling round us, members of the Oxford Groups want, as we all want, war and class conflicts to cease. To face the causes of war or the causes of class conflict is too great a strain for many of us. How much easier if God's message is that these problems can be solved by national unity, if we can throw our burden upon the shoulders of God-controlled experts under a God-controlled leader! I think I know the social and political movement of which the Buchmanite movement is unconsciously a part.

11 July 1936

New statesmanship entailed being in the forefront of the anti-racialist battle for the elimination of all discrimination against colour, race, religion. This tolerance, now generally accepted as the reasonable and intelligent attitude, if not as generally practised, by all but a few political imbeciles of no account, was by no means common in the Thirties. Paul Robeson, one of the great men of the age, here writing on the subject in the New Statesman, *embraced Communism because Communism embraced all races without discrimination.*

'Primitives'   Paul Robeson

When discriminating racially, popular opinion lays emphasis on the Negro's colour. Science, however, goes deeper than that and bases its arguments on the workings of the Negro mind.

Man, say certain of the scientists, is divided into two varieties – the variety which thinks in concrete symbols, and the variety which thinks in abstract concepts. The Negro belongs to the former and Western man to the latter.

Now the man who thinks in concrete symbols has no abstract conception of such words as 'good', 'brave', 'clever'. They are represented in his mind by symbolic pictures. For instance, 'good' in a concrete mind is often represented as a picture of a woman with a child. The drawing of this picture would be the way of conveying an idea of goodness to a person of the same mentality. Such pictures become conventionalized into a kind of written language. Now to the Western mind this may seem a clumsy way of going about things, but it is a method which has given the world

143

some of the most delicate and richest art, and some of the profoundest and most subtle philosophy that man has ever known.

For it is not only the African Negro, and so-called primitive people, who think in concrete symbols – all the great civilizations of the East (with possibly the exception of India) have been built up by people with this type of mind. It is a mentality that has given us giants like Confucius, Mencius, and Lao-tze. More than likely it was this kind of thinking that gave us the understanding and wisdom of a person like Jesus Christ.

It has given us the wonders of Central American architecture and Chinese art. It has, in fact, given us the full flower of all the highest possibilities in man – with the single exception of applied science. That was left to a section of Western man to achieve and on that he bases his assertion of superiority.

Now I am not going to try to belittle the achievements of science. Only a fool would deny that the man who holds the secrets of those holds the key position in the world. I am simply going to ask – having found the key, has Western man – Western bourgeois man (the reason for the distinction is made clear later) – sufficient strength left to turn it in the lock? Or is he going to find that in the search he has so exhausted his vitality that he will have to call in the co-operation of his more virile 'inferiors' – Eastern or Western – before he can open the door and enter into his heritage?

For the cost of developing the kind of mind by which the discoveries of science were made has been one which now threatens the discoverers' very life.

The reason for this lies in the fact that Western man only seems to have gained more and more power of abstraction at the expense of his creative faculties. There is not much doubt that the artistic achievements of Europe, as abstract intellectualism penetrated deeper and deeper into the people, have steadily declined. It is true that this decline is partly obscured by an output of self-conscious, uninspired productions, which have a certain artificial grace; but discriminating people have little difficulty in distinguishing these lifeless imitations from the living pulsing thing.

It may be argued that preference for live art over dead imitation may be simply a question of taste and is of no fundamental importance. Neither would it be if the change was something confined to that small minority usually described as artists, but unfortunately what shows amongst these is only a symptom of a sickness that to some extent is affecting almost every stratum of the Western world.

To understand this you need to remember that by 'creative ability' one means something more than the capacity of a few individuals to paint, to write, or to make music. That is simply the supreme development of a quality that exists in the make-up of every human being. The whole problem of living can never be understood until the world recognizes that artists are not a race apart. Every man has some element of the artist in him, and if this is pulled up by the roots he becomes suicidal and dies.

In the East this quality has never been damaged – to that is traceable the virility of most Eastern peoples. In the West it remains healthy and active only amongst those sections of the community which have never fully subscribed to Western values – that is, the exploited sections, plus some rebels from the bourgeoisie. For the rest, mathematical thinking has made them so intellectualized, so detached and self-conscious that it has tended to kill this creative emotional side. The result is, that as Western civilization advances its members find themselves in the paradoxical position of being more and more in control of their environment, yet more and more at the mercy of it. The man who accepts Western values absolutely finds his creative faculties becoming so warped and stunted that he is almost completely dependent on external satisfactions; and the moment he becomes frustrated in his search for these, he begins to develop neurotic symptoms, to feel that life is not worth living, and, in chronic cases, to take his own life.

This is a severe price to pay even for such achievements as those of Western science. That the price has not been complete, and its originators have so far survived, is due to the stubborn persistence, in spite of discouragement, of the creative side. Though European thought, in its blind worship of the intellect, has tried to reduce life to a mechanical formula, it has never quite succeeded. Its entire peasantry, large masses of its proletariat, and even a certain percentage of its middle class have never been really touched. These sections have thrown up a series of rebels who have felt rather than analysed the danger and cried out loudly against it.

Many of these have probably been obscure people who have never been heard of outside their immediate circle, but others have been sufficiently articulate to rise above the shoulders of their fellows and voice their protest in forms that have commanded world-wide attention. Of such persons one can mention Blake and D. H. Lawrence. In fact one could say that all the live art which Europe has produced since the Renaissance has been in spite of, and not because of, the new trends of Western thought.

I do not stand alone in this criticism of the Western intellect. Famous critics support me. Walter Raleigh, when discussing Blake, writes:

'The gifts with which he is so plentifully dowered, for all they are looked at askance as abnormal and portentous, are the common stuff of human nature, without which life would flag and cease. No man destitute of genius could live for a day. Genius is spontaneity—the life of the soul asserting itself triumphantly in the midst of dead things.'

In the face of all this can anyone echo the once-common cry that the way of progress is the way of the intellectual? If we all took this turning should we not be freeing ourselves from our earthy origins by the too-simple expedient of pulling ourselves up by the roots?

But because one does not want to follow Western thought into this dilemma, one none the less recognizes the value of its achievements. One would not have the world discount them and retrogress in terror to a primitive state. It is simply that one recoils from the Western intellectual's idea that, having got himself on to this peak overhanging an abyss, he should want to drag all other people – on pain of being dubbed inferior if they refuse – up after him into the same precarious position.

That, in a sentence, is my case against Western values.

It is not a matter of whether the Negro and other so-called 'primitive' people are incapable of becoming pure intellectuals (actually, in America, many have), it is a matter of whether they are going to be unwise enough to be led down this dangerous by-way when, without sacrificing the sound base in which they have their roots, they can avail themselves of the now-materialized triumphs of science and proceed to use them while retaining the vital creative side.

One does not go so far as to say that the West will not share in this new progress. Perhaps, even yet, it will find a way to turn the key. Perhaps the recognized fact that over-intellectualism tends towards impotence and sterility will result in the natural extinction of that flower of the West that has given us our scientific achievements, and to the rise of the more virile, better-balanced European, till now derided and submerged. Some people think that in the European proletariat this new Western man is already coming to birth.

It is some such solution as this which I imagine will solve the problem of the further progress of the world.

We, however, who are not Europeans, may be forgiven for hoping that the new age will be one in which the teeming 'inferiors' of the East will be permitted to share.

Naturally one does not claim that the Negro must come to the front more than another. One does, however, realize that in the Negro one has a virile people of many millions, overwhelmingly outnumbering the other inhabitants of a rich and undeveloped continent.

That, when he is given a chance, he is capable of holding his own with the best Western Europe can produce is proved by the quality of his folk music both in Africa and the Americas – also by the works of Pushkin, the Russo-African poet; or by the performance of Ira Aldrich – the actor who enslaved artistic Europe in the last century. Even a writer like Dumas, though not in the first rank, is a person who could hardly have been fathered by a member of an inferior race.

Today there are in existence more Negroes of the first rank than the world cares to recognize.

In reply, it will of course be argued that these are isolated instances – that the Negroes as a whole have never achieved anything. 'It may be true,' people will say, 'that the African thinks as Confucius thought, or as the Aztecs thought; that his language is constructed in the same way as that language which gave us the wonder of Chinese poetry; that he works along the same lines as the Chinese artist; but where are his philosophers, his poets, his artists?'

Even if this were unanswerable, it would not prove that – since he has the right equipment – the African's golden age might not lie ahead. It is not unanswerable, however. Africa has produced far more than Western people realize. More than one scientist has been struck by the similarity between certain works by long-dead West African artists and exquisite examples of Chinese, Mexican and Javanese art.

Leading European sculptors have found inspiration in the work of the West African.

It is now recognized that African music has subtleties of rhythm far finer than anything achieved by a Western composer. In fact the more complicated Negro rhythms cannot be rendered on Western instruments at all.

Such achievements can hardly be the work of a fundamentally inferior people. When the African realizes this and builds on his own traditions, borrowing mainly the Westerner's technology (a technology – he should note – that is being shown not to function except in a socialist framework) he may develop into a people regarding whom the adjective 'inferior' would be ludicrous rather than appropriate.

8 August 1936

Edited by a rationalist, a humanist, the New Statesman *in the Thirties was nevertheless not intolerant of religion; its agnosticism was urbane. But it was critical of the religious, as of the social and political, Establishments. H. G. Wells, who wrote a good deal for the paper from time to time, expresses a new statesmanly view of prelatical faith.*

147

Answer to Prayer   H. G. Wells

The Archbishop was perplexed by his own state of mind. Maybe the shadow of age was falling upon him, he thought, maybe he had been overworking, maybe the situation had been too complex for him and he was feeling the reality of a failure without seeing it plainly as a definable fact. But his nerve, which had never failed him hitherto, was failing him now. In small things as in important matters he no longer showed the quick decisiveness that had hitherto been the envy of his fellow ecclesiastics and the admiration of his friends. He doubted now before he went upstairs or downstairs, with a curious feeling that he might find something unexpected on the landing. He hesitated before he rang a bell, with a vague uncertainty of who or what might appear. Before he took up the letters his secretary had opened for him he had a faint twinge of apprehension.

Had he after all done something wrong or acted in a mistaken spirit?

People who had always been nice to him showed a certain coolness, people from whom he would have least expected it. His secretaries, he knew, were keeping back 'open letters' and grossly abusive comments. The reassurances and encouragements that flowed in to him were anything but reassuring, because their volume and their tone reflected what was hidden from him on the other side. Had he, at the end of his long, tortuous and hitherto quite dignified career, made a howler?

There was no one on earth to whom he could confide his trouble. He had always been a man who kept his own counsel. But now, if only he could find understanding, sympathy, endorsement! If he could really put things as he saw them, if he could simplify the whole confused affair down to essentials and make his stand plain and clear.

Prayer?

If anyone else had come to him in this sort of quandary, he would have told him at once to pray. If it was a woman he would have patted the shoulder gently, as an elderly man may do, and he would have said very softly in that rich kind voice of his, 'Try Prayer, my dear. Try Prayer.'

Physician heal thyself. Why not try prayer?

He stood hesitatingly between his apartments and his little private oratory. He stood in what was his habitual children's service attitude with his hands together in front of him, his head a little on one side and something faintly bland and whimsical about him. It came to him that he himself had not made a personal and particular appeal to God for many years. It had seemed unnecessary. It had indeed been unnecessary. He had of course said his prayers with the utmost regularity, not only in the presence

148

of others, but, being essentially an honest man, even when he was alone. He had never cheated about prayer. He had felt it was a purifying and beneficial process, no more to be missed than cleaning his teeth, but his sense of a definite hearer, listening at the other end of the telephone, so to speak, behind the veil, had always been a faint one. The reception away there was in the Absolute, in Eternity, beyond the stars. Which indeed left the church conveniently free to take an unembarrassed course of action. . . .

But in this particular tangle, the Archbishop wanted something more definite. If, for once, he did not trouble about style and manner. . . .

If he put the case simply, quite simply, just as he saw it, and remained very still on his knees, wouldn't he presently find this neuralgic fretting of his mind abating, and that assurance, that clear self-assurance that had hitherto been his strength, returning to him? He must not be in the least oily – they had actually been calling him oily – he must be perfectly direct and simple and fearless. He must pray straightforwardly to the silence as one mind to another.

It was a little like the practice of some Dissenters and Quakers, but maybe it would be none the less effective on that account.

Yes, he would pray.

Slowly he sank to his knees and put his hands together. He was touched by a sort of childish trustfulness in his own attitude. 'Oh God,' he began, and paused.

He paused, and a sense of awful imminence, a monstrous awe, gripped him. And then he heard a voice.

It was not a harsh voice, but it was a clear strong voice. There was nothing about it still or small. It was neither friendly nor hostile; it was brisk.

'*Yes,*' said the voice. '*What is it?*'

They found His Grace in the morning. He had slipped off the steps on which he had been kneeling and lay sprawling on the crimson carpet. Plainly his death had been instantaneous.

But instead of the serenity, the almost fatuous serenity, that was his habitual expression, his countenance, by some strange freak of nature, displayed an extremity of terror and dismay.

10 April 1937

George Barker was a new poet when his work first appeared in the New Statesman.

Lines Looking West   George Barker

Waking, like the walker into water,
Where did I wander but to Wales, where
The mountain wave, worse than the sea's wave,
Rose cold and suicidal over, soused
My pity in a snow shower, and I drowned.

The flower in glass or the fly in glue,
I lay in Wales watching the Welsh go.
Some went up Snowdon waving red flags, gay
Flourishing their hearts on sticks, to God.
Some descended the hell shafts to get to heaven.

The swan that lies perishing by the sea,
The city in the south, I heard sing:

Its sound was sorrow copied by the sea.
Then I was walking in an old garden's scum
Whose plague of leaves I recognised as human.

Where, I said, is the usual hoard of the west,
The Great Western Sun that polishes the rocks with
Grease of gold? Where is the waste,
I hear the hills repeat, but in the west.
Wait, they cry, for the summer's fortnight murmur!

Turning to return I met a man.
Wait, he said, I see what you mean.
Good, I answered, and so do many more
Gazing on the Welsh gap from the London moon.
They see the sunset, but not that the sun sets.

24 April 1937

---

*New statesmanship had two ways of striving against such vicious social
evils as the infamous Means Test which destroyed the self-respect of millions
of our fellow-countrymen in the Thirties. One was to keep presenting the
case against it in argument. The other was to use the talent of imaginative
writers, Orwell for one, to bring home to the more fortunate what it was like to
be a victim of the Thirties' economic imbecility, as in this piece by James Hanley.*

Means Test   James Hanley

He was an old man, short and heavily built, though the once broad
shoulders were now stooped. He was standing by the window in the little
kitchen. For some ten minutes now he had been standing there, looking
out, though what he stared at nobody could tell. Nobody really cared.
The old man seemed to be waiting for news. Behind him, seated on a low
black chair, was a young woman. She sat with her arms folded in her lap.
Her arms were bared to the elbow. Neither spoke. The old man's eyes
watered as freely as a ripe melon, and from time to time he took a large
white handkerchief from his pocket and dabbed rather than rubbed his
eyes with it. The fire in the grate had burned low, but the young woman

made no attempt to replenish it. This she would do from a arge-size child's sand-bucket. It was filled with all black-looking rubbish which he foraged for every morning. He called it 'back pay', she called it 'smalls'. A large wooden table in the middle of the floor contained the débris of the morning's breakfast. It gave the impression of being hastily left, as though one of the sitters had been hurriedly summoned to some task or other. The two other chairs were pushed in beneath it. Two cups and saucers with spilled tea, the morning newspaper splashed with it, broken bread, a large salt-cellar full of sugar, a cup without a handle containing milk. From time to time a gust of black soot blew down the chimney, filling the air with its acrid odour. Over the mantelshelf there hung a cheap oleograph of King Edward VII. An alarm-clock that never rang now and minus the hour hand, was the only other furnishing of the mantelshelf. The floor was stone, covered with a straw matting, much worn; its threads like feelers pawed across the stone flags. The old man coughed, moved from one side of the window to the other, rested on this leg, then on that, helped by a heavy stick.

He never once turned round to speak to the young woman, and she herself seemed quite indifferent. Indeed, her grandfather did not exist. Her orbit of vision was the stone floor; for some time she studied a crack in one of the cleanly scrubbed stone flags. People passed and repassed the window. The young woman never looked up, her grandfather just went on dabbing his eyes. Lying at his feet was a small oilcloth shopping bag. A worn tie hung out of it. The bag was full. It contained all his worldly belongings. They were both waiting. Once the young woman made an attempt as though she meant to re-stoke the fire, for she half rose in the chair, then with a curious expression upon her face, she sat down again, as though movement were painful, futile. The black cat came in through the open back-kitchen window, walked to the mat, lay down, stretched itself, looked up at the young woman, but she did not appear to see it. It went across to the old man, curled itself against his leg, walked round him, purring. It jumped on the table, smelt about, began lapping the milk in the broken cup. The woman in the chair looked at it as though horrified, but she did not move. Upstairs a room door banged loudly, its sound had a cavernous effect, it echoed and re-echoed through the house. A strong draught blew in through the kitchen door. In the street dogs were barking, fighting. The old man began fumbling with his vest pocket, and after a minute or two he dragged out a worn, well-rubbed gun-metal watch and noted the time. Half-past ten. It took him much longer to put the watch back in his pocket. It made him cough a lot. A loud knock came to the door. At last the woman got up, crossed the kitchen and opened the door. A little man, wearing a shabby overcoat, almost precipitated himself into the kitchen, a roll of cheap oil-cloth dragging at his heels. The woman quickly put out her foot, stopped him. She pushed the little man right back into the street. 'For Christ's sake,' the man said, as the door slammed in his face.

The old man seemed quite indifferent to anything and everything, he had not noticed the incident at all. He just went on looking out through the window at the grey, leaden sky, leaning heavily on his stick, hand-kerchief at the ready in his left hand. His lips were trembling, he slobbered a little, wiped this with a violently shaking hand.

The young woman went to the mantelshelf and picked up the alarm-clock, shook it violently, put its face to her ear, shook it again, banged it down on the shelf again, and a cloud of dust arose in the air. She resumed her seat by the wall. It was so silent she could hear the tick of her grand-father's watch. Her thick black hair, undone, hung slovenly about her ears and shoulders. The expression upon her face never changed, as though it were fleshed there for all time. She heard the old man's feet beginning to shuffle on the stone floor. It would be growing restlessness in him, she thought. She began looking at her hands, first one, then the other. They were very red, she flopped them about, they seemed lifeless. They were shaped by toil. As she began to bite her nails the back door opened and her husband came in. She did not look at him, even when he crossed to the table, and taking some coins from his pocket, placed them on it. The old man had not turned round, though he realized the man's presence by the rattle of the money. He turned suddenly now and stared across at the young man.

The husband was a young man about thirty. He had not worked for five and a half years. He wore a blue serge suit, the trousers of which shone like glass when they caught the light. A white scarf round his neck and a check cap pulled down over one eye completed his dress. His boots, heavily covered with dubbin, seemed to be made up of crude patches of varying kinds of leather. He took a white form from his pocket, also a ten shilling note, and crossing the kitchen, laid them in the young woman's lap. His wife looked up at him. Her expression was as wooden as before. She picked up the ten shilling note, straightened it out; it crackled in her rough hands. Then she picked up the coins, counted them, then let them fall noisily into her lap again. Her husband went up to the old man, patted him on the shoulder. She thought he would speak to her grand-father, but he said no word. He spat into the low fire, lit a half cigarette,

153

then put a shovel-full of 'back pay' on the dying fire. The hour had put a premium upon his tongue. He stood looking at the newly-stoked fire, hands in his pockets.

Now the old man turned away from the window. He looked at them both. His lips moved as though he were going to say something, and something like fear appeared in the young woman's face, for she picked up the money and the white form. She took a half-crown from the coins, closing her fist on the remainder. The old man lowered his eyes. They were standing face to face. He began scratching his chin, rubbing his lined forehead. He appeared to be trying to think. Of course, his going was a wrench, not to them, of course – he knew that – but then, if he went it would help them no end. Had he not seen her smile when the money fell into her lap? That secret smile he knew so well. Yes, and he could see that she had not far to go now. There was the child to think about. He felt a little sick in his stomach. It was the going, the step into the street, the separation from his chair, the little world of all his days, world of the past, many memories, yes, it was the stepping out from the quiet of the chair into lodgings, into the greater world, the jungle. But then times had changed. He knew that. The world had a bit of a crack in it, he had no doubt. By his going he helped. So now he would go. It meant a few shillings more to them. He could see by looking at her husband that he had been successful with the official this morning. He would say nothing. Go very quietly. Here she was coming towards him now, her husband with his back to both of them, for he was still staring into the fire. The woman took her grandfather's right hand, a thumbless hand – it had been blown off when he was a boy in the pit. She pressed the half-crown into his palm, closed his hand with her own, squeezed it. Through his bleary eyes he glimpsed the milk whiteness of her breast, she, prisoner of all that was grey. He wiped his eyes with the handkerchief, and walked slowly to the front door, leaning on his stick. She opened it for him. The husband heard it open but he did not look round. All feeling had dried up in him. He heard the shuffling step of the old man, and his heart gave a sudden thump in his breast, yet he knew not why. The old man was stepping down into the street. Soon they would be separated, worlds apart, he into the unknown amongst strangers, a few years yet to live, holding the secret dread of his kind, a morbid terror of unkindness. She to the grey fastness of her kitchen. Only now did she speak. Gripping her grandfather's two hands, she said, 'Ta! Ta!' He did not reply, did not look back, and as he stepped into the street she closed the front door on him. She went back to her chair. Her husband looked across at her. He, too, saw the milk-whiteness of her breast, like a bright flower after acres of mud. 'It will mean a few bob extra with his going', the man said.

The young woman rose from her chair, and with a sudden wild sweep of her hand cleared the table of its debris. 'It's hard lines,' the man said. She said no word, walked slowly from the kitchen. He heard her heavy tread upon the stairs.

2 October 1937

There are Bombers at the Bottom of My Garden
'Sagittarius'

There are bombers at the bottom of my garden,
But I'm not a teeny weeny bit afraid,
'Cause good Sir Samuel Hoare told us long before the war
What to do for home protection in a raid.
So we've made a lovely refuge with brown paper
On the Nursery-Anti-Gas-Precautions Plan –
I 'spect some people doubt poison gas can be kept out –
Well, it can.

There are bombers at the bottom of my garden,
But experts say they won't be there for long,
'Cause our air-arm (one to three) will chase them out to sea
And our anti-aircraft guns are going strong.
I'm not the leastest bit surprised to see them,
'Cause Baldwin told us bombers *must* get through,
And I think it's awful good that we've got Sir Kingsley Wood –
Well, don't you?

There are bombers at the bottom of my garden,
But Inskip says that home's the safest place,
So we'll just sit here and wait in our 10 × 10 × 8,
And my dolly's got a gas-mask, just in case.
And if *our* bombers bomb *these* bombers' countries,
Well, foreign countries have *their* A.R.P.,
So no little girls and boys need be gassed among their toys,
And I hope they'll all be just as safe as me.

11 June 1938

Of the Catholic novelists only Graham Greene found himself, from time to time, in a thoroughly new statesmanly state of mind; most of his contributions to the paper have been 'Books in General' essays. But here is an exception.

Twenty-four Hours in Metroland   Graham Greene

The little town always had an air of grit about it, as one came in under the echoing tin railway arch associated with shabby prams and Sunday walks, unwilling returns to Evensong – grit beside the watercress beds and on the panes of the station's private entrance which the local Lord had not used for generations. Now it appeared from the elderly lady's conversation and the furtive appearances in the lamplight that the grit had really worked in. Neither country nor city, a dormitory district – there are things which go on in dormitories. . . .

Sunday evening, and the bells jangling in the town; small groups of youths hovered round the traffic lights, while the Irish servant girls crept out of back doors in the early dark. 'Romans', the elderly lady called them. You couldn't keep them in at night – they would arrive with the milk in a stranger's car from Watford, slipping out in stockinged feet from the villas above the valley. The youths – smarmed and scented hair and bitten cigarettes – greeted them in the dark with careless roughness. There were so many fish in the sea . . . sexual experience had come to them too early and too easily. The London, Midland and Scottish Line waited for everyone.

Up on the hillside the beech trees were in glorious and incredible decay: little green boxes for litter put up by the National Trust had a dainty and doyly effect; and in the inn the radio played continuously. You couldn't escape it: with your soup a dramatized account of the battle of Mons, and with the joint a Methodist church service. Four one-armed men dined together, arranging their seats so that their arms shouldn't clash.

In the morning, mist lay heavy on the Chilterns. Boards marking desirable building lots dripped on short grass where the sheep were washed out. The skeletons of harrows lay unburied on the wet stubble. With visibility shut down to fifty yards you got no sense of a world, of simultaneous existences: each thing was self-contained like an image of private significance, standing for something else – Metroland, loneliness. The door of the Plough Inn chimed when you pushed it, ivory balls clicked and a bystander said, 'They do this at the Crown, Margate' – England's heart beating out in bagatelle towards her eastern extremity; the landlady had a weak heart, and dared not serve food these days in case she went off just like that in the rush. In a small front garden before a red villa a young girl knelt in the damp with an expression abashed and secretive while she sawed through the limbs of a bush, the saw wailing through wet wood, and a woman's angry voice called 'Judy, Judy,' and a dog barked in the poultry farm across the way. A cigarette fumed into ash with no one in sight, only a little shut red door marked Ker Even; 'the leading Cairn Terrier Farm' was noisy on the crest of the down, the dogs like the radio, never ceasing – how does life go on ? And at the newsagent's in the market town below the Chiltern ridge there was a shrewd game on sale, very popular locally, called 'Monopoly', played with dice and counters – 'The object of owning property is to collect rent from opponents stopping there. Rentals are greatly increased by the erection of houses and hotels. . . . Players falling on an unoccupied square may raise a loan from the bank, otherwise property will be sold to the highest bidder. . . . Players may land in jail.' The soil exacted no service and no love: among the beechwoods a new house was for sale. It had only been lived in a month: the woods and commons were held out by wire. The owners, married last December, were divorced this summer. Neither wanted the house. A handyman swept up the leaves – a losing fight – and lamented the waste. 'Four coats of paint in every room . . . I was going to make a pond in that dell – and I was just getting the kitchen garden straight – you can see for yourself.'

Kick these hills and they bleed white. The mist is like an exhalation of the chalk. Beechwoods and gorse and the savage Metro heart behind the Whipsnade wire: elephants turning and turning behind glass on little aesthetic circular platforms like exhibits in a 'modern' shop window, behind them dripping firs as alien as themselves; ostriches suddenly visible at thirty yards, like snakeheads rising out of heaps of dung. A wolf wailing invisibly in the mist, the sun setting at 4.30, the traffic lights out in the High Street and the Irish maids putting the door on the latch. In an hour or two the commuters return to sleep in their Siberian dormitory – an acre of land, a desirable residence for as long as the marriage lasts, no roots, no responsibility for the child on the line. 'The object of owning property .'

13 August 1938

In Michael Zoshchenko the Soviet Union produced a satirist of the first order. The State and Government being what they were did not like it. Many of Zoshchenko's brilliantly funny short stories appeared in the New Statesman.

The Crisis

Michael Zoshchenko

The other day, citizens, I saw a cart full of bricks going along the street. Yes, I swear to it!

My heart simply leapt with joy. Because you understand, citizens, it means building, no more or less! No one in his senses would cart bricks for nothing! It means that a house is being built somewhere. Building's begun in good earnest, touch wood!

Perhaps in twenty years' time, or even less, each citizen of our great country will have a room to himself. And if the population doesn't increase too rapidly, then everyone might get two rooms. Or even three to one person. With a bathroom!

That would be a fine life, citizens! We'd sleep in one room, entertain visitors in another, do something else, whatever it may be, in the third. We'd find a whole lot of different things to do when life's so free and easy!

But meanwhile the problem of where to live is not easy to solve. There isn't enough square metres of space to go round because of the housing crisis.

I've recently been to Moscow, friends. I've had a first-hand experience of this crisis.

When I arrived at Moscow, I began looking for a room. Up and down the streets I walked, carrying my things in my hands. Nothing doing. There was nowhere to leave my stuff, to say nothing of spending the night.

For a fortnight I wandered in this fashion about the streets, grew a beard and lost most of my things. And I continued looking for a room, unencumbered, so to speak.

At last in a block of flats I met a man coming down the stairs.

'For three hundred roubles,' he told me, 'I can fix you up in a bathroom. It's a gentleman's flat. Three lavatories and a bathroom. You can live in the bathroom. True, there's no window, but there's a door. And plenty of water. You can fill the bath with water,' he said, 'and swim in it all day long if you like.'

To this I replied:

'I'm not a fish, dear comrade. I don't want to swim all day. I'd rather live in a dry place. Can't you knock something off the price on account of the dampness?'

'I'd like to but I can't, comrade,' said he. 'It doesn't depend entirely on me. The flat's a communal flat. And the price for the bathroom has been decided upon communally.'

'Well,' said I, 'I call it robbery. But what is a man to do? All right. Take my three hundred roubles and let me in at once. I've been walking about the streets for three weeks. I'm getting a bit tired.'

Well, they let me in, and I soon settled down.

The bathroom was, in fact, a gentleman's bathroom. A marble bath with beautiful taps, a marble pillar supporting the ceiling and all that. But as it happens, there was nothing to sit on. Only the edge of the bath, and that, being marble, was very slippery. And you slipped off it straight down into the marble bath. . . .

I made a cover for it out of planks, and carried on.

A month later, as it happens, I got married.

I married a nice, good-natured young woman. She had no room.

I was a bit afraid that she'd turn me down on account of the bath, and that I'd never know the comfort and happiness of married life. But she did not turn me down. When she saw the bath, she just frowned a bit, and then said:

'Well, good people live in bathrooms as well as anywhere else. And if it comes to the worst, we could always put up a partition wall. F'r instance, we could make a boudoir here, and a dining-room there. . . .'

'To put up a partition wall is always possible, citizeness,' I told her. 'But the other tenants wouldn't allow it, the devil take them. The condition is: no alteration whatever.'

Well, we settled down to things as they were.

In a little less than a year a small child was born to my wife and me. We called him Volodia, and went on living as before. The bath proved very handy for bathing him.

In fact, it proved a very great convenience indeed. The child was bathed every day and never caught cold.

There was one inconvenience, though: in the evening the communal tenants insisted on taking their baths. And my whole family had to turn out into the passage while they did.

I tried to persuade them to take their baths on Saturdays.

'Citizens,' I told them, 'it isn't nice to bathe every day. Life is made very difficult for us by your habits of cleanliness. You must try and see our point of view.'

But they, the devils, were thirty-two men strong. And they used the worst possible language. They even threatened to smash my face for me.

What is a man to do? We had to put up with it. And so we went on living.

Soon after that my wife's mother arrived from the provinces. She settled down behind the marble pillar.

'I've been looking forward always to nursing a grandchild,' she told me. 'You cannot possibly deny me this pleasure.'

I said:

'I'm not denying it to you. Get on with it, old lady, nurse him as much as you like. You may, if you wish, fill the bath with water and dive in with your grandchild, if it please you.'

And to my wife I said:

'Perhaps you're expecting more relatives to come, citizeness? If so, tell me straight away. Don't keep a man in suspense.'

And she said:

'I'm not sure, but my little brother might come for the Christmas holidays perhaps. . . .'

Without waiting for the little brother, I left Moscow. And I'm sending money to my family by post.

Translated by Elisaveta Fen
3 September 1938

Time and the Fascist dictators having worked their ironical joke, new statesmanship was quicker than most to see in Winston Churchill the one effective leader against Hitler and Mussolini. A dialogue between Mr Churchill and Kingsley Martin at the beginning of the critical year 1939 reveals the basis of the alliance.

Mr Churchill on Democracy   Kingsley Martin and
                                     Winston Churchill

A famous journalist once told me of an alarming interview that he had with Mr Churchill some years before the last war. Mr Churchill happened to be in full Privy Councillor's uniform and emphasized his points with finely executed passes and slashes of his sword. Mr Churchill himself declares that this is a fairy tale; and certainly, when I went to see him the other day, he was wielding nothing more ferocious than the builder's trowel with which he was completing an arch in the house that he has built with his own hands this summer. He was not, however, too much absorbed to discuss very fully the problem of Democracy and Efficiency.

Kingsley Martin. The country has learnt to associate you, Mr Churchill, with the view that we must all get together as quickly as possible to rearm in defence of democracy. Now I am constantly asked whether this is a possible conception. In view of the strength and character of the totalitarian states, is it possible for a democracy to rearm without in the process surrendering its essential nature? Is it in your view possible to combine the reality of democratic freedom with efficient military organization?

Mr Winston Churchill. The essential aspects of democracy are the freedom of the individual, within the framework of laws passed by Parliament, to order his life as he pleases, and the uniform enforcement of tribunals independent of the executive. These laws are based on Magna Carta, Habeas Corpus, the Petition of Right, and others. Above all, they secure the freedom of the individual from arbitrary arrest for crimes unknown to the law, and provide for trial by jury of his equals. Without this foundation there can be no freedom or civilization, anyone being at the mercy of officials and liable to be spied upon and betrayed even in his own home. As long as these rights are defended, the foundations of freedom are secure. I see no reason why democracies should not be able to defend themselves without sacrificing these fundamental values.

K.M. One point people are especially afraid of is that free criticism in Parliament, on the platform and in the Press may be sacrificed. The totalitarian states, it is said, are regimented, organized and unhampered, as the Prime Minister suggested the other day, by critics of the Government 'who foul their own nest'.

W.C. I am aware that it has recently become fashionable to describe criticism of the action of the Prime Minister as fouling our own nest— a convenient thesis, if a dangerous one. Criticism may not be agreeable, but it is necessary. It fulfils the same function as pain in the human body; it calls attention to the development of an unhealthy state of things. If it is heeded in time, danger may be averted; if it is suppressed, a fatal distemper may develop.

K.M. Do you attribute the slowness in preparation of which you complain to any inherent defect in democratic institutions?

W.C. I am convinced that, with adequate leadership, democracy can be a more efficient form of government than Fascism. In this country at any rate the people can readily be convinced that it is necessary to make sacrifices, and they will willingly undertake them if the situation is put clearly and fairly before them. Naturally if the leaders of a Conservative Government insist that all is well, one can scarcely expect the Opposition leaders to press for increased armaments. But no one can doubt that it was within the power of the National Government at any time within the last seven years to rearm the country at any pace required without resistance from the mass of the people. The difficulty was that the leaders failed to appreciate the need and to warn the people, or were afraid to do their duty, not that the democratic system formed an impediment. In my view, short-sighted leaders are just as likely to come to the front in Fascist countries as in democracies.

K.M. You held great executive positions in the last war. Was it your experience that the Government was in any way hampered by the existence of parliamentary criticism? Should we have been better off with totalitarianism? Looking at the matter from a purely military point of view, should we have been more efficient if employers and employees had both been more regimented and less able to bargain? Would you attribute the scarcity of munitions in the early part of the war in any degree to the insistence of private manufacturers and employers on profits in wartime?

W.C. It may be that greater efficiency in secret military preparations can be achieved in a country with autocratic institutions than by the democratic system. But this advantage is not necessarily great and it is far outweighed by the strength of a democratic country in a long war. In an autocracy, when the pinch comes, the blame is thrown upon the leader and the system breaks up, as we saw in Germany and Russia. In a democratic country the people feel that they are responsible, and if they believe in their cause will hold out much longer than the population of Dictator States. Questions in Parliament and Debates, far from hindering the conduct of the war, frequently assist it by exposing weak points and give opportunities to clear up misunderstandings. Occasional difficulties arose with organized labour, but by working with and through the Trade Unions, these were all settled in a friendly manner. Of course the power to withdraw protection from military service lay in the background, but I do not think it was ever necessary to use it. I did not find that the existence of the profit motive on the part of manufacturers in any way hampered the production of munitions. It is true that in the early days orders were sometimes placed and accepted beyond the capacity of the factories to meet, and that the scarcity of munitions may be in part attributed to the undue optimism of the services and the manufacturers who had not sufficiently allowed for inevitable delays. But this was a question of inexperience rather than anything else.

K.M. I gather that you believe that Britain gained and did not lose from maintaining the structure of democratic institutions during the last war. Do you believe that these institutions could survive in another war? Could the Press maintain the measure of freedom that it then had? Would Parliament be able to function comparatively normally? How far do you think it would be necessary to compel labour and how far would the State need to go on taking over the control of industry.

W.C. The next war will presumably be entirely different from the last in that it will have to be carried on whilst the Capital and the greater part of the country are being disturbed by air raids. I see no reason why a censorship much more severe than existed in the last war should be imposed. Parliament would probably find it difficult, indeed dangerous, to meet regularly at Westminster. It might be asked to delegate a part of its day-to-day work to a number of large committees containing members of all the various parties, and to meet as a whole three or four times a year in suitable places to discuss the reports of these committees. Of course I am assuming that legislation would be in force 'to take the profit out of war'. The Americans have made a great study of this, and it would be easy to apply the same principles here. By 'taking the profit out of war' I mean that no one anyhow should come out of it richer than he went in. This could be achieved by assessing the value of undertakings at the outbreak of war on the basis of the information available to the Revenue Department, and insisting that nobody should be better off at the end of the war than at the beginning. Hardship would of course arise in the case of businesses just about to expand, but no man would have cause for complaint if he found himself at the end of the war as well off as he was at the beginning. I do not believe that this knowledge would in wartime in any way impair the enthusiasm and drive required from the employers, although it would in peace-time. As I have said, I feel certain that the knowledge that these measures would be effective would prevent in a great degree difficulties arising with organized labour.

K.M. May I go back now to the question of pre-war preparation which I think is more in people's minds? We should all agree on the necessity for many restrictions in wartime, but what about conscription and the compulsion of labour and capital in time of peace? Captain Liddell Hart has remarked that to have conscription to combat Fascism is like cutting our throats to avoid a disease.

W.C. I see no reason why any essential part of our liberties should be lost by preparations for defence. The demands of Somerset House are far more searching and disagreeable than any questions which could conceivably be put in producing a National Register. Yet nobody clamours against them as an infringement of liberty and privacy. I do not think we need a great conscript army on the continental model, but we should have besides our regular professional army a considerably larger body of Territorials available for home defence or foreign service in an emergency. If Parliament so decided, in case of war a great army could be built up around such a skeleton. I would not hesitate, if the numbers sanctioned by Parliament of the Territorial troops could not be obtained by the voluntary system, to fill up the gap by ballot among all the young men of the country of the appropriate age, allowing no substitute whatsoever. Nothing could be more democratic, or more likely to democratize the army. When one remembers that the democracy of France has voluntarily taken two years out of the life of each young man to safeguard its liberties, I cannot see that some such system, which would impose a sacrifice of only a few months on a small fraction of our population, could be regarded as a surrender to Fascism.

K.M. How much coercion of industry is implied in a Ministry of Supply with special powers? Will it involve State control of raw materials, and do you think that we need a system of State control to compete with the methods that the Nazis have so successfully employed in South-East Europe and South America?

W.C. As you know, I have long pressed for a Ministry of Supply. In my view this should have powers, if necessary, to compel industry to give priority as required to Government contracts for rearmament purposes, and to devote or turn over any necessary portion of its plant to such work. I do not believe these powers would have to be brought into play to any large extent, nor do I believe, if arrangements to limit profits such as already exist were efficiently brought into effect, that it would be necessary to mobilize the industrial worker. As to State trading, this is not part of a scheme of a Ministry of Supply, though I gather that the Board of Trade are seriously considering special methods to deal with abnormal conditions which State trading in other countries is producing in certain parts of the world.

K.M. May I pass on to another related subject—ARP? People write to me and say that the problem of defending London and other big cities in itself involves regimentation on an enormous scale. That you have to set up an army of petty officers with undefined powers, and that the only effect of preparing London psychologically for the possible ordeal of bombing is to make the East End sure that they will not be defended, while the rich will have the means of looking after themselves.

W.C. I think a great mistake has been made in spreading our ARP efforts over the whole country, instead of concentrating on what I should call the target areas and the paths to and from them. I do not believe any enemy will waste his bombs and effort on killing ordinary citizens just out of spite, when he could obtain a much greater military result by bombing docks, factories, Government offices and the like. I am certain that in the villages the risk will be infinitesimal. Our main effort should be to protect workers in the central parts of London, in the ports, and in the manufacturing districts which will be subject to attack. I should be inclined to consider the building of great underground roads, leading out of London and branching off to various points in the countryside, which would not only serve to evacuate the Capital in times of danger, but could be used as dormitories and refuges for those who were compelled to remain behind. In peacetime they would be of use either as garages, or probably in solving some of our traffic difficulties. That some steps should be taken in advance to prepare the population for the ordeal of war, seems to me essential. All other great nations have taken this line. If everybody knows that preparations have been made, and what to do, it seems to me there is less likelihood of inhabitants of the East End believing they will be left in the lurch while the rich look after themselves.

K.M. There is another question that I am often asked. People who are not necessarily pacifist are horrified at the idea that we may go into another war with the same kind of generals who were responsible for Passchendaele and other horrors in the last war. They say that they might be prepared to fight for democracy, as people are today in Spain, if they were democratically led; but that they are damned if they will be sacrificed again for the Camberley clique that was so horribly inefficient and wasteful in the last war. They fear not so much conscription as conscription under the old type of officer who was still thinking in terms of cavalry charges in 1916. Do you think it is possible to democratize the army?

W.C. It is quite true, I know, that many people consider that the cadre of officers is selected from too narrow a class. I have always taken the view that it should be possible for any man to rise from the ranks, and that merit should be rewarded by promotion in the army as in any other profession. I support this not only from the point of view of democratizing the army, but mainly because I think it leads to efficiency such as no other system can achieve.

K.M. May I ask one more question of a more general character? Most of us feel that if there is a war, whatever the efforts we may make to win it, or whatever efforts we may make to keep alive the ideals and essentials of democracy during war, nevertheless the war itself will be so destructive that the very substance of our civilization, let alone our democracy, is likely to be destroyed. Clearly the great object is to prevent war. Is it possible in your view still to regard these military preparations, not as the acceptance of inevitable war, but merely as a necessary complement of a policy which may keep the peace?

W.C. I fear that failure to rearm Britain is bound to lead to war. Had we strengthened our defences earlier, the arms race need never have arisen. We should have come to a settlement with Germany in good time, while she was still disarmed. But even now there are far more governments in the world anxious to preserve peace than to attack their neighbours. If these could be brought together under the aegis of the League of Nations to form a common front, I think it is still possible, with a strong Britain and France, to preserve the peace of Europe.

K.M. Is it not true historically that an armaments race leads to war? Do you believe that this period is exceptional?

W.C. To say that an arms race always leads to war seems to me to be putting the cart before the horse. A government resolved to attain ends detrimental to its neighbours, which does not shrink from the possibility of war, makes preparations for war, its neighbours take defensive action, and you say an arms race is beginning. But this is the symptom of the existence of the intention of one government to challenge or destroy its neighbours, not the cause of the conflict. In such circumstances, the side which has failed to keep up in the arms race may receive a set-back without a war, but it will never maintain its position or interests. The pace is set by the potential aggressor, and, failing collective action by the rest of the world, to resist him, the alternatives are an arms race or surrender. War is very terrible, but stirs a proud people. There have been periods in our history when we have given way for a long time, but a new and formidable mood arises. . . .

K.M. A bellicose mood?

W.C. A mood of 'Thus far, and no farther.' It is only by the spirit of resistance that man has learnt to stand upright, and instead of walking on all fours to assume an erect posture.

K.M. Do you think it possible, as people like Professor Haldane have recently suggested, to concentrate mainly on defence with the idea that we should be less afraid of attack and therefore able to stand up for ourselves without preparing to bomb other people?

W.C. I cannot subscribe to the idea that it might be possible to dig ourselves in and make no preparations for anything other than passive defence. It is the theory of the turtle, which is disproved at every Lord Mayor's Banquet. If the enemy can attack as and when he pleases without fear of reprisals, we should become the whipping-boy of Europe. We need shelters and tunnels, but crouching in a shelter is not a fighting posture. Quite apart from the fact that we could never defend our dependencies on such lines, we should be exposed to inevitable defeat. At any minute he pleased, the enemy could practically destroy any commerce and industry without danger to himself. Every nation of the world would have an incentive to have a free cut at the melon. War is horrible, but slavery is worse, and you may be sure that the British people would rather go down fighting than live in servitude.

7 January 1939

In October 1939 Bernard Shaw hoped that he could stop the war by publishing his arguments in favour of that course. In spite of a strong protest by Maynard Keynes, a New Statesman *director, the article was published. It made less stir than his 1915 contribution 'Common Sense about the War'.*

Uncommon Sense about the War   Bernard Shaw

Last week, in pursuance of our policy of making the N.S. and N. as much an open forum for the free expression of opinion as is possible in wartime, we published a number of 'communications' dealing with the position and policy of the Soviet Union. This week, in pursuance of the same policy, we publish Mr Bernard Shaw's provocative contribution. Manifestly, we are not to be taken as endorsing the views expressed by our contributors – for we shall leave them free to advocate widely divergent attitudes. Our own opinion on the issues raised by Mr Shaw will be gathered by our readers from our editorial columns. – Ed. N.S. & N.

The war in Poland is over. Every person in the country capable of seeing three moves ahead in the game of military chess has known this from the moment when the first Russian soldier stepped across the Polish frontier. Poland surrendered and laid herself at Herr Hitler's feet. He was able to say that as Poland's cause is lost we have no further excuse for continuing the war. Whereupon we threw off the mask of knight errantry and avowed flatly that we did not care two hoots about Poland and were out, on our old balance of power lines, to disable Germany, which we now called abolishing Hitlerism.

This left the Führer in a very dangerous position. The Axis had broken in his hands from the beginning, Italy and Spain having promptly deserted him. Turkey was definitely against him: Rumania and the Balkans generally were mortally afraid of him. America's neutrality was pro-British just as our non-intervention policy in the Spanish war was pro-Franco. 1918 had proved that Germany, though unconquerable and even victorious here and there in the field, could be starved into complete demoralization and defeat by the Allies. The situation was not pleasant even for a leader drunk with success. The encirclement was fairly complete. Except on one side, where Russia stood with an army of six million men eating their heads off. Those of us who were intelligent and knowledgeable enough to see that the balance of power was in the hands of Stalin had forced our Government to make overtures to Russia, and Mr Duff Cooper, a very favourable specimen of our reigning oligarchy, loosened his old school tie so far as to plead in the *Evening Standard* that Stalin, though of course a blood-thirsty scoundrel, was perhaps not quite so villainous as Hitler. Herr Hitler, having the tremendous advantage over Mr Duff Cooper of being a proletarian and knowing something about the world he was living in, courted Russia more sensibly.

Stalin, five hundred per cent or so abler and quicker at the uptake than all the dictators, including the Westminster Cabinet, rolled into one, had nothing to consider except which of them he should take by the scruff of the neck. Before deciding, he sent a handful of his six millions to take possession of White Russia, the Ukraine, and a substantial bit of Poland. Herr Hitler at once capitulated unconditionally, and was duly taken by the scruff of his neck; for Stalin could use Herr Hitler to keep Duff Cooperism out of the rest of Poland. He informed us in effect that since we could not even be civil to Russia we should not make Poland a gun emplacement for the obvious ultimate aim of our rulers (as far as they are capable of aims) of restoring the Romanoff Tsardom and once more dining happily with the Benckendorffs in Chester Square. And so the diplomatic situation stands. Nothing has happened since except that the French, whether after consultation with us or not I do not know, have most inopportunely started persecuting their Communists. . . .

Meanwhile we are enduring all the vagaries, from mere discomfort to financial ruin and the breaking up of our homes, of the ineptest Military Communism. Powers which no Plantagenet king or Fascist dictator would dream of claiming have been granted to any unqualified person who offered to assume them, including an enterprising burglar. Whatever our work in life may be, we have been ordered to stop doing it and stand by. Wherever our wives and children are they have been transported to somewhere else, with or without the mothers. Our theatres and cinemas have been closed; and our schools, colleges and public libraries occupied by the military bureaucracy. We have been bundled out of our hotels into the streets neck and crop, and our own houses simultaneously made into nests of billeted little evacuees, often unofficially described as little hooligans. Our bungalows, bought by us after a dreadful calculation of our ability to pay the mortgage interest and get to our place of business in a Baby Austin, have been put quite beyond our means by an appalling Budget, and by a rationing of petrol which aims at our being completely blind-folded from sunset to sunrise. When the bungalows and suburbs raise a bitter cry that they cannot pay the new taxes, Sir John Simon replies frankly that if they do not the Government will be forced to resort to inflation, thus reminding us that in Germany, when we forced the Reich to resort to it, a twopenny-halfpenny postage stamp cost £12,000, and the postman's wage rose to a king's ransom on which he could barely live, whilst annuities and insurances, on which unmarried elderly daughters and retired folk used to live in decency and comfort, became worthless. Our incomes depreciated from week to week through the rise in prices which the Government is pledged to prevent and cannot.

Such (and much more) is Military Communism in inexperienced hands, often the hands of fools who come to the top in wartime by their self-satisfied folly though nobody would trust them to walk a puppy in peace time. When we complain we are told that we must all make sacrifices, and that we had better buy white overcoats, carry our gas masks every-where, and take wildly impracticable precautions against high explosive blast and poison gas.

Naturally we cry 'Sacrifice! Yes: but what for?' You tell us to be resolute and determined; but we cannot be resolute and determined in the air about nothing. What are we suffering for? Upon what are we resolved? What have we determined? What in the devil's name is it all about now that we have let Poland go?

Mr Chamberlain, in reply, states our aim in peroration. Mr Winston Churchill echoes it in a broadcast with a certain sense of its absurdity which the microphone betrays. Our aim is first to deliver Europe from the threat and fear of war. And our remedy is to promise it three years more war! Next, to abolish Hitlerism, root and branch. Well, what about beginning by abolishing Churchillism, a proposition not less nonsensical and more easily within our reach? But, we are told, if we do not send Hitler to St Helena, he will proceed to annex Switzerland, Holland, Belgium, England, Scotland, Ireland, Australia, New Zealand, Canada, Africa, and finally the entire universe, and Stalin will help him. I must reply that men who talk like this are frightened out of their wits. Stalin will see to it that nobody, not even our noble selves, will do anything of the sort; and

Franklin Roosevelt will be surprised to find himself exactly of Stalin's opinion in this matter. Had we not better wait until Herr Hitler tries to do it, and then stop him with Stalin and Roosevelt at our back?

The Archbishop of York, in the next broadcast, rose finally to the occasion as became a great Christian prelate. Unfortunately he began not as a Christian prelate but as a righteously angry hotheaded Englishman by giving his blessing to our troops as 'dedicated' to the supreme immediate duty of lynching Herr Hitler and his associates. Now I cannot go into the question whether Herr Hitler deserves to be lynched without raising awkward analogies between his case and those of Signor Mussolini, General Franco, Stalin and his associates, and raking up events in India and Ireland which unfriendly pens have represented as somewhat dictatorial on our part. I simply remind the Archbishop that though we can easily kill a hundred thousand quite innocent Germans, man, woman and child, in our determination to get at Herr Hitler, we should not finally succeed in lynching him; and the killing of the Germans, and our own losses in the process, would produce a state of mind on both sides which would operate as a complete black-out of Christianity and make the Archbishop's sane final solution impossible. If we won, it would be Versailles over again, only worse, with another war even less than twenty years off. And if, as is desperately possible, we drove Russia and Germany into a combination against us to avert that catastrophe, which is just what our Stalinphobe Old School Ties and Trade Unionists are recklessly trying to do, then we shall indeed need God's help and not deserve it.

No: it will not do, however thickly we butter it with bunk and balderdash about Liberty, Democracy and everything we have just abolished at home. As the Archbishop nobly confesses, we made all the mischief, we and the French, when we were drunk with victory at Versailles; and if that mischief had not been there for him to undo Adolf Hitler would have now been a struggling artist of no political account. He actually owes his eminence to us; so let us cease railing at our own creation and recognize the ability with which he has undone our wicked work, and the debt the German nation owes him for it. Our business now is to make peace with him and with all the world instead of making more mischief and ruining our people in the process.

I write without responsibility, because I represent nobody but myself and a handful of despised and politically powerless intellectuals capable of taking a catholic view of the situation. One of these unhappy outcasts is my friend, H. G. Wells. He has written a vitally important letter to *The Times*, of which nobody has taken the smallest notice. I disagree with him on one point, and would fain comfort him on it. He warns us that we are risking not merely military defeat, but the existence of civilization and even of the human race. Dear H. G., let us not flatter ourselves. The utmost we can do is to kill, say, twenty-five millions of one another, and make the ruins of all our great cities show-places for Maori tourists.

Well, let us. In a few months we shall matter no more than last summer's flies. As two of the flies we naturally deprecate such an event; but the world will get on without us; and the world will have had an immense gratification of the primitive instinct that is at the bottom of all this mischief and that we never mention: to wit pugnacity, sheer pugnacity for its own sake, that much admired quality of which an example has just been so strikingly set us by the Irish Republican Army.

7 October 1939

John Betjeman, only best-selling poet of our time, published some of his work in the New Statesman.

Parliament Hill Fields   John Betjeman

Rumbling under blackened girders, Midland, bound for
    Cricklewood,
Puffed its sulphur to the sunset where that Land of Laundries
    stood.
Rumble under, thunder over, train and tram alternate go,
Shake the floor and smudge the ledger, Charrington, Sells,
    Dale and Co.,
Nuts and nuggets in the window, trucks along the lines below.

When the Bon Marché was shuttered, when the feet were hot
    and tired,
Outside Charrington's we waited, by the 'STOP HERE IF
    REQUIRED';
Launched aboard the shopping basket, sat precipitately down,
Rocked past Zwanziger the Baker's, and the terrace blackish
    brown,
And the Anglo, Anglo-Norman Parish Church of Kentish Town,

Till the tram went over thirty, sighing terminus again,
Past municipal lawn tennis and the bobble-hanging plane.

Soft the light suburban evening caught our ashlar-speckled spire,
Eighteen-sixty Early English, as the mighty elms retire
Either side of Brookfield Mansions flashing fine French-window
    fire.

Oh the after tram-ride quiet, when we heard, a mile beyond,
Silver music from the bandstand, barking dogs by Highgate
    Pond.
Up the hill where stucco houses in Virginia creeper drown;
And my childish wave of pity, seeing children carrying down
Sheaves of drooping dandelions to the courts of Kentish Town.

24 February 1940

---

*John Strachey, whose writings were what I may call creative new statesmanship,
turned to Communism when, with Oswald Mosley, he left the supine Labour
Party rendered helpless by Ramsay MacDonald's waffling leadership in 1931.
Avoiding the mistakes of Mosley, however, he was to make a brilliant come-
back into a new statesmanly state of mind and opinion. Here is a sample of his
literary talent in a wartime* New Statesman *piece.*

Digging for Mrs Miller   John Strachey

Miss Sterling said: 'Post D has rung through to say that you are to go to
Slaney F at 8.00. They have more incidents than they can cope with.'

Ford had been on from 4.00 a.m. to 6.00 a.m., and was lying by. The
light of Miss Sterling's torch woke him. He disentangled his slept-in
clothes from the blankets and mattress on the basement floor of the sub-
post. He swilled water over his face, finding it cold out of the hot tap.
Apparently the gas had gone again in the night. He took a bus down the
Queens Road to the next ARP district, Slaney. When he got to the Slaney
F Post the Senior Warden was out; fetched, he hesitated between various
tasks. Then Rumbold, another Post D Warden, came. Finally they were
both told to go down to Beaton Street.

A bomb, or bombs, had hit the last five houses in Beaton Street, where it
joins the river, and a small tenement that forms the last block on the
embankment. These buildings had been destroyed. Where they had stood
there was a crater, with two mounds of debris on each side of it, one some
25 feet, and the other some 15 feet, high. The debris of the five houses and
the tenement was completely mixed in the mounds; there was no trace of
separate structures.

Ford and Rumbold found rescue squads working on each mound. After wandering about a little they found the Warden in charge. He seemed unable to think of anything he wanted done. 'Just keep them from coming down the streets,' he said. He evidently felt vaguely that it must be right to stop people doing something. But nobody was coming down the streets. Between ten and twenty oldish men and women, and one or two untidy girls were standing about in the doors and on the area steps of the more or less shattered, but still standing, houses round the incident.

Ford and Rumbold saw no one to stop doing anything; so they just waited about. It was a squally October morning. As usual on the embankment, you suddenly became conscious of the weather, almost as if you had been in the country. The tide was low: gulls stood on the mud flats. The wind flickered the surface of the channel. A biggish collier, looking inappropriate so far up the river, was moored fifty yards further on beside the Power Station. The Power Station's chimneys stood over them. People glanced at them, and then at the mounds.

Ford began watching what the rescue squad on the nearest mound was doing. They had evidently been at work for some hours already. They had fixed a plank walk up the side of the mound, and a knot of them was concentrated near the top, apparently moving the debris about with their hands, and putting bits of it into wicker baskets. When the baskets were filled they took them to other parts of the mound and emptied them. It looked aimless. Ford climed on to the debris to try to see what they were at. As soon as he got on to the mound he found that it was made up of an extraordinary texture of brick and plaster rubble, more or less shattered lengths of floor joists and beams, pieces of broken furniture, rugs, carpets, linoleum, curtains, pieces of crockery, often unbroken, all made into a homogenous, tight pressed pudding. It was rather difficult to climb up on to.

When Ford got to the top he was gradually able to make out what the rescue squad was doing. They were sinking a small shaft vertically downwards through the mound from its top. They worked much in the same way as archaeologists open up the debris of millennia; but this was the debris of seconds. The rescue men had blue overalls and white steel helmets, instead of the brown overalls and black helmets of the Wardens, such as Ford was wearing. The Rescue men took no notice of him. They had only sunk their shaft about 5 feet down into the mound. They seemed to Ford to be working in an incredibly primitive and inefficient way – with their bare hands, and without any tools even, let alone any mechanical appliances.

One of them began to let himself down into the shaft, which was encumbered by ragged ends of floor joists and beams. He got to the bottom and then wormed his body round till he was lying in a knot with his head down by a crack, where some tattered rubble was held up an inch or so by a joist end. Ford moved to the edge of the shaft to see. The Rescue men stood still, and one of them called down to the people by the mound to be quiet. Ford heard the river waves lap the mud. The Rescue man down the shaft put his mouth to the crack and said: 'Are you there, chum?' Everybody kept really still. But they heard nothing. The man down the shaft put his ear to the crack. The Rescue man at the top, who had called to the people to be quiet, said: 'Can't you hear him any more, Smith?' Smith said: 'Yes, but he's getting very faint.' Then he began to get out of the shaft. It was 9.30 a.m. Ford had not realized before that there were people alive under them in the mound.

The Rescue squad went on digging, no faster but steadily, filling wicker baskets with rubble, passing them from hand to hand to the edge of the mound and emptying them.

The one who called down to the people to be quiet said: 'Cut away some of that stuff,' pointing to one edge of the shaft, 'the weight'll be coming down on Smith otherwise.' A couple of Rescue men took up shovels and began trying to use them on that edge of the mound, pushing rubble down into the central crater. Ford felt restless. He saw a pick lying about, so he took off his coat, put down his gas mask and torch, and began to loosen the rubble so that the men with shovels could really get at it. The Rescue men neither warned him off – as he feared they might – nor welcomed him. Rumbold came and worked with another shovel.

For about a foot down his pick made good progress; it was easy to loosen the broken brickwork, plaster, and the rest of the indescribable mixture of which the mound was made. Then his pick stuck in something tough and sticky. Using all his strength, he got it out. At the next stroke it stuck again. He got it out. Forewarned, he made smaller strokes, only attempting to loose tiny bits of the new material. He wondered what it was. He picked a bit up in his hands, and recognized it as the clay which is the universal sub-soil of London. If you dig down, say, 10 feet almost anywhere in London this is what you come to. But he was working more than 10 feet above street level. The bomb had picked up layers of the sub-soil and somehow spread them above the layers of obliterated houses.

After some little time the Rescue man who had put them on, who was evidently called Frank, said, 'That's enough.' Ford was glad. His arms ached, and he had very slightly scorched his hand the night before, having been clumsy in putting out an incendiary; the pick rubbed it. But he didn't fancy standing about. So he got a place taking the filled baskets as the men in the shaft passed them out to be emptied. The Rescue men still neither welcomed nor repulsed him. He could now see that their apparently primitive method of work with their hands was in fact the only possible way of dealing with the material of which the mound was made. It would have been quite impossible to swing a pick or shovel in the shaft, partly because it was too narrow. But even if they had dug it wider, as soon as you got a few feet down a network of half-shattered woodwork would have prevented the use of any tool which Ford could think of. As it was, they were continually having to stop to saw through a wedged joist or beam. They used absurdly small, flimsy saws – they looked as if they had been bought at toy shops, and perhaps they had – in order to be able to get them into the corners of the shaft.

They began to smell gas – not poison gas, but ordinary domestic gas. As the shaft progressively opened up the mound, the shattered gas pipes of the houses permeated it with gas. 'Nobody must strike a match,' said Frank. But the Rescue men went on smoking just the same.

Every now and then a Rescue man would call out 'Warden,' and Ford or Rumbold would go over and take charge of some bit of personal property that had been unearthed. Ford got several pots and pans, a china dish, unchipped even, two ration books in the names of Andrews and Miller, and a lady's handbag, undamaged and full of its owner's make-up equipment. When he had collected a small heap of these he took them over to a partly ruined, but still standing house on the other side of the street. Here a dump of miscellaneous and trival possessions had been established. A man, a boy in his teens, and a girl who was crying a little, stood in the doorway of this house. Ford was surprised to see them, because the police had twice moved away onlookers from under this house, owing to the evident danger of more of it falling down. As Ford put down his handful of dust-encrusted possessions, the man said: 'Don't matter about those. What I want you to get out is my boy.' Ford didn't say anything. 'Is there any hope – for him?' said the man, jerking his head towards the mound, and speaking more gently. 'I don't know,' Ford said, shaking his head. He went back to the mound. 'Is it a boy under there?' he said to one of the Rescue men. 'Lad of about fifteen, we're told. Some say there's two, some says there's three of them,' he replied.

Smith wormed his way down again to the bottom of the shaft, which was now several feet deeper. He put his mouth to another and larger crack, and said rather softly, 'You there, chum?' Again they were silent, while Smith put his ear to the crack, screwing up his face at the stench of the gas. After a little he began to worm up again. 'Can't hear nothing now,' he said.

They went on filling the wicker baskets. The morning wore on. Once a doctor came. Work on the shaft was stopped and Frank and Smith, who were in it, came out. But the doctor couldn't see what was below the bottom of the shaft any better than they could. He stood quite still, peering down it – a big, very well turned out man, with a spotless mackintosh and black soft hat, and a rather arrogant face. There was a point in the doctor's *tenue* amidst the encrusted grime of the rest of them, Ford noticed. It actually did give confidence. However, the doctor said nothing and went away.

Frank said, 'Warden, telephone for a mobile canteen.' Rumbold went to the nearest telephone box and got through to the Town Hall. About half an hour later a canteen, drawn by a private car, arrived. After that the Rescue men, and everybody else, went to it for a cup of tea at intervals.

The sirens went. The next arrival was a smallish, quick-moving man who said, 'Where's my rabbits?' He received no answer. 'Four I 'ad,' he said, 'kept 'em in the Anderson, and this morning I saw two of 'em up the top of Beaton Street.' Ford wondered if his Warden's training should have included elementary rabbit catching. But one of the Rescue men said unexpectedly that he had seen a rabbit on the embankment. 'There,' said the small man, 'how they do stray!'

But he didn't demand that the Wardens should institute a hunt. He wanted to talk. 'It's my belief,' he said, 'that this 'ere was done by one of them 'igh explosive bombs.' Frank said, his face not moving a muscle, 'You may be right at that, chum.' But irony was lost on the rabbit keeper. He nodded his head. ' 'igh explosive,' he said. 'I was up the other end of the street with my lad Bert, and Bert had just said "Good-night" to this poor lad here underneath when it comes down. Bert was blown through the door of No. 12 and I were blown through No. 11. "Come on, Bert," I says, and we went down to the shelter to find the Missus and my little boy Sam, what I couldn't send away on account of his 'ealth. When we got there the Anderson wasn't to be seen under earth and bricks. But we soon found it, and tapped on the steel. As soon as they 'eard us, my little boy Sam, what we 'ad to keep here on account of his 'ealth, calls out, "Come on, Dad, be quick and take this earth off." So Bert and I digs 'em out and not a penny the worse they were.' Ford said nothing. The rabbit keeper went off.

The morning wore on. The 'All Clear' went. The shaft was imperceptibly deepened. The gas stank. An ambulance drove up. The driver came up and asked Ford where she was to park it. Ford said, 'I'm afraid you won't be wanted.' The driver said, 'Oh,' but she backed the ambulance up to the mound.

Ford spent some time taking an old lady, who was pretty badly shocked, to the Post. The old lady was shaking all over and kept repeating, 'Find me somewhere to go before to-night: before to-night: before to-night.' Ford put the First Aid people on to her; they were glad to have something to do, and finally took the old lady off to hospital.

Ford went back to the mound and emptied more baskets. Smith and Frank could now both work at the bottom. It was now 12.00 noon. Frank said to Smith, 'You're finished. Go up and have a cup of tea at the mobile.' Smith came up, all in. Ford talked to him while he stood on the mound. 'Do you think they can still be alive?' he asked. 'No,' said Smith. Then Smith said to Ford and Rumbold, 'I wish other bloody civilians helped like you.' Ford was shocked to hear Wardens called civilians by a Rescue man. But he appreciated a compliment from Smith.

The other Rescue men went on filling baskets. The shaft got lower. It was about 10 feet deep now. The atmosphere of the group working round it began to change. Everyone began peering at the bottom of the shaft. But there was still only the rubble, the bits and bats of broken furniture, the joists and beams, the twisted gas and water pipes, to see. Then Frank and the Rescue man who had taken Smith's place straightened up, stopped filling, and looked round. Ford peered at the bottom of the shaft. There seemed to be nothing there except one more greyish-yellow joist, which ended in a curiously grooved knob. But after looking at it for some time Ford saw that it was a rubber-coated fist and arm, bare to the elbow. It seemed far too big a hand for a boy of fifteen. The Rescue men filled a few more baskets with rubble from the very bottom of the shaft and sawed through several more joist ends. They uncovered a large, untorn and apparently new, though intensely grimy, blanket. Ford noticed that it had a narrow light blue stripe in it at the ends, exactly like the one on his own camp bed at the post. So that's what it would have looked like if 'he' had let go his stick ten seconds earlier, flying East to West, or ten seconds later, flying West to East, he thought.

A smallish man in brown plus-fours with no uniform, nor badge, nor armlet of any description appeared. Frank and the other Rescue men called him, 'Sir.'

'How are they lying?' he said. 'Directly at the bottom here, Sir,' said Frank.

'Well, get them out then; what are you waiting for?' said the man in plus-fours sharply. But the Rescue men did not want to pull off the blanket at once. They moved about, collected their saws, took off their gloves, wiped their faces. Smith came back from the canteen. He looked down the shaft. 'Which way are they lying, Frank?' he said. 'Head here, legs here, body bent round here,' said Frank. 'Very awkward,' said Smith. Then he got down the shaft again and pulled off the blanket. Ford could not instantly see anything underneath it except a good deal of white and red, and a good deal of white and blue, striped material. Then he realized that these were the pyjamas of two bodies, lying face down, on top of each other, or, rather, with their arms and legs intermingled both with each other, and with the network of boards, joists, bits of bedsteads, and the omnipresent rubble, which made up the bottom of the shaft. There was no blood nor gross mutilation. But the bodies had become part of the debris; they had become one constituent of the many constituents of the mound. They had been crushed and pressed into the decomposed raw material of the five houses. Like the clay of the London sub-soil, their clay, now quiet, had lost its individual existence and become indissolubly a part of its environment.

'Well, get them out; come on!' said the man in plus-fours again. But again the Rescue men paused. Then Frank took hold of the edge of the white and red material, and pulled an arm up from under the two bodies. He began putting this arm down beside the white and red material, straightening it. He had to use a good deal of force. 'None too soon,' said Smith, noticing this. His meaning was that they would never have got the bodies out of the narrow shaft if they had had time to stiffen thoroughly. Gradually the contours of human forms began to take shape as Frank folded arms and legs down beside the main mass of white and red, and white and blue, pyjamas.

'Now lift, get on with it,' said the man in plus-fours. Frank and Smith got their arms under the main white and red mass and lifted. Immediately the two bodies became distinguished from each other by their outlines instead of merely by the colour of their pyjamas. Ford saw that they were those of a woman, in the white and red, and a man in the white and blue, pyjamas. The bodies had been driven, whether by the blast itself or by the falling debris, not only into the material of the houses, but also into each other. They were locked in a reluctant intercourse. Frank and Smith got the woman's body a couple of feet up. But they could not move it any farther; so they put it down again. Frank took up one wrist round which was an identity disc. 'Mrs Miller,' he read off. Mrs Miller had been a very big, strong, and vigorous woman.

'Get a rope,' said the man in plus-fours. When the rope came Frank took it. 'Pass it under the buttocks,' said the man in plus-fours. With some difficulty they did. 'Now pass the blanket under her,' he ordered. Ford noticed that he seemed to know his business. 'Now raise her.' Frank and Smith got their arms under her again and pushed upwards. Mrs Miller's body seemed to loll for a moment on the blanket. Her black hair was mingled and matted with the brick rubble. Her face was covered thick with it, like an actress in her dressing-gown, taking her make-up off with cleansing cream. She bled a little at the mouth, as her head sagged.

'Cover her up,' said the man in plus-fours. They got the blanket wrapped over her as well as under her. 'Heave on the rope and pull the corners of the blanket.' Ford got on to a ledge halfway down the shaft and took the weight of one corner of the blanket. Two men pulled on the rope. Gradually Mrs Miller's heavy body came up. They had a light metal stretcher ready at the top of the mound and put her down on to it.

The sirens went. They straightened themselves and looked up, before tackling the man's body. Before the sirens stopped they heard planes. A gun or two wuffed. One cracked nearer. Between two clouds they saw the raiding squadron pass, high, aloof, preoccupied, flying fast across the river to the South. The stretcher party began to carry the body down from the mound. There was a heavy thump as a big bomb fell somewhere South of the river. The mound shuddered. So they took Mrs Miller away, and the sounds of the new raid were her only requiem.

Ford stayed to help get the man's body out of the shaft. When they had done so Smith said to him, 'It's a funny thing, but you hardly ever find what you're looking for in this game. I expect that lad who was talking is in another part of the mound altogether. Dead, of course, by now. Shouldn't wonder if they all died of the gas in the end. Hope so. It's quietest that way.' It was one o'clock and another Warden came down from the Post to relieve Ford. So he went home to wash. He found two people whom he had asked to lunch just going away, after waiting for him half an hour. He washed, got out his uniform, and they all went out to lunch at a restaurant in Soho. Ford thought that this was the first peculiar thing that had happened that morning.

9 November 1940

Arthur Koestler's influence as a journalist and publicist had first a good deal to do with the new statesmanly blindness to the faults of Stalinism, subsequently with the opening of new statesmanly eyes to those faults.

The Crank   Arthur Koestler

The one entirely self-revealing sentence he wrote has never been exactly translated. The original says: *In der Groesse der Luege liegt immer ein Faktor des Geglaubtwerdens*. An exact rendering is difficult because the sentence has no logical structure; it is a mystic's proposition in his own grammar. The nearest approximation would be: 'The greatness of a lie always contains an element of being believed.' Note that the verb 'contains' is related not to 'lie' but to 'greatness'. 'Greatness' here has a mystical double meaning: it stands both for quantity (a big lie) and for grandeur, majesty. Now this majestic lie, the apothesis of the Absolute Untruth, is said to *contain* the quality of being believed; it is born by intuition and its very greatness auotmatically compels adoration. This is one of the keys to the Crank's mysticism; actually the one which opened for him the door to power. Obviously, if the key was strange, the lock must have been even stranger.

But the lock is a problem for historians; we are only concerned with the key. The Crank in his unhappy youth knocked at many doors, and was always refused. He tried his hand as an artist, but his sunsets in aquarelle did not sell. He worked on a building site, but was refused the fraternity of his fellow workers because he drank milk instead of beer, and made crankish speeches. He joined the Army, but never got further than his first stripe. He lived in Salvation Army shelters, under bridge-vaults, and in casual wards; he mixed with the *Lumpenproletariat*, the nomadic outcasts in the no-man's-land of society. This period lasted for several years; it was a unique experience for a future statesman. Here the master-key began to take its first rough shape, the shape of sovereign contempt for the people. True, he mistook the refuse for the substance, but his mistake proved to be an asset not a liability. He divined that the mentality of the crowd is not the sum total of the mentality of the individuals which form it, but their lowest common denominator; that their intellectual powers are not integrated by contact but bewildered by the interference of their minds – light plus light resulting in darkness; that their emotional vibrations, however, increase by induction and self-induction like the current in a wire coil. By descending into the bottom strata of society the Crank made the discovery of his life: the discovery of the lowest common denominator. The master key was found.

Its magic worked first on its owner. The frustrated Crank became the inspired Crank. His face in those early years, an unshaped pudding with a black horizontal dot, came to life as the lights of obsession were switched on behind the eyeballs. The features of it retained their crankish ridiculousness, with the black dot under the upturned nose and the second black dot pasted on the forefront, but it now assumed the grotesque horror of a totem-mask worn at ritual dances where human sacrifices are performed. His shrill voice became even shriller, an entranced incantation, while the catchwords it conveyed were simple in their ever-repeated monotony, like the rhythmical beating of the tom-tom in the bush. He knew it and in those early days called himself the Drummer.

He first spoke at small meetings and tried the formula: disintegration of the intellect by interference, increase of the crowd-emotion by induction. It worked. Now those were the days after his nation's defeat, when certain powers were on the search for useful cranks to divert the energies of the embittered populace, and they discovered that this was a very useful crank. Though its effect became visible only later this was a historic event: the key had met the lock.

History is always written in terms of keys and locks; the keys are shaped by subjective individual factors, the locks by objective constellations in the structure of society. If the course of history is determined in its broad outlines, there is always a margin left for undetermined. It is the margin of chance in all probability calculations; the chance of a given lock constellation meeting a key which fits, and vice versa. How many potential Wellingtons died as retired Colonels in Cheltenham we cannot know. And vice versa: if the Gracchi had been a little less dilettanti, Rome might have survived; and if this Crank had been killed in time, Weimar might have survived and the present war postponed or even avoided. As it is, men must die with open eyes to fill in the blind margin of chance; and the danger that this may happen again, that another future Crank may discover the master-key to the masses, will persist – until the lowest common denominator of men has gradually been lifted to a level beyond his reach. This, perhaps, is the basic issue between Democracy and the Crank.

17 October 1942

1939–45 was less rich in war poetry than 1914–18. Among the few Second War poets was C. Day Lewis.

Will it be so again?   C. Day Lewis

Will it be so again
That the brave, the gifted are lost from view,
And empty, scheming men
Are left in peace their lunatic age to renew?
Will it be so again?

Must it be always so
That the best are chosen to fall and sleep
Like seeds, and we too slow
In claiming the earth they quicken, and the old
                                   usurpers reap
What they could not sow?

Will it be so again –
The jungle code and the hypocrite gesture?
A poppy wreath for the slain
And a cut-throat world for the living? that stale
                                   imposture
Played on us once again?

Will it be as before –
Peace, with no heart or mind to ensue it,
Guttering down to war
Like a libertine to his grave? We should not be
                                 surprised: we knew it
Happen before.

Shall it be so again?
Call not upon the glorious dead
To be your witnesses then.
The living alone can nail to their promise the ones
                                 who said
It shall not be so again.

                                 1 May 1943

1943: F. Kuznetsov joins Chekhov, Gorky, Zoshchenko as one of the Russian contributors to the New Statesman.

High Boots   F. Kuznetsov

Ivan Ivanovitch Krutilkin entered the Post Office and went up to the window where letters were left to be called for. He waited in the queue. Soon he found himself in front of the window, peering through the grille at a handsome ginger-haired girl.

'Your identity card,' said the girl, scanning and flinging back his factory pass.

Ivan Ivanovitch lost his courage. 'Well, you see, it's like this, I'm here for the May Day festivals, and I'm waiting for letters from home. I . . .'

'Have you your identity card on you?'

'Yes, I have.'

'Well, hand it over, comrade.'

'I can't.' Ivan Ivanovitch pushed his head through the window and, bending towards the girl, said in a low voice: 'I've hidden it in my boot.'

'That's nothing to do with me. No letters without showing your card.'

'Citizen – please – reconsider it.'

'I can't. It's regulations.'

'So it means that I've got to take my boot off.'

Ivan Ivanovitch moved away from the window. He looked despairingly round the big hall. There was not a single seat vacant.

He took off his coat and swept the floor with it. Then he sat down, laid his portfolio down beside him and began to pull at his right boot.

Very soon a crowd gathered round him, firing questions.

'What's the matter? Why's he taking his boot off?'

'He's dislocated his ankle and he's trying to pull it back.'

'Nonsense,' added a gloomy citizen, 'it's corns.'

'Corns? No, he's got something stuck in it!'

The ginger-haired beauty stuck her head through the window and watched Krutilkin with interest – and amusement. He was sitting on the floor with perspiration running down his face. The boot would not come off. Then, with his left foot resting on the heel of his right boot, he pulled, and the boot began to move. Krutilkin was triumphant, but on the last lap the boot suddenly stuck fast at the heel.

'Bad luck,' said someone. The crowd began to give him further advice.

'Press on the toe – on the toe!' shouted a citizen in a bowler hat.

'On my toe!' shouted Krutilkin back. 'It's the heel that's the trouble.'

'It's a pity you can't undo the bootlaces,' chimed in the girl.

Ivan Ivanovitch was perspiring profusely and felt completely worn out. His efforts had been in vain. The boot wouldn't come off, and that was that. He looked round at the crowd with pleading, anguished eyes.

'Citizens!' he said. 'Comrades!' he cried. '*Help!*'

Someone wearing pince-nez and carrying a small walking stick came up to Ivan Ivanovitch, and, taking hold of the latter's boot, began to pull. He pulled and puffed and blew, but nothing came of it, except that his glasses fell off. Then he gave up, and moved away. Another fellow tried to help Ivan Ivanovitch, but that was in vain, too. Next, out of the crowd came a big man with hands like spades and very thick fingers. He began to have a go at the boot. The crowd was silent, watching. Everybody could see that the man would either pull off the boot or the leg – or both. Ivan Ivanovitch closed his eyes in horror. The big man, still pulling at his leg, dragged him along the floor by it. Each time he tugged the same thing happened again.

'Get a vice!' he shouted hoarsely.

Ivan Ivanovitch rested with his left foot on a board. The man pulled him up and then flung him down again.

'Get a vice!' he shouted again. 'A piece of wood, anything to keep him still!'

But there was nothing of the kind in the Post Office. So for ten minutes he dragged Ivan Ivanovitch round the floor. The crowd watched them. They had already made two rounds of the building, when at last the man sat down exhausted.

'You can't do it without a vice of some sort,' he said, wiping the sweat off his forehead. Five people came out of the crowd and, holding each other round the waist, hung on to Ivan Ivanovitch. The big man was delighted. 'Now, that's different,' he said, catching hold of Ivan's foot and pulling it against himself. The chain of people moved after him. He pulled again, and the same thing happened again. 'Citizens!' cried out the man. 'We want another two volunteers!'

Three more people joined in. The man once more caught hold of Ivan Ivanovitch's foot. The boot creaked but still refused to come off. He then pulled again with all his might and suddenly fell back with the boot in his hand. The crowd sighed with relief. Ivan Ivanovitch jumped up from the floor, ran towards the man, and put his hand in his boot. He peered right into the boot, turned it upside down and shook it out, but there was nothing there.

'Not this one – not this one,' he muttered.

'What isn't?' said the man desperately.

'You've taken off the wrong boot.'

The man turned pale. 'What do you mean?'

'You'll have to pull the left one off!'

'The *other* one, you mean,' gasped the man with fright, and promptly rushed out of the Post Office. Ivan Ivanovitch sat down on the floor again. He felt so tired that he couldn't move. But the ginger-haired girl rallied the crowd.

'What are you standing like that for? Why don't you help him?'

Out of the crowd appeared another man, a little one this time. He went up to Ivan Ivanovitch, pulled up his sleeves and caught hold of the boot. The crowd watched intently. The little man gave one pull and the boot came off. The crowd gasped. The little man eyed them with disdain, and without further explanation made his way proudly towards the door.

'What strength!' said one of the citizens who came up to Ivan Ivanovitch. 'What interests me is, how did it happen that the right came off with such difficulty, whereas the left – one, two, three and it's off!'

'Because the right is size 39 and the left is 41,' replied Ivan.

'How's that?'

'I made a mistake in the shop.'

Ivan Ivanovitch, holding his boots under his arm, walked barefoot to the window, flourishing his card.

'My letter!'

The girl examined the identity card – looked through the letters – and remarked indifferently: 'There's nothing for Krutilkin.'

Translated by Musia Renbourn
7 August 1943

Kathleen Raine is another of the major poets of the period whose work appeared in the New Statesman.

Transient Gods   Kathleen Raine

Strange that the self's continuum should outlast
The Virgin, Aphrodite and the Mourning Mother,
All loves and griefs, successive deities
That reign supreme within the human breast.

Abandoned by the gods, woman with an ageing body
That half remembers the annunciation,
The passion and the travail and the death
That wore the mask of my humanity.

I marvel at the soul's indifference.
For in her theatre the play is almost done,
The tears are shed; the actors, the immortals,
In their eternal manifestation, elsewhere gone.

And I who have been virgin, and Aphrodite,
The mourning Isis and the queen of corn
Wait for the last mummer, dread Persephone
To dance my dust at last into the tomb.

29 May 1948

Though I says it as shouldn't, it is easier for an editor to find good serious writers than good comic writers, and a touch of comedy is always to be welcomed. Anthony Carson and Claud Cockburn (see beyond) are brilliant exponents of new statesmanly comedy. Another is Honor Tracey: here is her handling of Buchmanism to contrast with Kingsley Martin's, followed by a contribution of my own.

Absolutely Frank   Honor Tracey

Five thousand people of seventy-one nations have passed through Caux-sur-Montreux this summer. They come to study Moral Re-Armament, the theory of inspired democracy which, Mr Paul Hoffman says, is the ideological counterpart of the Marshall Plan. During their stay, they live in Dr Frank Buchman's three luxury hotels, for, as is well known, it is impossible to be morally rearmed in anything else; and, if you wonder a little at the lavishness of everything, Frank will explain that, by providing a material perfection, he sets your minds free to dwell on spiritual things.

In the great assembly room at Mountain House, you may see people of every race, class and creed. That little woman over there is Princess Alice von Hohenzollern, as no time is lost in letting you know. These are two repentant Communists from the Ruhr, Max and Paul: they are full of praise for a kind gentleman called Kost, the General Direktor of the Ruhr Coal Board, who is paying their wages and expenses while they are here.

Shake hands with the daughter of the Duke of Montrose! There goes Princess Lieven: and there, Comrade Jones of the Rhondda valley. The small dark person, whose face wears such a look of simple piety, is Mr Mitsui, of the Mitsui Zaibatsu, before the war a giant money clique in Japan. There is a Swedish admiral; a German chief of police; an American diplomat; and a little bevy of British generals (retired). Mom is present in force; and there is a bunch of those shrewd, hard-headed industrialists and

businessmen who always seem to fall for everything. Catholic priests are quietly making notes, and Lutheran pastors are loudly making speeches. And Germans, Germans, everywhere, nattering in corners, wailing, criticizing, protesting. Only at meal times, when they rush to the cafeteria and munch away for dear life, does a relative silence fall.

Everything up here is a little larger than life. Smiles are wider and toothier and handshakes positively cripple. The success of MRA, as described, is so brilliant that one cannot understand why the world is still in such a mess. The people attending the conference, too, are apt to be presented as rather more important than they are; from hearing the officials talk, you would suppose that this was the cream and flower of Europe.

I drew the attention of the Press Officer to what looked like over-optimism in some of his handouts, and taxed him with having on one occasion told me a plain fib. He hung his head.

'I'm not Absolutely Honest yet,' he groaned. 'Sorry!'

A remark of this kind immediately makes one a friend for life; but it would be helpful if MRA prefaced its publicity material with a note to say that, as the editors are still in the process of Change, the contents should be taken with a grain of salt.

Meetings are held morning and afternoon, when two or three speakers each make a statement. Every speech is doubled in German from the platform, and other languages are relayed through earphones, by courtesy of International Business Machines, Inc. In between the statements a chorus of youths and maidens, wearing a specially designed fancy dress of folksy cut, their faces stretched in a beaming smile, sing catchy numbers like 'The Good Road' and 'Deutschland, unser Vaterland.'

There are some very fine people among the speakers. A French woman Socialist, for example, whose son was tortured before her eyes by the Germans, tells how MRA helped her to overcome hatred: she is a little, grey, motherly body and, as she speaks, quietly and without emotion, a great silence comes over the room. Less spiritually advanced, but engaging, is the Member for West Ham, who organized a strike at the Savoy Hotel and lay down in front of a lorry: pink, round, dimpled, very *bébé* and deliciously coy, he tells us how hard it will be for him, on his return to London, to go and say 'Sorry' to the Savoy Manager.

There are the usual exhibitionists, and the ex-Indian Army officers who are tired of mowing suburban lawns, and the cosy married couples ('I never feel quite so much in love with Agnes as when we've had a good fight to bring the truth to someone'). Each is warmly applauded, but what we like best is a man who has left the Communist Party. Then we rise to our feet with one accord and give him a real ovation.

Get God the Buchman way, and fix Communism, settle industrial disputes, step up production and go down big with the family! It is curious that thousands of people who have been deaf to the voices of the saints and seers and martyrs all their lives, should now be stirred to their depths by a few peppy slogans; but it is so.

In this classless society (see prospectus) there are two places to eat: the cafeteria, seating a thousand, and the dining-room, seating two hundred. The food in the cafeteria is excellent, but it is in the dining-room that you get the *Méringues Chantilly*. Here, too, is Frank's Table, where, surrounded by all the nobs, sits Frank himself, grinning affably like a big-hearted fish.

To get the real flavour of the thing, however, you must go and work a shift with the angels in Frank's kitchen. Girls, what you say we make a fig *soufflé* just for Frank's Table? Pass me that tin, labelled For Frank Only. See that cherry jam? Made specially for Frank, by the King of Siam's mother. Hurry up with the fried chicken, Frank's Table has finished soup! More cream for Frank's Table! Butter for Frank's Table! Pudding for Frank's Table! This is none of Frank's doing: it's just how these devoted ladies show their gratitude for being allowed to work for him.

(Memo: Shall I tell Frank I stole a spoonful of his private Siamese cherry jam?)

Forty years have passed since Frank said 'Sorry' to God for having been a materialist; and today, lying in the sun on a *chaise longue* and gazing dreamily at the snowy peaks of the Dent du Midi across the lake, my room filled with flowers, a bowl of grapes, peaches and pears at my elbow, I am sorely tempted to follow his example.

15 October 1949

Riding to Hounds   Edward Hyams

I used to ride a horse that was supposed to be vicious, but really it was just independent. It was said to come from the Argentine, was enormously tall, and had the air of a cavalry charger. A number of retired military men, using the same livery stable, always treated the horse very firmly, because of its reputation: they insisted on riding it on a curb, would mount with a grave, determined air, clamp their knees in like a vice, handle the bridle with a look of thin-lipped mastery. The horse used to wait until it was in the middle of the main road, which had to be crossed on the way to the common, and then stand on its hind legs and waltz, like a circus pony. Ex-polo-playing officers were unlikely to be unseated by that caper, but then the horse used to try to stand on its head, and the military men often fell off. But if they didn't, the horse would wait until it was on the nice soft grass and then either roll over, or just sit down like a recalcitrant mule, and refuse to move.

It never did any of these things to me because I was no horseman. I just sat on its back, spoke to it in a respectful manner, rode it on a snaffle, and merely suggested the direction to be taken, or the pace to be adopted, by a very gentle hint with bridle, knee or heel. Quite often the horse did not care for my suggestions, and took its own way, but as a rule it fell in with my wishes, and even when my hints were so diffident as to be confusing, it would stop and look round, as much as to say: *For goodness sake, make up your mind.*

I was fortunate in discovering that the horse was partial to a pint of a mixture of old ale and draft Bass, called Harley Street, which I used to drink myself and had the happy idea of sharing with him. After a pint of Harley Street, the horse was always uncommonly placable, but there was this disadvantage, that we had to begin every day's hacking by going to the pub; until that had been done, all my suggestions were ignored, and it was sometimes inconvenient to go so far out of our way.

I knew that there was some sort of Hunt in the neighbourhood, but however much my instincts might lead me to enjoy the idea of blood-sport, I had a strong conscientious objection to it; and in any case I was not nearly good enough a horseman to think of riding to hounds. But one morning when I was out on the common with my horse, about a mile to the west of a coppice of silver birch, we heard hounds give tongue, and the horse, which must have had hunting antecedents, responded with all the fervour of Mr Jorrocks himself. It was useless to protest: we covered the mile to the coppice and cleared two ditches in a time which would have interested a National trainer, and were presently among the trees – and the hounds.

Whatever hunting antecedents the horse may have had, its hunt manners were very bad. It got in among the hounds and trod on several, and although I was ignorant of fox-hunting, I realized that this was undesirable. I should have realized this in any case, because the Master was very explicit on the subject. I knew him by sight, he was an enormously wealthy manufacturer of drugs, not the kind of drugs the trade oddly calls 'ethical,' but, I should imagine, excessively profitable. He was passionately desirous of countrifying himself, and by lavish expenditure of money had bought control of the Hunt and the village cricket team. He was a little, grey-faced, bilious-eyed creature, with a snarling, metallic voice, and he looked terrible on a horse. However, he had great courage, for he had not learnt to ride until he was forty, and he usually stayed on his horse grimly, or fell off without complaining.

When he saw my horse trampling on his hounds, he became angry and abused me in language which was very mortifying. The Hunt listened to him with respect. Naturally, in that suburban county, there were no actual countrymen present – a couple of market gardeners perhaps – but even if there had been they could never have appreciated the Master's *tour de force* of invective as much as the immaculately dressed brewers, stockbrokers, film magnates, novelists and journalists who gathered round to listen. Meanwhile, the hounds had prudently moved out of the way of my horse.

Round the fringes of a denser part of the coppice, about two hundred yards down an open ride, a number of persons, led by a man in a pink coat, were fossicking about, with several hounds making excited, whining noises. Suddenly something happened, for the hounds all streamed away as if they had been sucked up by a gigantic vacuum cleaner, the huntsman and his assistants went after them, the Master and his cronies after the huntsman. My horse was a trifle slow in starting, but he quickly made up for that. He went at a gate, neck and neck with the Master's horse, and took me over with my knee under the Master's. Then we drew away, and really settled down to race. We overtook the huntsman at the next hedge, knocked him off his horse going over some wire, crossed a ploughed field and were among the tail of the pack. Naturally the hounds were alarmed at the reappearance of the formidable animal which had treated them so carelessly before, and began to lag behind, apparently much discouraged.

We came round on to a corner of the common and I found I could see a long way: in fact, I could see the fox going like a red streak, running low across heather, the three leading hounds fifty yards behind him, and the rest of the pack, excepting those we had overtaken, trailing after the leaders like the tail of a kite. I did not have much time to enjoy this spectacle, because we had soon passed most of the hounds and were up with the leaders, and still going with plenty of reserve in hand.

I had no idea what my horse had in mind, but it seemed to know what it was doing. The country was vaguely familiar, so I had no anxiety about being lost. True, I had been under the impression that there was a correct order in the procession of the hunt, with the horsemen following the hounds, so that I was a good deal surprised to find that we had passed the leaders and were rapidly gaining on the fox. But I was not nearly so surprised as the fox, which turned its head as we drew level, looked absolutely astounded, swerved aside into a gully, and was lost to me. For it now appeared that the fox had not been our object at all, we just kept going in a stretched gallop, across the rest of the common, over a road about four inches in front of a tradesman's delivery van, over a low fence and into somebody's back garden. We then dropped to a canter among this person's winter greens, pushed ourselves through the garden gate, trotted down a lane and stopped at the back door of the pub.

There is only one thing to be done with an accomplished fact – accept it.

I dismounted and led the horse round to the door of the public bar, which the publican was in the act of opening. He asked me if I'd caught a glimpse of hounds, and I said I had. 'I wonder you don't hunt,' he said, as he drew our two pints of Harley Street, 'that horse'd carry you nicely to hounds.'

I said I didn't care for blood sports.

'Come to that,' he said, 'this 'Unt don't often kill.'

I said I was glad to hear it.

27 January 1951

Like other writers of talent who have made names for themselves, John Braine was known to New Statesman *readers before he shot into fame with* Room at the Top. *In the Fifties, with the publication of work by the young men from the provinces, the* New Statesman *was encouraging the new movement and this policy was confirmed when, in the early Sixties, Karl Miller was appointed Literary Editor, a Literary Editor very much alive to the results for literature of the grammar-school revolution.*

Number Nine Rock   John Braine

If you've lived in Blackersford you know where Number Nine Rock is. It's at Ripley Glen, a threepenny tram ride out of Blackersford. It's one of the main features of the Blackersford district, as much a part of it as its textile mills. And it's just as important as the mills, perhaps more so. It's important because it's an aspect of something bigger – happiness.

The happiness can be pinpointed, a line starting at the top of Edward's Way, the broad avenue which leads into Ripley Glen, past Ripley Memorial Hospital, past the Albert Institute with its four stone lions (unsuccessful entrants in the Trafalgar Square competition), past the fire-station which looks like a Methodist chapel and over the canal to the huge sprawling hulk of Ripley Mills. Ripley Mills haven't changed much since 1850 when Seth Ripley first built them. Nor has Ripley, which he designed as a model industrial village. It's this changelessness, this sense of the past as nourishing and bland as milk stout, which soothes and quietens the nerves, which abolishes neurosis; Ripley is fixed permanently in the Victorian age. But in one of its bright patches: Ripley, with all its faults, was built for human beings to live in; it was designed as a village, a living community; it's not just a sprawl of mean houses, a huddle of rent-books. The happiness isn't an accident, for it doesn't have to fight for survival here; Ripley holds it like a sponge, it's cumulative, a kind of benign lead acetate accumulating ever since 1850.

The road to the Glen and Number Nine Rock begins at Ripley's green belt, a few hundred yards past the mill. It's narrow and rough and almost perpendicular, but if you can't face the climb there's the Glen Tramway. The Tramway's so important a feature of the Glen that it's hard to say whether the Tramway's there because of the Glen or the Glen because of the Tramway. It's cable-run, with open cars, and there's just enough room for two on a seat; and, the side-rails being inadequate, it's considered positively ungallant in Blackersford not to put your arm firmly around your girl.

The shops begin where the tramway ends and the road broadens. The goods they sell have hardly changed since the Glen first began to be called the Glen instead of the Goit (the local term for any wooded valley). The papers are local ones – the *Sporting Pink*, the *Observer Budget*, the *Blackersford Independent* – and in the little dark wooden shops their fresh sharp smell seems to have special excitement, a holiday in ink. The sweets are unsophisticated and long-lasting – Bottomley's mint rock, Judy Barratt's humbugs, gelatine snakes, jelly babies, and wine gums with their flavours stamped on them.

Farther on are the Glen Nurseries – roses and vegetable marrows, carnations and pots of jam. And the Japanese Gardens – zig-zag paths, monkey-puzzle trees, tiny ponds, bridges which look like toys, a willow-pattern world. And the fairground, on the same miniature scale – civilized, the amusements simple – a merry-go-round, shove-halfpenny stalls, a zoo with half a dozen monkeys and an iridescence of canaries and budgerigars, a coconut-shy, a shooting-range, slides and swings for the children, and an elevated railway which is simply a bosun's chair travelling at a very moderate speed round some hundred feet of rail. It's a daylight fair, a ginger-bread and pink ribbons fair.

Inside the fairground there's a tea-garden where they don't mind you bringing your own food. Few take advantage of this now, but before 1914 most visitors brought doorstep sandwiches and huge home-made pasties to eat with their pint-pots of tea. Here pleasure was made out of the simplest materials: food, drink, the view of the Glen. And the greatest luxury was the fresh, clean air; for in a mill the temperature and humidity of the atmosphere must suit the wool, not the workers; men have been sacked for opening a window without permission. The Glen was, and is, the lungs of Blackersford. And, before paid holidays, the Glen was the only place the majority of mill-workers could afford for a holiday or, indeed, be able to reach. But this has left about the place no bitterness, only a solid happiness, a sense of infinite leisure.

There aren't many people in the tea-garden now, only an old couple and a young couple sitting at opposite tables. The old couple sit very still, immobilized in contentment. The man has a stiff blue suit and a gold watch-chain festooned with little badges across his waistcoat; his thick-soled brown boots glitter with polish, and his bowler, set firmly on his head, is as dignified as a cardinal's hat. Even the white cricket-shirt, open at the neck and spread out Byronically over his jacket, cannot destroy this dignity, the strange indestructible quality which comes unasked and unawares at the end of a lifetime's hard and ill-paid work. His wife, mountainous in flowered cretonne and a red hat with a green feather, sits with her hands folded in her lap, a look of quiet enjoyment on her face. They have about them a humbleness which makes one almost angry; they look as if they were frightened someone would take the evening away from them.

The young couple are an exact definition of what Wilfred Pickles means by Courting. The boy wears the summer best of the working-classes – a check jacket with plain flannels of the same colour, and thick-soled brogues – a fashion ten years out of date and worn with a morning-coat stiffness instead of casually. His girl with her neat, mousy hair and make-up applied with such odd, frightened discreetness that it makes her look ten years older than she really is, wears a pink rayon dress and a beige coat, both in those strange Blackersford shades which never show the dirt but never look clean. She's that most respectable of institutions, the Young Lady who is about to become a Fiancée. And her young man, though he can't be more than twenty, has already settled down: one can see at a glance that when they're married they'll call each other Mother and Father. But not yet; tonight they're not respectable, they hold hands shamelessly and look into each other's eyes; the dark is waiting for them.

The old couple don't stare at them, they don't speak to them, yet one can sense an infinite indulgence, an almost pagan approval. The young couple suddenly rise and leave the tea-gardens, their arms around each other's waists. 'Ah knaw wheer they're going,' the old man says, and laughs comfortably. 'Number Nine Rock,' says his wife. They nod like mandarins and the old woman's huge bosom jiggles with amusement. 'Too late for us nah, Josh,' she says. 'Nay, doan't say that, lass,' he says, and squeezes her waist. 'Well, Ah nivver. Thar't a fond 'un,' she says tenderly, and he assumes a doggish air.

The young couple walk towards the Glen. There are other young couples there too, interlaced behind the rocks, in the bracken, in glades in the woods the other side of the valley. The family parties are going home, the plump housewives have finished their knitting, the light is too dim for cricket, the cool breeze from the moors makes the men put their jackets on and fold up their newspapers; and high tea and the current 'Dick Barton strip' will bring the children home from their first cigarette behind the rocks, from fording the stream and making campfires, from piracy and war and mastery of empires, from the huge cosiness of dreams.

A huge cosiness: that is the phrase for the Glen. It's a combination of space and warmth, a room that is always exactly the size you want. It's part of the moors; from here you can walk to Ilkley and never have anything but springy turf beneath your feet and have only the curlews and sheep for company – the Glen is freedom and space, claustrophobia is abolished. And it is the river, the Tramway, the walking-sticks and hum-bugs, the merry-go-round, the gossip over knitting, the leisured reading of the newspaper – there's shelter and company, everything is man-size, the rocks aren't big enough to be oppressive, the stream isn't deep enough to drown in, the slope isn't steep enough to break your neck. And now that evening is coming it is, above all, Number Nine Rock. There's no signpost to Number Nine Rock, but now is the time when it most easily can be found. For it is simply the place where you take your girl; for a hundred years it's been a joke in Blackersford, the reality behind teasing and blushing and clock-watching and dreaming at the loom—an odd, industrial name for Cytherea, but one which doesn't make it Cytherea any the less.

The Glen Tramway makes its last journey of the day. The tram is held up whilst a young man scrabbles frantically through his pockets. 'What's up, lad?' says the gnome-like booking-clerk. ' 'As shoo spent all tha brass?' The passengers laugh, and, surrounded by that laughter, the tram glides into the green and gold twilight and the smell of the woods – cool and fresh, hot and musky all at once. The children are half-asleep with the wind on their faces, their mothers holding them and Thermos flasks and knitting and beach balls firmly to their bosoms. 'Little muck-tub,' says one mother in front of me, wiping the child's running nose. 'Ee, thar't a bonny little muck-tub,' the love in her voice so deep that one's almost embarrassed.

An empty tram passes on its way up. When one goes down the other one is automatically sent up: theoretically the Tramway could go on for ever. As the heart would have the moment go on for ever – the mother with her strange endearments, the children drugged with sun and fresh air, the couple remembering Number Nine Rock; but the moment is absorbed into Ripley, into the common stock of happiness; and already dance music spills into the night from the Albert Institute and the neon lights of the cinema advertise other and more garish Number Nine Rocks.

29 March 1952

John Wain was another of the new poets whose work appeared in the New Statesman.

Clinical Report   John Wain

The early stages were quite commonplace.
It was, in fact, the mixture as before;
Just that they loved and that he fell from grace,

And found himself outside a bolted door.
It was not difficult to diagnose
His state, nor guess the anguish that he bore.

But these things last, as everybody knows,
And soon the case departed from the norm;
Unusual developments arose.

His pain at first took the expected form,
We thought his balance sure to be preserved;
He was no Lear to wander in the storm,

And cases more acute have been observed.
But symptoms then arose which gave concern:
He seemed to think his punishment deserved,

And when the season caused it to return,
Rejected pity, asked for no relief,
When balm was offered, said he chose to burn,

Because (these were his words) 'she left me grief
And nothing else; so be it; this is mine.
Who takes it from me shall be called a thief.'

So, living in a world of strange design,
He finds in pain his true magnetic pole;
And we conclude from such a morbid sign

That this disease has passed from our control.

31 May 1952

– and so was Gavin Maxwell

The Scapegoat   Gavin Maxwell

Now, all ritual performed in order,
I drive you from the fold with whip and goad;
through wilderness where I cannot follow
you bear my shed intolerable load.

Groping after you, my purpose wanders
through dry defiles upon the world's roof;
on dimly-lit Saharas of unknowledge
I trace the double imprint of your hoof.

Goat calls to distant goat across the mountain,
the outcast taint is rank upon the air;
the herd forms; defiant horns turn outward,
possessive of the Calvary they share.

There, in the smell of sin, you will discover
that my shed load held more than guilt and pain,
and in those banished herds may mate another
with love that I cannot recall again.

28 June 1952

'Please can Gilbert come out to pray?'

Angus Wilson's strong commitment to a liberal humanism and the deep seriousness which underlies his wit makes him a new statesmanly writer. The paper's 'attitude' to the royal family and the Monarchy lies somewhere tween that of two of its contributors, Malcolm Muggeridge and Angus Wilson, here writing on the Coronation of Queen Elizabeth II as it was celebrated 'throughout the country'.

Throughout the Country   Angus Wilson

'Throughout the country,' the faintly contemptuous, ascetic voice of the BBC news reader has told us so often in the last week, people have been doing this or that – 'hoping against hope that the weather', 'accompanying the Queen in their thoughts,' rejoicing, and then, somewhat solemnly, 'taking their well-earned rest', or 'going once more about their daily business', or, somewhat facetiously, 'nursing the inevitable headache.' The phrases are so stale that they probably evoke no image. Or, if they do, it is at the most a fleeting, slightly uncomfortable remembrance of that vast, disquieting body of people who do not live in London and whose

198

actions, therefore, are at once 'so important a social factor' and so improbable. A quick succession of visual images – provincial town halls, streets with trams, market crosses, slag heaps and seaside piers – may pass across one's mind like the horrible intimations of a thousand private lives outside our own that make an express train's progress through the London suburbs so disquieting an experience.

The whole thing is not a private London dream, sweet or nightmarish according to taste, not just yours and mine, but of all those familiar figures of 'Housewives' Choice' and 'Family Favourites'. This time, indeed, I did not try to preserve the comfortable, little Londoner's view of England's rejoicings. Urged perhaps by some innate Republicanism, but far more probably by my foolish failure to secure a seat on the Procession route, I spent Coronation day in the most beautiful of Essex towns, and, undeterred by the rain that had swept the market square so carefully prepared for Olde Tyme Dancing and had dripped from the thatched roofs of a hundred stockbrokers', journalists' and publishers' country cottages, I returned there again last weekend to see the celebrations that closed this week of festivity.

The Trust hotel had been careful to provide television, so that Coronation day passed for us as it did for most others. Perhaps if I had viewed the ceremony in my home, I should have been able to preserve my scepticism, my innate Republicanism. Soothed by the familiarity of my own surroundings, the comments of my own small world, I should have sunk easily into my comfortable prejudices. As it was, I sat in a draught, surrounded by the uneasy comments of the saloon bar gang. Never have I seen Good-Scoutery less at ease; they had come with that Rotarian, have-the-next-one-on-me-old-boy jollity that they had found so infallible at a thousand business dinners, Legion reunions and family gatherings. It was a big, British occasion, and no people, of course, were more British than they. It was fascinating to see them fight the strange beauty, the formal Byzantinism of the ceremony that appeared upon the screen. They were prepared, of course, for an occasional catch in the throat, a moment of lowered head, but the elaborate grace before them demanded less perfunctory reverence. There is no English *milieu* less sympathetic than that of the Frothblowers' Anthem; it was nice to see the 'gang' so put out when they least expected it.

It was a people, then, dazed with ritual that poured out at the afternoon's end into the Essex countryside, itself lush and sodden with rain, but lit with those strange grey and lemon lights that are a peculiar East Anglian beauty. We were promised dancing (modern) on the town square and dancing (Olde Tyme) in the Exchange. The same ubiquity of police, so peculiar in face of the much advertised inadequacy of the Force, reigned here as in London. The policemen, who forbade the few cars that ventured out to park in the space reserved for dancing, would have served to protect a minor Tito or Akihito. As it was, they helped to move the piano indoors, when it was finally decided to abandon outdoor dancing. It is usually said that youth today likes its pleasures machine-processed, ready made. I suspect that this means that they take pleasure for granted, which seems to me excellent; at any rate, it worked very well on a wet Coronation evening. They just went indoors and danced to an extremely good pair of dance bands, neither the typical BBC genteel 'sweet' band, nor its phoney idea of 'hot', but first-rate rhythm, which to my delight was amplified so that I could hear 'Bye, Bye Blues' in my bedroom well after midnight. It was Mum and Dad who were lost, not the young. For the older 1914 generation, of course, fun on such occasions has to be spontaneous, which means the old stereotyped singing of 'A Long, Long Trail' and 'Knees-up, Mother Brown'. A few sad matrons and their British Legion men tried to keep up the tradition, but even their hearts of oak were eventually daunted by the drizzle. As they departed, dejected, the strains of 'Pat Him on the Boko' could be heard triumphant from the dance hall. The moral of which is that old English fun may be all very well, but the Palais de Dance lasts forever.

The only peculiar feature of these Coronation celebrations occurred during the firework display. I was busy dissociating myself from the children, who in face of all police prohibitions were determined to get in the line of fire, when I turned to see a line of dwarfs drawn up black and threatening on the edge of the common against the skyline. Who could they be? Martians, no doubt. What better time and place for an interplanetary invasion? But no, I was informed that this was a nearby private school come to observe the pyrotechnics, drawn up at a safe distance from the town's possible infection. It cannot be said that the townspeople objected. They were used no doubt to the private school headmaster's medieval belief that they were infected with bubonic.

In short, the Coronation celebrations, though pleasant, were quiet. The real festivities, we were told, would come at the weekend. And so Saturday morning found us speeding beneath an Essex sky less impressionistically impressive but more promising. At Dunmow, the usual collection of commuting gentry in careful tweeds and yellow waistcoats were saying 'Here's how,' while their wives discussed Princess Margaret's dress over double gins. They had all 'had seats'. But as we passed through the villages, stands and marquees gave promise of the day's entertainment.

We prepared for the festivities by lunch at Long Melford, where some of the best food in England may be eaten. (This is not an advertisement, for there are two hotels in the village.) We then set off for the pageant at Castle Hedingham. On a green sward before the Norman Keep – curiously unreal and like a Victorian stage set – Queen Elizabeth received addresses from Will Shakespeare, Edmund Spenser and Lord Burghley dressed – God knows why! – as a clergyman. If the Keep was Victorian, so indeed were the actors, dressed in Elizabethan costume of that curious frumpy kind that recalls photographs of Ellen Terry as Viola and Beerbohm Tree as Wolsey. The high note, perhaps, was reached when Thomas Morley introduced Her Majesty – always and entirely like Joyce Grenfell – to the madrigal singers, who proceeded to give us that sort of Elizabethan part-singing that belongs irrevocably to Edward German's Merrie England. However, the Pageant was certainly the big draw for the gentry, mostly the commuting barristers and stockbrokers in their shooting brakes and Land-Rovers. There were, however, one or two of that fabulous species – the really rich – busy with field glasses on the steps of their Rolls. I was particularly pleased with an elderly lady who showed her high Nancy Mitford station by a flashing array of diamonds worn with a tweed suit. She had carefully enamelled, inches thick, that disappointed, sulky face which only the very wealthy former beauties wear. For myself, I was happier in the lovely village of Finchingfield where sports were in progress run by the villagers for the villagers. But England is a class-conscious country and, after watching the under-tens bob for apples and the over-sixteens joust over a stream, we suddenly felt intruders and left for Thaxted, the Mecca of all intellectuals.

Already, as our car came down the hill, we could see the jolly-jack-tar hats and ribbons that mark the merry morris, and there indeed it was, the annual festival, with more than fifty schoolmasters sitting cross-legged in coloured braces, some earnest and hearty, others like Sir Stafford Cripps. A large crowd contained a sprinkling of first-rate Osbert Lancaster intellectuals, including an old lady with grey earphones, purple ribbons round her hair and throat, a purple cloak, and a flatly benign expression that smiled at once upon a Co-operative Guild future and a Maypole past. In a very short time, however, the charm both of the music and steps banished my sense of patronage. The truth was that I thoroughly enjoyed the morris. Indeed, so much so, that the pageant at Toppesfield was almost over when we reached there, too far gone, at any rate, to do more than register the look on all faces that means 'the afternoon has been a success'.

Afterwards at supper at a nearby house I was told that the hostess had been a great success as Roxana; another guest told me he had been playing Wamba the Jester; while a lady who arrived late explained how exhausted she was 'what with the rehearsal of Benjie's opera and playing Katharine Howard.' Roxana, Wamba and Katharine Howard, a combination that nicely expresses the eclectic, faintly mysterious note of our English countryside festivities.

13 June 1953

All the Sitwells have appeared, from time to time, in the New Statesman.

The Queen of Scotland's Reply to a Reproof from John Knox　　Edith Sitwell

Said the bitter Man of Thorns to me, the white Rose-Tree:
'That wonted love of yours is but an ass's bray –
The beast who called to beast,
And kicked the world away!
(All the wisdom of great Solomon
Held in an ass's bray.)

When body to body, soul to soul
Were bare in the fire of night
As body to grave, as spirit to Heaven or Hell,
What did we say?
'Ah, too soon we shall be air –
No pleasure, anguish, will be possible.
Hold back the day!'
For in this moment of the ass-furred night
You called the hour of the Beast, was born
All the wisdom of great Solomon
From the despised clay!
All the wisdom of Solomon
Held in an ass's bray.

20 June 1953

Dame Edith Sitwell [*23 Jan. 1954*]

'... it is a living body you are about to examine.' – Aneurin Bevan
by Vicky [11 June 1955]

Of the New Statesman's *comedians Anthony Carson has become the best known and is the most consistently successful.*

Playing the Game   Anthony Carson

I went to stay with some friends at a village in Wiltshire called Cowbright Minor. It is a long thin village, with groups of huddled houses standing like cattle lost on the way to market. It begins nowhere in particular and ends at a duck pond and a grey angry church muttering at the heathen hills. It has one pub called the One-Armed Adventurer. The saloon is a medium-sized room with a piano, skittle table, shove-halfpenny board and dart board. Besides drink, you can buy tobacco, cigarettes, aspirin, tomatoes and hairpins. Mr Badgers, publican, has the face of an Ancient Egyptian.

204

He suffers from hay-fever, and only drinks a sort of purple lung-tonic out of a sherry-glass. A quarter of an hour after closing time, Mr Badgers always looks at the clock and says 'Time, gentlemen, please.' Inaudibly. The clock rarely goes.

At the other end of the village is Cowbright Major, with its own public house, the Stag. Although the Stag and the One-Armed Adventurer play each other at darts, they are different worlds. The Stag is 'gentry', mostly brand-new and talking too much about money. The One-Armed Adventurer is the 'people', darkly traditional and tough as brambles. The Squire drops in for a pint. Any foreigners to be found there are staying with my hosts at Widgeon Mill, visitors from the neurotic brick village of Soho, quick to subside in the mist of shag and bury their faces in pints of cider. The pub beckons to the wayfarer with warmth, music and out-of-tune harmony.

But I soon found there was little harmony. The village was united only in its hatred of Cowbright Major, which it had hated steadily, for some reason, since 1253. The clients of the One-Armed Adventurer were split into complicated groups with networks of conspiracy and feud. George, the Widgeon Mill gardener, hated William, the hedger. George's father had hated William's father. Stanley, the shepherd, turned his back on Phil, the odd-job man. Stanley's grandfather had turned his on Phil's grandfather. Only the Squire, Mr Badgers and the Londoners could talk to everybody.

Once I was helping George at Widgeon Mill. He was turfing over a burial ground of beet, as neat as a chapel. 'Let's go and snare a renyer,' he said. 'A what?' I asked. 'A renyer. A fox. I've found his run in the hedge. I've got some wire for him. It's more decent than the way that William shoots them. He's no good is William.' Both George and William were always on hand for every meet of the West Wiltshire, and offered voluble advice to the huntsmen. 'Can't think where they foxes got to,' they would say at the end of an unsuccessful hunt.

William was a sprig. He travelled to his hedges by motor bicycle. One night, after a tea-and-cake hop at the school house, I heard a whistle and found him behind a hedge. He had a companion with him, and they shared a gun, a torch and a sack. The gun was equipped with a silencer. 'Come for a stroll,' said William, ''tis a fine night.' We set off and covered about four miles across ploughed fields, kale and pasture. Then we came to the corner of a wood. 'We'll have a rest here,' said William. 'Never start anything before three o'clock. Folks are decently in bed then.' So we lay down on the grass and had a few smokes. All around us lights were flickering.

'Rabbit poachers,' said George. 'Netters. Or ferrets or dogs. It's real scandalous.'

We set off for the wood. Presently William's mate shone his torch up into a tree, and there were three fat pheasants glowing like coals. 'We'll fill the sack easy,' whispered William. 'There's nothing to worry about the farmer who owns the wood. I've been filling him up with whisky all night. He even lent me this gun. Mind you, he's a poacher himself. He let the shooting rights a month ago.' William fired the gun and missed, fired and missed again. 'The bastard beggared up the sights of his gun before he lent it to me,' he said. 'A man couldn't hit a horse with it.'

After some more futile shooting, we left the wood and returned towards Cowbright Minor. The night was hollow with owls and cocks were fretting up the dawn. 'Does everybody poach here?' I asked George. 'Everybody,' he said. 'We all live above our means, in a manner of speaking. Always been the same, folk say.' We climbed over a fence and crunched on to the road. A figure approached us, and William slipped the gun under a bramble bush. It was Mr Stales, the policeman. 'Hullo,' he said. 'Out late, aren't you?' 'Early,' said William. 'We're just starting.' Mr Stales stood there, undecided. He was new, and could only sense the long dark lanes of misrule which didn't begin and didn't end. 'Well, goodnight,' he said, sludging away. William felt for the gun.

'Everybody in Cowbright Minor acts as though nobody knew his business,' said my host next day over stacked plates of pheasant pie. (The larder was bulging with game.) 'They hate tale-bearers and are shocked by people who openly admit they know that others know about them. If a farmer had a drink in the One-Armed Adventurer and said he knew who poached his game, no one would speak to him. Or take the Squire. Everybody has known for the last year that when he leaves the Manor for a week in London and waves good-bye to his wife, he doesn't actually go to London at all. He drives off to a cottage, ten miles away, where he has installed the postmistress's daughter, Ruby. All in order, as long as he behaves as though he thinks nobody knows. And the Squire has deer in his woods. For a week the village is bristling with venison, and all's above board. But one day he walked into the pub with Ruby on his arm and ordered drinks all round. They were outraged. They even stopped raiding the deer for a time.'

A few days later we all went over to the Stag at Cowbright Major for the Cowbright dart match. There was George, William, Stanley, Phil and the rest of our team and the Soho set from Widgeon Mill. We dribbled sluggishly into the public bar and the publican greeted us like an advertisement for Inns. He wore heavy tweeds and smoked a pipe. He smelt strongly of

Oxford Street, gins and lime, the car trade. 'Who's going to win?' he shouted heartily. But the air was thick with feuds. Mr Badgers brought out a bottle of lung tonic, asked for a glass and ostentatiously poured out a thumbful. 'Here's luck,' he said to the rival publican.

Through the hatchway I could see a man in the saloon bar. He was smoking a cigar and waving a glass. A sudden silence fell in the public, and we could all hear what he was saying. 'Should be good sport, the deer . . . The Squire's gone off to London for a fortnight and he's let me his woods. . . .' It took a little time for the dart match to get going again. Our team didn't seem to be able to keep their minds on this game. They shot wild and lost the match.

3 April 1954

V. S. Pritchett was for many years Literary Editor of the New Statesman *and both during that time and thereafter he wrote that remarkable series of 'Books in General' which constitutes in itself an important body of critical writing on the literature of our time. From time to time he also wrote for the paper on what he saw and experienced as well as on what he read.*

An Encounter   V. S. Pritchett

There are people and there are cases. From a writer's point of view the latter are stultifying. They tell one too much. They infect one with theories of human conduct; they become puzzles with one piece missing. Attempt to supply the piece and there is the certainty of being wrong; give them up and they haunt you for years with your failure and their plausibility. Every writer has these recalcitrants sketched out abortively in his notebooks. For sixteen years I have been tormented by one I call the blue-eyed captain.

The blue-eyed captain torments because he is a case and he is most active at this time of the year which is the anniversary of our short encounter. I met him one evening in the dining car of a West Country train in the first mad months of the war in 1939. Like love, war is a sickness in its beginnings. It falsifies everything. Towns change their appearance, time goes to pieces, journeys drag on light-headedly; above all, people let out their private madness. We drop through a trap door into other periods of our lives. The day I met the captain, a middle-aged clerk at my bank went down with nettlerash, an illness he had not had since he was under canvas at Le Havre in 1914. Myself, I had reverted to my fourteenth birthday, stared at soldiers and was full of the dramatic war scenes I could remember when I was a boy. For this reason I stared at the captain as he sat opposite to me in the train.

The captain was a lithe, good-looking man in his forties, young for his age. A few months before he would have been one of those men who look like smart game in their tweeds and who one sees at race meetings, point-to-points, at parties on small estates. What these men do is mysterious. They talk of hunting, fishing, horses, dogs and land. They may run a farm for a rich man or sell expensive agricultural machinery in a gentlemanly way. Coveys of them meet in bars at hours which suggest idleness and anxiety. The captain was one of these. Agriculture was a poor thing before the war. He was delighted by the pleasure of being in uniform once more.

'I've seen this war coming a long time,' he said with a small sententious stammer and reproaching the world. 'We ought to have had it before.'

Personable, the ready picker up of acquaintance, the captain might have been any other officer of his age who suddenly felt the world had meaning at last.

Any other officer – except in one startling private respect: his eyes. They were blue; one could see their blueness the length of the dining car away. They were unsubmissive to the sunburn and the uniform. In a hard-faced, sporting figure they had the effect of an ornament or an elegance. They were set in a mesh of fine lines, though not puddled, and were like two dead china blue stones, opaque and semi-precious. When his lids moved, they had the indifference of an artifice.

This was one of the crack trains of the Great Western but now, because of the war – troop trains or air raid rumours – it stopped and crawled and stopped again. We sat in an oddly disembodied collection of human voices cut off from travel, as if a film had broken and the sound was going on from a blank screen.

'Are you going back to the depot?' I asked.

'No,' he said. 'I'm on leave.'

'That must be a relief.'

'I'm on sick leave.'

'That must be a relief in a way too,' I said.

'As a matter of fact,' the captain said, 'it isn't. I'm going blind.'

How does one suddenly tell a stranger one is going blind? The captain did so in the quiet confident voice of one who had backed a winner yesterday. He was pleased. He was even quietly boastful. To me, of course, the blue eyes at once became the whole man: serene in their hurt, their very intensity, the tired dilation of things blooming too full. I noticed now they were yellowing in the whites.

'I've just been up to see a specialist in London,' he said. 'He's messing me about. I've been going to him for a month and he thinks if he can check it for a while he'll cure it altogether. He says the nerves are engorged with blood. I get black-outs. Damned awkward when you are driving a car on the road. I never had anything wrong with my eyes in my life before this. That is how I knew something was wrong. I blacked out on the road a mile from the camp.'

It wasn't at all funny; it was damned lucky, the captain said. He had slowed down because he thought he saw some fellow he knew – people you knew years before were always trickling into the camp – and the next thing, he was on the pavement, blind. He was a bit shaken. There was nothing to do at Headquarters, everything was at sixes and sevens there. 'All the chaps I used to know in the regiment from 1918 and – you know "Have a drink old boy!"' There had been sessions. He thought he'd been lifting the elbow too much. Then, it happened again and this was not funny at all. Taking a bend on the Bath Road at fifty. He had his batman with him, giving him a lift home.

'I might have killed him,' the captain said. 'It's about the most frightening thing there is.'

The captain's voice was drawling and vain.

'They tell you it's all psychological,' he said in the falsely amused manner of one who has just been dumped at the edge of a tropical jungle after sunset.

A fatal remark to make to a writer. I looked at the captain's startling eyes. So featureless, their shutters of blueness down. What – I asked myself the question that was to change him from a human being into a trick case – what was it the captain did not wish to see?

'Whatever it is,' the captain said, 'it put the wind up me and I'm not easily frightened. I went through the whole of the 1914 war, spent three years in France and I never had anything like that.'

The subject was ended. I looked out of the window. The train was still standing in the sad silence of the water meadows. Slowly trundling towards us was an endless goods train which became a procession of guns when it passed.

'I would have thought three years in France was enough war for a lifetime,' I said.

'I enjoyed it,' said the captain.

'I don't think many people did,' I said.

'You'd be surprised,' said the captain. 'Lots of fellows cracked up, people you would think would never break. Others didn't. I'm not shooting a line but it never worried me once. I was three years in the line and I can honestly say I was never once afraid. People were pulled out and sent back to the base; I wasn't. I don't take any credit for it. From the beginning of the war to the end, nothing touched me.'

'The noise alone. . . .'

'I know. Nothing. Noise never bothered me.'

'And you were never afraid ?'

'Never,' said the captain. 'Never thought of it.'

The captain's manner had become spacious and enthusiastic. As if it had caught his confidence, our train began to move and the voices in the dining car lost their isolation and became merged in the general slurring of time.

'The only time that I was frightened in France,' he said, 'was in the last month of the war. There was a German attack and I suddenly found myself alone with a German coming at me with his bayonet. I saw him. I stood there. I had a revolver in my hand. I couldn't lift it. I was paralysed. If my batman hadn't seen it and got the fellow first I should have been dead. He just rushed at him and got him. Saved my life. I can see it now. Nice fellow. He wiped his bayonet afterwards, as naturally as anything, as good living a fellow as you'd ever see. Yes,' said the captain. 'I was afraid then.'

It was funny, the captain said, joining the regiment again. A bit of a strain, after the first few days. Everyone was older, you forget that. The brigadier was past it. Some of those old fellows were still fighting the 1914 war. There were a lot of small quarrels.

'When I get my eyes right I shall probably put in for a transfer,' he said.

I said goodbye to the captain. It was not, as I have said, a real goodbye. I talked about him to my friends, I discussed his case with one or two doctors. Yes (they agreed) it was probable that the new war had brought back to him some incident he did not want to see again. Yes (they agreed) it was odd that his old batman had been in the car with him at the time of the black-out. If (they said) his batman had really been in the car with him! If (they added) he himself really had had a black-out when he was driving! The strong probability was (they said) that his blindness had started one morning when he was sitting on the lavatory. It was on the cards that his old batman had never rejoined the regiment. Or, in the terms of his story, had never existed at all. But obviously (they said) there was *something* the matter with the captain's eyes.

24 September 1955

Norman MacKenzie worked for the New Statesman *for twenty years; at editorial meetings he had a sure feeling for the right new statesmanly line; it is hardly too much to say that he was the keeper of the paper's conscience. He wrote almost every feature of it at some time or other. Here he is on Paul Robeson.*

The World Well Lost   Norman MacKenzie

As the lights go down in Madison Square Garden, leaving only ten thousand cigarettes glowing like stars in the darkened tiers, Paul Robeson stands on the dais under the floodlamps. Right hand cupped to his ear, he sings – is it 'Ballad for Americans', or 'Water Boy', a Russian, a Chinese, a Spanish song? Or is it the inevitable encore, for which the galleries are already shouting: 'Last night I dreamed I saw Joe Hill, alive as you and me'? For whatever the title of the show, the scenery and the producers are the same. It is Spanish Aid, The Yanks Are Not Coming, the Second Front, the Wallace campaign, Civil Rights, here in the Garden, or Chicago or Los Angeles, or at the Peekskill riot, with Paul in the spot before the collection.

Just so do we remember him in pre-war England – the warm-hearted champion of the common people in their fight for freedom, the most moving singer this generation has heard or is likely to hear. The difference was that when he sang for the Popular Front he did not need to decide whether or not he was a Communist. Fascism was the enemy of freedom, and, above all, of racial equality. In England there was no racial discrimination to narrow the scope of Paul's sympathy with Left causes.

Somewhere about the time of Munich, a pacifist who was also a resolute anti-fascist argued with Robeson about the coming war. He at first puzzled Paul by boggling about taking part in war against the Nazis. He explained that he had a prior loyalty – deeper even than his hatred of Fascism. Robeson's face lit up. 'I understand now,' he said. 'You feel as I should if fighting against Hitlerism meant, by some accident, that I had to fight against my own Negro people? I just couldn't do it, however good the cause.'

In America Paul feared the taunt that he was willing to compromise about the Negro cause; he would not, like some other successful Negro artists, merely appease his conscience by supporting respectable liberal organizations for Negro emancipation. He must join the ranks of the fighters, and that, he believed meant the Communists. So he gave them his great talents, singing, speaking, marching with them down every inch of the Party line.

And for that he has lost his passport and his livelihood. Since 1950 he has been unable to travel outside the United States, refusing, on principle, to sign an affidavit that he does not belong to the Communist Party. His most recent legal action has brought yet another rejection from the State Department. Given permission to visit Canada, he is still unable to accept a Soviet offer to make a film version of *Othello*, as well as concert engagements in England, invitations to Paris and Rome and Prague. The State Department has not forgiven his speeches on previous journeys abroad and, at home, no one will hire him as a professional entertainer. At the beginning of August an English visitor asked a San Francisco radio station why it did not play Robeson's records. The station president, Mr Cisler, replied: 'We consider him a disgrace to the American scene for his long-standing feud with our way of life, and hence no need to publicize his name for any further public income to him from concerts or recordings.' The boycott is complete. For, in any case, as Mr Cisler added, 'he has not recorded any material on the new and better long-playing records which we now use exclusively.' Therefore, 'considerations of good taste and discrimination do suggest his omission from programme planning.' Paul Robeson has not been tried by due process, but 'good taste' has sentenced him to unemployment in a country he cannot leave.

As witch-hunting intensified he became more extreme, more outspoken. Former friends recanted, turned informer, ran for cover, but Robeson took to the stump. Though he has never revealed whether he holds a party card, he refers to himself as a Communist, and at union halls and picnics, at rallies and on picket lines, he has spoken up for the Communists 'who have done a magnificent job.' With pride he received the Stalin Peace Prize in 1952, and listened with emotion as Howard Fast pinned on his coat the medal which Fast called 'the highest award the human race can bestow upon one of its members.'

Paul is courageous but not sophisticated about politics. At the White House, in 1946, he told President Truman to his face that there was 'little to choose between the crimes of the men on trial at Nuremburg and recent US lynchings.' In 1949 he insisted that countries which received aid under the Marshall Plan 'had nothing to give the US except the raw materials to be found in their African colonies – and that means further exploitation and abuse of Africans.' At the same time, he announced that 'the struggle in Greece is again noble testimony to the courage of the Communists, who have always been the first to fight and die for the freedom of all peoples.' And this was in the same year that he told a civil rights conference that Trotskyists were Fascists and therefore had no claim to civil liberties.

Robeson's conversion, absolute and unquestioning, is the more remarkable because it has no obvious impulse from his personal experience. He was famous, popular and rich. He had never himself suffered from serious discrimination as a Negro. Of his own free will he bears on his shoulders the accumulated sufferings of his people; as the greatest of American Negroes he feels that he must be a self-appointed sacrifice on the altar of racial freedom and equality. It is this quality in him that has aroused such hostility among other leaders of the Negro community, jealous perhaps, certainly embarrassed by him, and bitterly critical of his refusal to see that the battle against segregation can be waged in other ways than by the head-on and often unscrupulous tactics of the Communists. 'If only,' they will say, 'if only Paul were on our side,' as he contemptuously dismisses them as reformists and Uncle Toms.

Robeson's contempt is harsher, possibly, because of all Negroes he has had to steel himself most against the blandishments of success, to cultivate his sense of injustice. In Princeton, New Jersey, where he was born in 1898, his father was the minister at the Witherspoon Presbyterian Church, much respected by Negroes and Whites. His mother, who died tragically when he was six, came of a mixed Indian-Negro family of Quaker belief, and her great-grandfather – an acquaintance of Benjamin Franklin – helped found the Free African Society in 1787. In this liberal tradition, young Paul grew up, a brilliant boy, popular and mixing freely with both White and Negro schoolfellows. Princeton University at that time was closed to Negroes, and Paul was only the third to enter Rutgers. There he continued to prove himself as a scholar, and, what was a more certain path to social acceptance, one of the outstanding athletes of his day. Years later, when he was playing Othello, he said that to catch the tension of Othello's rage he recalled the only time in his life when he felt a similar emotion. As a freshman, he was trying to get into the college football team. At practice, each of the team was playing for his place against the newcomer, hating the thought of making room for a Negro: the whole team made a set at Paul. A broken nose and a dislocated shoulder put him out of practice for ten days. When he returned to the field, one player brutally kicked the finger nails from his hand. Paul lost his temper, charged down the field like a mad bull, and then, gripping the last man to approach him, he swung the wretched player above his head, and was about to smash him to the ground when the coach shouted from the touchline, 'Robeson, you're in the team.' He became one of America's greatest football players.

Moving to Columbia Law School, and living in Harlem, Paul was still scarcely aware of his colour. He made friends easily; he even managed to get a job in a White firm, something that few Negro lawyers had yet done. But he left the job when some of his White colleagues protested against working with a Negro, and after drifting for a while, struck up a friendship with the Provincetown Theatre Group, and especially with Eugene O'Neill. He was cast as Emperor Jones, as Jim Harris in *All God's Chillun Got Wings* – he had barely set foot on the boards when he was beginning to dream about *Othello* – and then, with the backing of his Greenwich Village friends, came his first concert in April, 1925, the first concert ever given in the U.S. which consisted entirely of Negro music.

Success, but what Paul felt to be increasingly limited success, came after. *Show Boat* made him, in New York and London. But the songs, the stage parts, were Negro songs, Negro parts. The London production of *Othello*, at the Savoy Theatre in 1930, was the beginning of his escape into a wider field. New York producers were still afraid of it; even in London, there was doubt. Hannen Swaffer asked whether the theatre public would take to seeing a Negro make love to a White woman and throw her round the stage. 'It didn't bother most people,' Paul said afterwards, 'but it sure bothered me. For the first two weeks in every scene I played with Desdemona, that girl couldn't get near me. I was backing away from her all the time like a plantation hand in the parlour.' New York had to wait until 1943 to see Robeson as Othello, but – as the *New York Times* wrote of the opening night – it then gave him 'an ovation that has not been equalled along Broadway in many years.'

By then, however, Paul Robeson was more than a great singer and a magnificent actor: he himself said that he had come 'to see my work as a social weapon, not as art for art's sake.' He had become dissatisfied with 'singing to the same audiences of comfortable people.' And the climax of his discontent came shortly after he appeared in the film *Sanders of the River*. He said that he put everything he had into his part: 'I thought that I was doing a good job for my people.' Then some of his Leftist friends told him that the film was imperialist propaganda, that he had played up to the White stereotype of Black. In anger, Paul gave away all the money he received from the film to Negro relief organizations, and repeatedly tried to buy up the negative.

About this time he made his first visit to Russia. In 1948, he told a Senate Committee how he then felt and why he sent his son Paul to school in the Soviet Union. 'I walked the earth there for the first time in complete dignity.' The minority peoples had 'infinitely more opportunity than I would have in Mississippi.' So the regular visits began. The Robesons preferred Europe to the US, Russia to Europe; and but for Paul's conviction that, having seen the light, he must communicate his conversion, he and his wife Essie would have settled in Moscow.

In the years when the Popular Front made Leftism acceptable on both sides of the Atlantic, Paul could earn a great deal of money, and he could be a propagandist too. He moved happily through a whirl of meetings, plays, concerts: it could be the Albert Hall one night and Unity Theatre the next. His personal warmth and generosity, his bigness and his kindness, made him everybody's friend – and many of those friendships have lasted despite the naïveté of his political activities in recent years. Even today, when Paul makes some outrageous statement, one which would seem silly or vicious in the mouth of a hard-boiled party official, one feels more embarrassment than anger. For he has stood up to be counted when others were running away, spending his energies prodigally for the truth as he sees it, counting the world well lost. In 1948, when he made five hundred free appearances, most of them political, he was giving away the equivalent of $750,000 at the box-office to help win votes for Henry Wallace. By cutting himself off from the mainstream of American life, he may have been guided along tortuous paths and done less than was in him to help his people towards equality. If so it was from no fault but lack of political judgement. Now, perhaps, as the mood changes, he can find his way back.

24 September 1955

Malcolm Muggeridge first appeared in the New Statesman *in the early Thirties. He has contributed to the paper for thirty years, during which time the astringency of what he says and the urbanity with which he says it have become more marked. He is one of the writers over fifty who still find themselves at home with the younger new statesmanship as it is emerging under the Editorship of John Freeman. This piece appeared six months before Suez.*

Leadership is always apt, even under universal suffrage. Government is seldom imposed, except for brief periods, and in politics there are never any Guilty Men. It is not by chance that a Baldwin or a Neville Chamberlain, an Attlee or a Roosevelt, or for that matter a Hitler or a Mussolini or a Stalin, emerge. Governors and governed seek and find a *modus vivendi*; the collectivity expect those set in authority over them to manifest, in a recognizable manner, the *zeitgeist* to which they belong. Otherwise they get rid of them.

Thus, today, we have in Sir Anthony Eden an eminently suitable prime minister, conveying, as he does so exactly in appearance and in personality, the benevolent intentions and earnest purposes whereby an almost extinct ruling class seeks to protract itself a little longer. His somehow slightly seedy good looks and attire, his ingratiating smile and gestures, the utter nothingness of what he has to say – does it not all provide an outward and visible manifestation of an inward and invisible loss of authority and self-confidence? Yes, it is entirely fitting that this tedious, serious Etonian, on whose lips are the last dying echoes of the late nineteenth-century concept of progress without tears, should have his moment in the middle of the turbulent and cruel twentieth century. He is a Disraeli hero who has moved into a service flat, or perhaps a deep shelter; a Bertie Wooster who has turned from the Drones Club to Toynbee Hall. As has been truly said, he is not only a bore but he bores for England.

Why, then, does he arouse, particularly among some of his ostensible supporters, a frenzy of irritation, if not of positive dislike? After all, there are plenty of bores and nonentities among politicians of all parties. No one gets furious with Lord Woolton because he is not a dazzling conversationalist. Nor has a heavy hand in ladling out the spoken word prevented Lord Waverley or Lord Halifax from enjoying a reasonable measure of public esteem. Lord Alexander of Hillsborough is no Sidney Smith, and Mr Griffiths' oratory is more notable for sound and fury than for sense. Yet these, and many like them, patiently tread the political mill, receiving in due course their due award.

The simple fact is that there is nothing in Sir Anthony either to admire or to abhor. He is just empty of content, like his television appearances in which a flow of banalities is presented in the persuasive manner of an ex-officer trying to sell one a fire extinguisher at the front door. His writings are the same. There is nothing wrong with them except that they are unreadable. One has to fight one's way through them; only dogged determination and a series of pauses to get one's breath for a fresh assault will carry one on to the end. When, as in the case of the recent Washington communiqués, President Eisenhower also takes a hand, with Mr William Clark doubtless putting in the finishing touches, the result is a brew which makes Coca-Cola seem, by comparison, like Imperial Tokay.

Even so, quite a lot of Conservatives, particularly among his parliamentary and even ministerial colleagues, find it very hard to enthuse over Sir Anthony, and next to impossible to praise him. At best they put up with him. It was the same with Ramsay MacDonald during the second Labour government. Labour ministers and MPs for the most part just could not abide him, and at the same time they felt they had to endure him because he 'had a large following in the country,' because he 'spoke with authority in the counsels of the nations', and so on – the self-same reasons, in fact, which induce Conservative MPs to endure Sir Anthony. If there had been a Gallup poll when MacDonald was a Labour prime minister it would have shown, I am sure, as overwhelming a majority in favour of his leadership among the Labour Party rank-and-file as it has lately shown in favour of Sir Anthony's among rank-and-file Conservatives.

The two men – MacDonald and Sir Anthony – have, as a matter of fact, a great deal in common, down to the small but significant detail of frequently referring to us, the public, as 'my friends'. In the United States MacDonald was greatly esteemed, and so, it is said, is Sir Anthony today. Again, MacDonald had no more idea of how to deal with unemployment, the chief domestic problem confronting his government, than Sir Anthony has of how to deal with inflation, which is the chief domestic problem confronting his government. In his rather more shaggy, William Morris sort of way, MacDonald was as consciously elegant in appearance as is Sir Anthony, and their diction bears many points of resemblance – a note of almost whimpering persuasiveness combined with a lack of precision which, in MacDonald's case, degenerated into total incomprehensibility.

In a sense, too, their roles are the same, though in reverse. MacDonald's role was to convince the then much more powerful middle and upper classes that they had nothing to fear from a Labour prime minister, and Sir Anthony's is to convince the now much more powerful lower classes that a Conservative prime minister is really on their side. Such a role cannot but give a touch of ribaldry to those who undertake it, and though neither MacDonald nor Sir Anthony can be regarded as greatly dowered with humour, there is something inherently comical about both of them. In the pages of history they are likely to appear as Don Quixote figures, whose earnest intentions and high aspirations bear no valid relation to the actual circumstances of their times, and therefore in retrospect seem funny.

It is, of course, true that MacDonald did not run out his time as leader of the Labour Party. Sir Anthony might be well advised to follow his example in this respect. When the inflation crisis reaches its peak, what possible recourse will he have but to join up with Mr Gaitskell, as Mac-Donald did with Baldwin, and appeal to the country for a Doctor's Mandate? Many Conservatives would doubtless refuse to follow him and would, in consequence, lose their seats; but the Gaitskell-Eden government would be returned with a huge, and largely Labour, majority. *The Observer*, under J. L. Garvin, said of MacDonald, when he formed his national government with Baldwin: 'Thank God for him!'; *The Observer*, under Mr David Astor, would probably make a like observation about Sir Anthony if he were to form a national government with Mr Gaitskell. Just as there was a minute Labour opposition under George Lansbury in 1932, so there would doubtless be a minute Conservative opposition under, say, Mr James Stuart, when Sir Anthony and Mr Gaitskell had appealed successfully to the country. Mr Bevan would then make forays from the left as Churchill did from the right. Otherwise the two situations would be identical. In due course Mr Gaitskell and Sir Anthony could change places as Baldwin and MacDonald did.

Without some such arrangement it is difficult to see much future for Sir Anthony as a purely Conservative leader. Conservative MPs, certainly, are more docile than Labour MPs, but even they will scarcely go on enduring with equanimity the surrender, one after another, of all their cherished positions at home and abroad. Fate, and Sir Winston Churchill, have given them, just at their moment of recovery from the 1945 débacle, a general whose instinct is always to retreat, and whose words of command have about as much dynamism as a Third Programme talk on the place of the potato in English folk-lore.

None of this is Sir Anthony's fault. He is but a victim of history. The ship of state was already hopelessly water-logged and incapable of responding to the tiller when he took over command. What was there, then, for him to do but to bend his efforts to soothing down the increasingly apprehensive passengers? Like the Republicans in the United States under President Eisenhower's leadership, the Conservatives under his have been unable to find any *raison d'être* except to continue the policies of their opponents. They asked for a leader and were given a public relations officer; here is the news, and this is Anthony Eden reading it.

11 February 1956

Leonard Woolf, as he says in this account of his association with the New
Statesman, *was in at the birth of the paper and is by far its oldest inhabitant,
as it were. His influence, as a friend and adviser of Kingsley Martin during
Martin's thirty years as Editor, was important. He is a director of the New
Statesman company.*

The Prehistoric 'N. S. & N.'   Leonard Woolf

The *Nation* was born before I became conscious of journals and journalism. But I was in at the birth of the *New Statesman* in the Webbs' house
in what was then Grosvenor Road. Beatrice and Sidney Webb, being the
midwives, and the famous luncheons of leg of mutton and milk pudding
ensured that the childbed was austere, hygienic, antiseptic. It was in 1913
and the Webbs had just 'taken me up'. In 1911 I had come back on leave
after seven years in the Ceylon Civil Service; in 1912 I resigned and
decided to try to earn my living in England by writing. One of the first
things which I wrote was an article for the *Manchester Guardian* on the
co-operative movement, and Mrs Webb, who was the authority on the
movement at that time and was always on the look-out for potential
Fabians, asked me to come and see her and Sidney. They were in the
throes of launching the *New Statesman* and were therefore on the look-out
not only for potential Fabians, but also for potential contributors, and it
was as a potential contributor that I was asked to what must have been,
I think, the first Tuesday *N.S.* lunch at Grosvenor Road after it began
publication.

Clifford Sharp, the Editor, Jack (now Sir John) Squire, the Literary
Editor, and Desmond MacCarthy, the dramatic critic, were of course
there; also Shaw and, I rather think, S. K. Ratcliffe. After that I went
fairly often to these Tuesday lunches to which more than once only
Sharp, Squire and I came. Meals with the Webbs always had a hard,
metallic, sombre brightness, but the *New Statesman* lunch had a peculiar
grimness of its own. This was mainly due to Clifford Sharp, who insisted
on discussing 'subjects' and 'situations' in the abstract and not as potential
copy for the *New Statesman*.

I was never on the staff of the *New Statesman*, but Sharp asked me to
come and suggest an article to him whenever I thought I had a good
subject, and Jack Squire sent me enormous packages of 'war books' and
books on foreign affairs for review. I therefore saw a good deal of the inside
of that curious, poky, little newspaper office in Gt Queen Street. It was

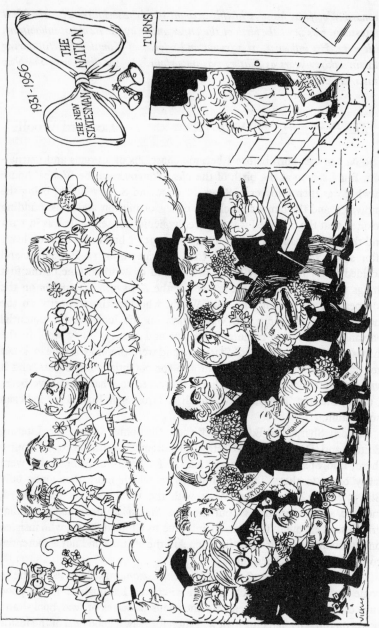

Kingsley Martin – twenty-five years as Editor by Vicky [12 May 1956]

dominated by the Editor. I acquired an affection for Clifford Sharp, but it was the kind of affection which one sometimes gets for an old, mangy, bad-tempered, slightly dangerous dog. One is rather proud of being among the few whom he will with a growl allow to pat him gingerly on the head. Sharp had been trained as an engineer, and it always seemed to me that he brought to human relations, to politics, to journalism the attitude of the engineer, of a sanitary engineer or super-plumber. When he stood in his room – he was nearly always standing – listening to what one had to say, there was an atmosphere about him of intellectual Jeyes' Fluid, moral carbolic soap, spiritual detergents – to such an extent that one sometimes had the illusion that he himself smelt strongly of soap and his room of disinfectants. Temperamentally and fundamentally he was a conservative of the Rule Britannia, Disraelian, 1878 vintage; but he was also, as the Webbs used to point out with quiet enjoyment, a collectivist. Indeed, collectivism and drainage – material or spiritual – were the only things Sharp believed in. He liked to think of himself as the hard-boiled tough, without sentimentality, without illusions, without emotions – the realist and no damned nonsense; and his face, particularly the eyes and nose, which always made me think of a hooded falcon, helped him to sustain this chracter. In fact he had the sentimentality of those who make a fuss about being anti-sentimental.

He was a first-class editor within the limits which he prescribed for his paper and his contributors. He knew what he wanted said and he got it said in the way he wanted it said. He thus gave the *New Statesman* a very marked character, an air of highly efficient political plumbing and sanitation. His editorial limitations were shown when he would not print Shaw's articles even when they were signed. As a beginner in journalism, I found his methods rather disheartening, until I came to know him better. He was one of those editors who believe in keeping his contributors up to the mark by a liberal use of cold water (perhaps another instance of his sanitation complex). When I nervously went to suggest an article to him, he would make me say what I proposed to write and then for five or ten minutes pour buckets of icy water down my back. When he saw that I had become sufficiently despondent, he would say brightly: 'Well, Woolf, you may as well go off and see what you can do. I don't say it won't make an article.' I think he always did take the article and occasionally I even got a word of unexpected praise.

In my experience, the literary side of weekly papers is almost always the exact opposite of the political, and the *New Statesman*, all through its glacial period, was no exception to this rule. To go from Sharp's room into

Jack Squire's or Desmond MacCarthy's was to step from a refrigerator straight into a sun loggia. Here you could be sure to find good company, endless talk, and plenty of laughter. Squire as Solomon Eagle, and MacCarthy as Affable Hawk, each gave to the literary part of the paper an individuality as strong as Sharp gave to the political; and the cheerful and charming urbanity of the Literary Editors, so different from the toughness of the Editor, spread all over the last half of the paper.

I cannot end my reminiscences of the primeval *New Statesman* without a word about the short interregnum between the editorship of Sharp and the editorship of Kingsley Martin. During the interregnum C. M. Lloyd sat in the editor's chair and I used to go in and help him with proofs and odds and ends. Mostyn Lloyd deserves to be remembered as having done a great deal of good work for the paper. When you knew him you found him to be a charming man. He was congenitally pessimistic – possibly because of ill-health – but even his pessimism had its charm and seemed to fit the *New Statesman* at that time, when someone is reputed to have remarked about it that Lloyd grumbles, Martin snarls, and Woolf bites.

The atmosphere of the *Nation* was always very different from that of the *New Statesman*. During the 1914 war I occasionally wrote an article for the *Nation* under Massingham. When Brailsford became editor of the *New Leader*, in 1922 I think, Massingham asked me to take his place on the *Nation*. This meant writing every week a political leader and some notes. On Monday morning I used to go and see Massingham in order to decide what I should write about. The editor, the spacious office in Adelphi Terrace overlooking the river, the staff, the atmosphere, were all a complete contrast to Sharp and Gt Queen Street. Massingham was a brilliant editor in so far as, without writing very much himself, he was able to distil the essence of a very strange personality into every crevice of his paper. He was an emotional sentimentalist but with a small central hard core of toughness. When I went to him of a Monday morning, he usually began by talking about something unconnected with a potential article. Then he would drift into the most violent abuse of Lloyd George, against whom he had turned, and of Scott of the *Manchester Guardian*. His language was remarkably foul and his charges against them fantastically lurid. After a while, he would ask me whether I had thought of a subject to write about. I would suggest one and explain what I proposed to say. He rarely said much himself, but was always very appreciative and encouraging. I used to go away in good spirits and write an article which, when I read it through, I found to my astonishment was written not in my, but in Massingham's style.

The atmosphere of Adelphi Terrace was extremely friendly, civilized, and distinguished after the bleakness of Gt Queen Street. Unlike the *New Statesman* of those days, it had a remarkable staff of writers whom one continually met on the premises. Hammond, Nevinson and Hobson all wrote regularly and H. M. Tomlinson was literary editor. They were all humanists and made good company at a *Nation* lunch. But it lasted, for me, a very short time. Suddenly one day Massingham told me that he had been 'given notice' and that the paper would be sold. After a period of short and painful indecision the *Nation* was acquired by a group of which Maynard Keynes was an important member. Hubert Henderson became editor and I became literary editor. It was a queer revolution, for the *Nation* of Keynes and Henderson was again completely different from the *Nation* of Massingham and the *New Statesman* of Sharp. Unlike Massingham and Sharp, Henderson was not a natural journalist, nor a born editor. He had an absolutely first-class Scottish logician's brain. Right or wrong, he could always defeat anyone – even Keynes – in any argument on any subject. But his victories were logical and academic. His leaders on politics and economics were extremely able and much admired by Liberals, but it may be that they were a symptom, if not one of the causes, of the rapid decay of the Liberal Party and of political liberalism during the nineteen-twenties.

I resigned the literary editorship of the *Nation* a year or two before its marriage with the *New Statesman*, and I cannot therefore say anything about its last days as an independent paper under the editorship of Harold Wright. But before I end this article there is one thing which I should like to say because it is never said about the history of weekly journals. All through the history of the *New Statesman* and the *Nation*, as I knew them, there has always been a secretary to the Editor, a woman, who played an extraordinarily important part in the fortunes of the paper. Mrs Mason of Sharp's *New Statesman*, Miss Crosse of Massingham's *Nation*, Mrs Jones of Henderson's, all deserve to be mentioned when one is praising famous men and women. Without Mrs Mason, Sharp's *New Statesman* would never have survived, for, when Desmond was literary editor, there would have been too many blank pages. Mrs Jones played the same kind of part on Henderson's *Nation*, and as for Miss Crosse she was the dominant figure in Adelphi Terrace. Indeed, when I got my *Nation* on Saturday morning and read my article in it, I used often to think that we were all – Massingham, Tomlinson and I – under a delusion, that it was Miss Crosse who had really edited and written the paper, including my own article.   *12 May 1956*

Poets of distinction are born new statesmen: the policy of publishing their work has been maintained consistently by all the paper's Editors for half a century.

Plea for the Hated Dead Woman   Doris Lessing

Wrath sank her waterstopped in weed.
Nor ever can those silences
Compel the sympathy we need
To thaw our frozen consciences.

'Mourn that hag-riding harridan!
Mourn her whose monument is grief
She did not die when needed, in
Good time to save our sweet belief!

God stops the young beloved and fair.
Five sons and daughters must receive
Her heritage of hate and fear.
Had she died sooner they might grieve.

The world's steel-slaughtered innocents
Plead dumbly for their grudging share
From our strained stores of pity, whence
You ask us to find more for her!'

But wait! You pity those five yet
Who live hate-wrung as she was wrung.
Each generation pays that debt
Contracted first with Adam's young.

And do not bombs and bullets start
From that same root where sprang, perverse,
The poisoned blossoms of her heart?
And who may say which bane is worse?

But, if you will, deny that debt:
Then so far stretch your sympathies;
That salt-scoured face and grim was set
No less unflinching than it is.

Wrath sunk her waterstopped in weed.
With weed she lies, unfleshed, alone.
With quickflesh contest if you need:
There is no argument with bone.

30 June 1956

Claud Cockburn's various journalistic enterprises, notably the famous The Week, *the one paper, run on a shoe-string, which was said always to have the inside story, are too well known to need explaining. He is probably the only Communist ever to approach politics in the spirit of John Wilkes . . . a serious conviction and purpose covered by a wittily frivolous manner which was his reader's delight. He contributed irregularly to the* New Statesman.

Days on the 'Worker' Claud Cockburn

There was a time during Franco's siege of Bilbao – Guernica period – when *The Times* ran serious risks of getting no news out of Viscaya at all; its brilliant Special Correspondent there, passionately *engagé*, was a lot busier than some of our generals organizing and seeking effectively to direct the Basque defences against Navarrois and Moors. And in Madrid at about the same time Ernest Hemingway was similarly occupied. Some of the generals sneered, fumed and threatened to have such over-participant journalists arrested. Non-participant journalists sneered too.

In my experience, uninvited civilian advisers were right quite as often as the generals. And in any case the urge to put the cover on the typewriter for a bit and man the barricades is irrepressible among many newspapermen. At the *Daily Worker*, when I functioned there, the urge to direct action was so widespread among our reporters that it became quite a hazard to smooth newspaper production. Came an important industrial dispute in, say, Lanarkshire or Glamorgan, and we were kept on tenterhooks all evening wondering whether Our Representative would make the deadline before being locked up by the police or beaten senseless in a battle with blacklegs.

Quite early in my stint for the *Worker* I went out on a story with a veteran staff member – a former textile worker from Lancashire of rather bookish appearance, fluently didactic manner and long training in the dialectic. The idea was that he would captain our team of two, directing my inexperienced attention to the kind of points that would be of special interest to *Worker* readers. The occasion was a rally of Mosley's Black-shirts in – if I recall rightly – West Ham Town Hall, and its special importance was that this was the anti-semites' first major, and vastly provocative, invasion of the East End.

There were big, furiously hostile crowds around the hall when we got there, and I paused to scribble a note of the badge-numbers of a posse of police who seemed to be acting as a sort of bodyguard for the Fascist cordon round the hall – allied with them, apparently, against the locals. Separated momentarily from my mentor by this delay, I heard him shouting to me imperiously from the thick of the crowd ahead. Fearing that I was already missing the main story, I fought my way forward.

'Give a hand here, mate,' he said as, sparkling with energy and excite-ment, he began to pry loose from a stationary tramcar one of the indicator boards which at that time were suspended along the sides of tramcars and were a favourite utensil of the under-privileged in London at moments of emergency such as this. An ill-protected side-door of the hall had been reported by someone, and with this board as a battering-ram and the help of one or two others, we might cause havoc in the rear of the enemy. We never actually had a chance to swing the thing against the door because before we could reach it we were set upon by men with truncheons and driven from our objective.

We got into the meeting somehow, and I was dutifully taking a note or two on the speech of some blackshirted ruffian, when my colleague rose in his place to shout some questions about concentration camps and German democracy, and roar out three times 'Oop Dimitrov!' We were beaten where we stood, then dragged into the gangway and kicked violently into the street.

By this time – since the *Worker* necessarily had a very early bedtime – we had to think about finding a telephone booth from which to ring in a preliminary story. As we hurried through the outskirts of the crowd my companion gave me advice.

'The proper political perspective on this,' he was saying, when out of an alley-way or garage entrance came chugging across our path a Blackshirt motor-cyclist – patrol or courier. Interrupting his remarks, the head of our little team hurled himself forward in a flying tackle, and brought the machine, the Blackshirt, and himself banging to the ground. I was really surprised when we finally reached the telephone with ten minutes or so to spare before our deadline.

After a number of months, part of which I spent participating to some extent in the revolt of the miners of Asturias in north Spain, I too, began to

226

feel a small itch to get out and about in Stanley Baldwin's England and add, to news stories, features and other arrangements of the printed word, a more direct attempt to break through the heavy fog of silence and humbug which, as it seemed to me, had descended upon our land. I filled in such spare time as I had from *The Week*, the *Daily Worker* and the Council for Civil Liberties – then a rather noisy adolescent – by helping to organize what was known with occasionally affectionate and occasionally shocked derision to my friends as 'Claud's Terror Troupe'.

It wasn't at all a Terror Troupe, but rather a very small publicity gang – there were never more than eight or nine people in it – devoted to doing things that would advertise our various Causes, and doing them in such a way that the newspapers would have to take notice even if it choked them. Since these were instances of 'individual action' – if not exactly of that 'individual terror' condemned by the orthodox – the Communist Party could not lend them its countenance. It could only go to the length of not automatically expelling people suspected of taking part in such illegal activities. We had to work on our own. And we did produce quite a number of incidents which got things printed that never would have been printed otherwise. It was all rather small-time stuff, but it was interesting work to organize and was, in the oppressive atmosphere of the time, occasionally exhilarating.

The episode of the banner in Fleet Street, however, was interesting both in itself and because it accidentally demonstrated how easy it would have been for real terrorists to have blown up most of the Royal Family and many other leaders of State, Church and Armed Forces all at once at eleven o'clock in the morning in the sight of thousands in the middle of London. This all occurred on Jubilee Day, 1935. With the Great Depression barely over and World War II visibly looming, it seemed that every effort, however puny, should be made to attract maximum attention to the seamy side of the Jubilee brocade.

For quite a while before Jubilee Day the streets of London had begun to be decked with banners – often of the kind that are strung from one side of the street to the other, displaying to the cavalcade presently to pass beneath them messages of loyalty and joy. Our little group constructed a banner of unusual design, though it outwardly looked like any other Jubilee banner. It was like an enormous handkerchief folded across the middle, and hung on a rope, and then the bottom half of each hanging side was folded back and up. In that position it displayed to the gaze innocuous sentiments. But at the twitch of a pulley the hooked up sides would be released, the innocuous slogan would vanish and instead everyone

227

would see, in huge letters, the words 'Twenty-five Years of Hunger and War'.

The next problem was how to get it prominently slung. We selected the lower part of Fleet Street as the site and, hiring a small, sober-looking van in which the huge banner lay furled, we called at a couple of offices facing one another there, and explained that, as officials of the Office of Works making an ultimate inspection of decorations along the morrow's royal route, we had noticed that just at this point there was an unsightly gap between the otherwise regularly spaced banners. Would they, we asked, permit that we use their windows for the purpose of slinging an auxiliary banner?

The occupants were proud and privileged to have us do so.

The banner was infernally heavy, and although for this occasion we had included in the party a couple of merchant seamen who understood ropes and could climb on window ledges like cats, there was the ever-present danger that the wrong string would somehow get pulled. This was the very eve of Jubilee, and already – at about 6 or 7 of that evening – people were squatting on the pavements in preparation for what the newspapers were terming their all-night vigil. Just as all seemed fairly well, the banner sagged, and a bus nearly hit it. What was our relief when a policeman, observing the difficulties of us fellows from the Office of Works, held up all two-decker traffic until such time as we had the main rope taut and the banner in line with the others.

So far, so good. But the final problem was how to release the banner at precisely the correct moment next morning – a moment, that is to say, when it would unfurl about ten yards ahead of the King's motor-car and thus in full range of the newsreel camera-men. Judging it too risky to hope to have a man lurking in one of the two offices to pull the string at the right time, we brought the vital string out of the window and round into the little court which at that point runs southward out of Fleet Street. Here the string was hooked, with a bent nail, high on the wall.

Next morning the group resolved itself into an organization of tick-tack men, and at the proper moment the signal reached us and we pulled the string. Thereupon the banner opened. We knew it had because we heard an angry roar of the loyal crowds who, the moment the King and followers had passed, dashed into the roadway and tore it to pieces. (The horrified office-holders had already cut the main rope.) We had not waited to see this for fear that we should be torn to pieces too.

The intra-mural and internecine row between various branches of the Security Services was the more violent because nobody could tell anybody else whodunnit. It was bad enough that the subversive slogan appeared on the newsreel screens of half the world. Worse was the realization that the folds of that banner could have held enough dynamite to blow the whole Jubilee procession to blazes.

18 August 1956

Many of the Directors of the New Statesman, *beginning with Beatrice Webb, Sidney Webb, and Bernard Shaw, were also contributors, although Editors were always free to refuse their work and did so. Arnold Bennett was another 'writing' director. So is Sir Charles Snow, a director of the present holding Company, who introduced his Two Cultures theme in the* New Statesman.

The Two Cultures   C. P. Snow

'It's rather odd,' said G. H. Hardy, one afternoon in the early Thirties, 'but when we hear about "intellectuals" nowadays, it doesn't include people like me and J. J. Thomson and Rutherford.' Hardy was the first mathematician of his generation, J. J. Thomson the first physicist of his; as for Rutherford, he was one of the greatest scientists who have ever lived. Some bright young literary person (I forget the exact context) putting them outside the enclosure reserved for intellectuals seemed to Hardy the best joke for some time. It does not seem quite such a good joke now. The separation between the two cultures has been getting deeper under our eyes; there is now precious little communication between them, little but different kinds of incomprehension and dislike.

The traditional culture, which is, of course, mainly literary, is behaving like a state whose power is rapidly declining – standing on its precarious dignity, spending far too much energy on Alexandrian intricacies, occasionally letting fly in fits of aggressive pique quite beyond its means, too much on the defensive to show any generous imagination to the forces which must inevitably reshape it. Whereas the scientific culture is expansive, not restrictive, confident at the roots, the more confident after its bout of Oppenheimerian self-criticism, certain that history is on its side, impatient, intolerant, creative rather than critical, good-natured and brash. Neither culture knows the virtues of the other; often it seems they deliberately do not want to know. The resentment which the traditional culture feels for the scientific is shaded with fear; from the other side, the resentment is not shaded so much as brimming with irritation. When scientists are faced with an expression of the traditional culture, it tends (to borrow Mr William Cooper's eloquent phrase) to make their feet ache.

It does not need saying that generalizations of this kind are bound to look silly at the edges. There are a good many scientists indistinguishable from literary persons, and vice versa. Even the stereotype generalizations about scientists are misleading without some sort of detail – e.g. the generalizations that scientists as a group stand on the political Left. This is only partly true. A very high proportion of engineers is almost as conservative as doctors; of pure scientists, the same would apply to chemists. It is only among physicists and biologists that one finds the Left in strength. If one compared the whole body of scientists with their opposite numbers of the traditional culture (writers, academics, and so on), the total result might be a few per cent more towards the Left wing, but not more than that. Nevertheless, as a first approximation, the scientific culture is real enough, and so is its difference from the traditional. For anyone like myself, by education a scientist, by calling a writer, at one time moving between groups of scientists and writers in the same evening, the difference has seemed dramatic.

The first thing, impossible to miss, is that scientists are on the up and up; they have the strength of a social force behind them. If they are English, they share the experience common to us all – of being in a country sliding economically downhill – but in addition (and to many of them it seems psychologically more important) they belong to something more than a profession, to something more like a directing class of a new society. In a sense oddly divorced from politics, they are the new men. Even the staidest and most politically conservative of scientific veterans, lurking in dignity in their colleges, have some kind of link with the world to come. They do not hate it as their colleagues do; part of their mind is open to it; almost against their will, there is a residual glimmer of kinship there. The young English scientists may and do curse their luck; increasingly they fret about the rigidities of their universities, about the ossification of the traditional culture which, to the scientists, makes the universities cold and dead; they violently envy their Russian counterparts who have money and equipment without discernible limit, who have the whole field wide open. But still they stay pretty resilient: they are swept on by the same social force. Harwell and Winscale have just as much spirit as Los Alamos and Chalk River: the neat petty bourgeois houses, the tough and clever young, the crowds of children: they are symbols, frontier towns.

There is a touch of the frontier qualities, in fact, about the whole scientific culture. Its tone is, for example, steadily heterosexual. The difference in social manners between Harwell and Hampstead, or as far as that goes between Los Alamos and Greenwich Village, would make an anthropologist blink. About the whole scientific culture, there is an absence – surprising to outsiders – of the feline and oblique. Sometimes it seems that scientists relish speaking the truth, especially when it is unpleasant. The climate of personal relations is singularly bracing, not to say harsh: it strikes bleakly on those unused to it, who suddenly find that the scientists' way of deciding on action is by a full-dress argument, with no regard for sensibilities and no holds barred. No body of people ever believed more in dialectic as the primary method of attaining sense; and if you want a picture of scientists in their off-moments it could be just one of a knock-about argument. Under the argument there glitter egotisms as rapacious as any of ours: but, unlike ours, the egotisms are driven by a common purpose.

How much of the traditional culture gets through to them? The answer is not simple. A good many scientists, including some of the most gifted, have the tastes of literary persons, read the same things, and read as much. Broadly, though, the infiltration is much less. History gets across to a certain extent, in particular social history: the sheer mechanics of living, how men ate, built, travelled, worked, touches a good many scientific imaginations, and so they have fastened on such works as Trevelyan's *Social History*, and Professor Gordon Childe's books. Philosophy the scientific culture views with indifference, especially metaphysics. As Rutherford said cheerfully to Samuel Alexander: 'When you think of all the years you've been talking about those things, Alexander, and what does it all add up to? *Hot air*, nothing but *hot air*.' A bit less exuberantly, that is what contemporary scientists would say. They regard it as a major intellectual virtue, to know what not to think about. They might touch their hats to linguistic analysis, as a relatively honourable way of wasting time; not so to existentialism.

The arts? The only one which is cultivated among scientists is music. It goes both wide and deep; there may possibly be a greater density of musical appreciation than in the traditional culture. In comparison, the graphic arts (except architecture) score little, and poetry not at all. Some novels work their way through, but not as a rule the novels which literary persons set most value on. The two cultures have so few points of contact that the diffusion of novels shows the same sort of delay, and exhibits the same oddities, as though they were getting into translation in a foreign country. It is only fairly recently, for instance, that Graham Greene and Evelyn Waugh have become more than names. And, just as it is rather startling to find that in Italy Bruce Marshall is by a long shot the best-known British novelist, so it jolts one to hear scientists talking with attention of the works of Nevil Shute. In fact, there is a good reason for that: Mr Shute was himself a high-class engineer, and a book like *No Highway* is packed with technical stuff that is not only accurate but often original. Incidentally, there are benefits to be gained from listening to intelligent men, utterly removed from the literary scene and unconcerned as to who's in and who's out. One can pick up such a comment as a scientist once made, that it looked to him as though the current pre-occupations of the New Criticism, the extreme concentration on a tiny passage, had made us curiously insensitive to the total flavour of a work, to its cumulative effects, to the epic qualities in literature. But, on the other side of the coin, one is just as likely to listen to three of the most massive intellects in Europe happily discussing the merits of *The Wallet of Kai-Lung*.

When you meet the younger rank-and-file of scientists, it often seems that they do not read at all. The prestige of the traditional culture is high enough for some of them to make a gallant shot at it. Oddly enough, the novelist whose name to them has become a token of esoteric literary excellence is that difficult highbrow Dickens. They approach him in a grim and dutiful spirit as though tackling *Finnegan's Wake*, and feel a sense of achievement if they manage to read a book through. But most young technicians do not fly so high. When you ask them what they read – 'As a married man,' one says, 'I prefer the garden.' Another says: 'I always like just to use my books as tools.' (Difficult to resist speculating what kind of tool a book would make. A sort of hammer? A crude digging instrument?)

That, or something like it, is a measure of the incommunicability of the two cultures. On their side the scientists are losing a great deal. Some of that loss is inevitable: it must and would happen in any society at our technical level. But in this country we make it quite unnecessarily worse by our educational patterns. On the other side, how much does the traditional culture lose by the separation?

I am inclined to think, even more. Not only practically – we are familiar with those arguments by now – but also intellectually and morally. The intellectual loss is a little difficult to appraise. Most scientists would claim that you cannot comprehend the world unless you know the structure of science, in particular of physical science. In a sense, and a perfectly genuine sense, that is true. Not to have read *War and Peace* and *La Cousine Bette* and *La Chartreuse de Parme* is not to be educated; but so is not to have a glimmer of the Second Law of Thermodynamics. Yet that case ought not to be pressed too far. It is more justifiable to say that those without any scientific understanding miss a whole body of experience: they are rather like the tone deaf, from whom all musical experience is cut off and who have to get on without it. The intellectual invasions of science are, however, penetrating deeper. Psycho-analysis once looked like a deep invasion, but that was a false alarm; cybernetics may turn out to be the real thing, driving down into the problems of will and cause and motive. If so, those who do not understand the method will not understand the depths of their own cultures.

But the greatest enrichment the scientific culture could give us is – though it does not originate like that – a moral one. Among scientists, deep-natured men know, as starkly as any men have known, that the individual human condition is tragic; for all its triumphs and joys, the essence of it is loneliness and the end death. But what they will not admit is that, because the individual condition is tragic, therefore the social condition must be tragic, too. Because a man must die, that is no excuse for his dying before his time and after a servile life. The impulse behind the scientists drives them to limit the area of tragedy, to take nothing as tragic that can conceivably lie within men's will. They have nothing but contempt for those representatives of the traditional culture who use a deep insight into man's fate to obscure the social truth – or to do something pettier than obscure the truth, just to hang on to a few perks. Dostoevski sucking up to the Chancellor Pobedonostsev, who thought the only thing wrong with slavery was that there was not enough of it; the political decadence of the *avant garde* of 1914, with Ezra Pound finishing up broadcasting for the Fascists; Claudel agreeing sanctimoniously with the Marshal about the virtue in others' suffering; Faulkner giving sentimental reasons for treating Negroes as a different species. They are all symptoms of the deepest temptation of the clerks – which is to say: 'Because man's condition is tragic, everyone ought to stay in their place, with mine as it happens somewhere near the top.' From that particular temptation, made up of defeat, self-indulgence, and moral vanity, the scientific culture is almost totally immune. It is that kind of moral health of the scientists which, in the last few years, the rest of us have needed most; and of which, because the two cultures scarcely touch, we have been most deprived.

6 October 1956

233

Rising literary stars have been found in the New Statesman *for the last fifty years, often when they had only just lifted above the horizon, and nearly always long before they had come to their zenith.*

Bridewell Revisited   Brendan Behan

Our Matron told us to get down to the library and she would pick her cast for the nativity play.

A bloke from Saint Andrew's was picked for Saint Joseph. He was doing His Majesty's Pleasure for driving a motor car into his father; and, though he was very good looking and well spoken in the English way, most of the blokes thought he was a bit balmy.

For the matter of that they thought most of the H.M.P. blokes were balmy; in different ways.

Clarke croaked a soldier that he caught with his mum; and he was balmy, too, and went round the place on his own when he wasn't up on the heath minding his sheep, and ran out in the middle of the blitz one night, and they thought he'd scarpered. But he was found in the morning with his sheep round him, where he'd been minding them from the air-raid.

But though he liked sheep, you couldn't have had him for Saint Joseph. He was bandy as a barrel. You'd have thought he spent his time riding pigs to hounds instead of chivvying soldiers, and they called him Gordon Richards – though I'd have thought he was more like Johnny Dines.

The H.M.P. bloke from Saint Andrew's that was acting Saint Joseph was called Kenneth Large. He was balmy, they reckoned, because he recited poetry at the concerts. He recited 'my head is bloody but unbowed' and was choked when I beat him in the essay competition at our Eisteddfod in May. The boys were delighted with me. The fact of my being Irish didn't weigh with the Elephant boys. Kenneth Large was a toff, while I was a scruffhound like themselves and knew about the pawn on Monday morning, and the old woman on the next floor fighting over who choked the cawsy by pitching cinders down the pot, and bunking into the pictures. For the North Circular Road, Dublin, was no different from Mile End.

So they took it as a victory for the lot of us, and they said that Kenneth Large and some of the other geezers that had been to grammar schools and colleges were choked – doing their nut over being beaten in an essay competition by a Paddy.

Joe Marcantonio looked over at him when he came into the library.

'That there Kenneth – 'e shouldn't be Saint Joseph,' said he; ' 'e shouldn't be Saint Joseph – 'e's a C. of E.'

'You silly born bastard,' said Charlie, 'we got Saint Joseph and Jesus Christ and the lot in the C. of E. church, same as you 'ave.'

'Mary' Williams came in, and sat down with his timid grin near the Matron who passed him her dogend. He drew on it, gratefully, and looked round the room, contented.

'That bleeding puff,' said Joe, ' 'e'd do for Judas.'

'Well, to tell the truth of him,' said I, 'I never heard of him shopping anyone.' Neither I didn't; neither was he a puff, but that accusation was of no importance.

The door opened, and Charlie whistled in a whisper.

'My, My,' said Joe, 'get on that.'

A girl of about nineteen had come in. Some of the blokes made room for her beside the Matron.

'She's the wife of Mister Hackbell, the young screw over the farm machinery,' said a Welsh bloke behind us. He worked a tractor himself. 'She is going to act the Virgin Mary.'

'I'll be the the Holy Ghost,' said Joe.

The Welshman looked away, shocked.

I looked away from him myself. Not that I was shocked. God knows, but I was afraid I'd burst out laughing and that we would embarrass the girl, who was one among a lot of strange blokes, and Borstal boys at that. You wouldn't mind the Matron, she was a Borstal Boy herself, damn near, but it would also be letting her down before the girl.

'Come along, dear,' said the Matron, 'we have only just begun.'

The blokes stood up and nodded politely to her, and murmured 'Excuse me' as she went towards the place where the Matron and Kenneth Large stood.

'She's a smasher all right,' said Joe.

'She is that,' said I.

Charlie looked at her and nodded, and looked back again at her. 'She's in the play – she's the Virgin Mary.'

'I know,' said Joe, 'I wish I could be the Baby.'

The Matron called us round her then to give us our parts.

Joe and I were picked for two of the Wise Men, and the third Wise Man, the Black King, was a real black bloke called Christian, from Tiger Bay, near Cardiff. He got done for chopping the right arm off a Norwegian sailor. Now I come to think of it, I think it was the sailor's name was Christian – I could never remember.

'That's all for now,' said the Matron, 'you can go now, you blokes, except for 532 Jones' – that was the Welsh bloke who was singing a hymn in the play – 'and Kenneth Large here.'

Going along the corridor Charlie said to Joe, 'That girl would get a nice idea of us if she'd heard you.'

'Why, you fancy her yourself,' said Joe. 'Just look at 'im blushin'.'

'It's all equal to you whether he fancies her or not,' said I. 'I suppose he wasn't got in a foundry any more than the rest of us; but you can fancy her without passing remarks on the girl and she good enough to come down amongst us and act in the play. Though I don't mind saying, that Kenneth Large has a soft job.'

'He's kept back and all,' said Charlie.

'Probably practising clinching with her,' said Joe. 'Why didn't they pick me for 'er spouse? I am Joseph, anyway, and always 'ave been. In real life.'

'You'd have been a bit too much like real life,' said I, 'for a play.'

8 December 1956

If we select this out of J. B. Priestley's very numerous contributions to the New Statesman *it is because, with this article, he, the paper and Kingsley Martin started one of the most important of the great pressure movements which have for centuries played a part in enabling the citizen to drag his leaders kicking and screaming out of the past and into the present –* CND.

Britain and the Nuclear Bombs   J. B. Priestley

Two events of this autumn should compel us to reconsider the question of Britain and the nuclear bombs. The first of these events was Mr Aneurin Bevan's speech at the Labour Party conference, which seemed to many of us to slam a door in our faces. It was not dishonest but it was very much a party conference speech, and its use of terms like 'unilateral' and 'polarization' lent it a suggestion of the 'Foreign Office spokesman'. Delegates asked not to confuse 'an emotional spasm' with 'statesmanship' might have retorted that the statesmanship of the last ten years has produced little else but emotional spasms. And though it is true, as Mr Bevan argued, that independent action by this country, to ban nuclear bombs, would involve our foreign minister in many difficulties, most of us would rather have a

'Apologize!' by Vicky [*28 May 1960*]

bewildered and overworked Foreign Office than a country about to be turned into a radio-active cemetery. Getting out of the water may be difficult but it is better than drowning.

The second event was the successful launching of the Soviet satellite, followed by an immediate outbreak of what may fairly be called *satellitis*, producing a rise in temperature and signs of delirium. In the poker game, where Britain still sits, nervously fingering a few remaining chips, like a Treasury official playing with two drunk oil millionaires, the stakes have been doubled again. Disarmament talks must now take place in an atmosphere properly belonging to boys' papers and science fiction, though already charged with far more hysterical competitiveness. If statesmanship is to see us through, it will have to break the familiar and dubious pattern of the last few years. Perhaps what we need now, before it is too late, is not statesmanship but lifemanship.

One 'ultimate weapon', the final deterrent, succeeds another. After the bombs, the inter-continental rockets; and after the rockets, according to the First Lord of the Admiralty, the guided-missile submarine, which will 'carry a guided missile with a nuclear warhead and appear off the coasts of any country in the world with a capability of penetrating to the centre of any continent'. The prospect now is not of countries without navies but of navies without countries. And we have arrived at an insane regress of ultimate weapons that are not ultimate.

But all this is to the good; and we cannot have too much of it, we are told, because no men in their right minds would let loose such powers of destruction. Here is the realistic view. Any criticism of it is presumed to be based on wild idealism. But surely it is the wildest idealism, at the furthest remove from a sober realism, to assume that men will always behave reasonably and in line with their best interests? Yet this is precisely what we are asked to believe, and to stake our all on it.

For that matter, why should it be assumed that the men who create and control such monstrous devices *are* in their right minds? They live in an unhealthy mental climate, an atmosphere dangerous to sanity. They are responsible to no large body of ordinary sensible men and women, who pay for these weapons without ever having ordered them, who have never been asked anywhere yet if they wanted them. When and where have these preparations for nuclear warfare ever been put to the test of public opinion? We cannot even follow the example of the young man in the limerick and ask *Who does what and with which and to whom?* The whole proceedings take place in the stifling secrecy of an expensive lunatic asylum. And as one ultimate weapon after another is added to the pile, the mental climate deteriorates, the atmosphere thickens, and the tension is such that soon something may snap.

The more elaborately involved and hair-triggered the machinery of destruction, the more likely it is that this machinery will be set in motion, if only by accident. Three glasses too many of vodka or bourbon-on-the-rocks, and the wrong button may be pushed. Combine this stock-piling of nuclear weapons with a crazy competitiveness, boastful confidence in public and a mounting fear in private, and what was unthinkable a few years ago now at the best only seems unlikely and very soon may seem inevitable. Then western impatience cries 'Let's get the damned thing over!' and eastern fatalism mutters 'If this has to be, then we must accept it.' And people in general are now in a worse position every year, further away from intervention; they have less and less freedom of action; they are deafened and blinded by propaganda and giant headlines; they are robbed of decision by fear or apathy.

It is possible, as some thinkers hold, that our civilization is bent on self-destruction, hurriedly planning its own doomsday. This may explain, better than any wearisome recital of plot and counter-plot in terms of world power, the curious and sinister air of somnambulism there is about our major international affairs, the steady drift from bad to worse, the speeches that begin to sound meaningless, the conferences that achieve nothing, all the persons of great consequence who somehow seem like puppets. We have all known people in whom was sown the fatal seed of self-destruction, people who would sit with us making sensible plans and then go off and quietly bring them to nothing, never really looking for anything but death. Our industrial civilization, behaving in a similar fashion, may be under the same kind of spell, hell-bent on murdering itself. But it is possible that the spell can be broken. If it can, then it will only be by an immensely decisive gesture, a clear act of will. Instead of endless bargaining for a little of this in exchange for a little of that, while all the time the bargainers are being hurried down a road that gets steeper and narrower, somebody will have to say 'I'm through with all this.'

In plain words: now that Britain has told the world she has the H-bomb she should announce as early as possible that she has done with it, that she proposes to reject, in all circumstances, nuclear warfare. This is not pacifism. There is no suggestion here of abandoning the immediate defence of this island. Indeed, it might well be considerably strengthened, reducing the threat of actual invasion, which is the root fear in people's minds, a fear often artfully manipulated for purposes far removed from any defence of hearth and home. (This is of course the exact opposite of the views expressed

239

at the Tory conference by Mr Sandys, who appears to believe that bigger and bigger bombs and rockets in more and more places, if necessary, thousands of miles away, will bring us peace and prosperity.) No, what should be abandoned is the idea of deterrence-by-threat-of-retaliation. There is no real security in it, no decency in it, no faith, hope, nor charity in it.

But let us take a look at our present policy entirely on its own low level. There is no standing still, no stalemates, in this idiot game; one 'ultimate weapon' succeeds another. To stay in the race at all, except in an ignominious position, we risk bankruptcy, the disappearance of the Welfare State, a standard of living that might begin to make Communist propaganda sound more attractive than it does at present. We could in fact be so busy, inspired by the indefatigable Mr Sandys, defending ourselves against Communism somewhere else, a long way off, that we could wake up one morning to hear it knocking on the back door. Indeed, this is Moscow's old *heads-I-win-tails-you-lose* policy.

Here we might do well to consider western world strategy, first grandiloquently proclaimed by Sir Winston in those speeches he made in America just after the war. The Soviet Union was to be held in leash by nuclear power. We had the bomb and they hadn't. The race would be on but the West had a flying start. But Russia was not without physicists, and some German scientists and highly trained technicians had disappeared somewhere in eastern Europe. For the immediate defence of West Germany, the atom bomb threat no doubt served its turn. But was this really sound long-term strategy? It created the unhealthy climate, the poisonous atmosphere of our present time. It set Russians galloping in the nuclear race. It freed them from the immense logistic problems that must be solved if large armies are to be moved everywhere, and from some very tricky problems of morale that would soon appear once the Red Army was a long way from home. It encouraged the support of so-called peoples' and nationalistic and anti-colonial wars, not big enough to be settled by nuclear weapons. In spite of America's ring of advanced air bases, the race had only to be run a little longer to offer Russia at least an equally good set-up, and in comparison with Britain alone, clearly an enormously better set-up.

We are like a man in a poker game who never dare cry 'I'll see you'. The Soviet Union came through the last war because it had vast spaces and a large population and a ruthless disregard of losses, human and material. It still has them. Matched against this overcrowded island with its intricate urban organization, at the last dreadful pinch – and party dictators made to feel unsure of their power can pinch quicker than most democratic leaders – the other side possesses all the advantages. If there is one country that should never have gambled in this game, it is Britain. Once the table stakes were being raised, the chips piling up, we were out. And though we may have been fooling ourselves, we have not been fooling anybody else.

This answers any gobbling cries about losing our national prestige. We have none, in terms of power. (The world has still respect and admiration for our culture, and we are busy reducing that respect and admiration by starving it. The cost of a few bombs might have made all the difference.) We ended the war high in the world's regard. We could have taken over its moral leadership, spoken and acted for what remained of its conscience; but we chose to act otherwise – with obvious and melancholy consequences both abroad, where in power politics we cut a shabby figure, and at home, where we shrug it all away or go to the theatre to applaud the latest jeers and sneers at Britannia. It has been said we cannot send our ministers naked to the conference table. But the sight of a naked minister might bring to the conference some sense of our human situation. What we do is something much worse: we send them there half-dressed, half-smart, half-tough, half-apologetic, figures inviting contempt. That is why we are so happy and excited when we can send abroad a good-looking young woman in a pretty new dress to represent us, playing the only card we feel can take a trick – the Queen.

It is argued, as it was most vehemently by Mr Bevan at Brighton, that if we walked out of the nuclear arms race then the world would be 'polarized' between America and the Soviet Union, without any hope of mediation between the two fixed and bristling camps. 'Just consider for a moment,' he cried, 'all the little nations running, one here and one there, one running to Russia, the other to the US, all once more clustering under the castle wall . . .' But surely this is one of those 'realistic' arguments that are not based on reality. The idea of the Third Force was rejected by the very party Mr Bevan was addressing. The world was polarized when, without a single protest from all the noisy guardians of our national pride, parts of East Anglia ceased to be under our control and became an American air base. We cannot at one and the same time be both an independent power, bargaining on equal terms, and a minor ally or satellite. If there are little nations that do not run for shelter to the walls of the White House or the Kremlin because they are happy to accept Britain as their nuclear umbrella, we hear very little about them. If it is a question of brute power, this argument is unreal.

It is not entirely stupid, however, because something more than brute power is involved. There is nothing unreal in the idea of a third nation, especially one like ours, old and experienced in world affairs, possessing great political traditions, to which other and smaller nations could look while the two new giants mutter and glare at each other. But it all depends what that nation is doing. If it is still in the nuclear gamble, without being able to control or put an end to the game, then that nation is useless to others, is frittering away its historical prestige, and the polarization, which Mr Bevan sees as the worst result of our rejection of nuclear warfare, is already an accomplished fact. And if it is, then we must ask ourselves what we can do to break this polarity, what course of action on our part might have some hope of changing the world situation. To continue doing what we are doing will not change it. Even during the few weeks since Mr Bevan made his speech the world is becoming more rigidly and dangerously polarized than ever, just because the Russians have sent a metal football circling the globe. What then can Britain do to de-polarize the world?

The only move left that can mean anything is to go into reverse, decisively rejecting nuclear warfare. This gives the world something quite different from the polarized powers: there is now a country that can make H-bombs but decides against them. Had Britain taken this decision some years ago the world would be a safer and saner place than it is today. But it is still not too late. And such a move will have to be 'unilateral'; doomsday may arrive before the nuclear powers reach any agreement; and it is only a decisive 'unilateral' move than can achieve the moral force it needs to be effective.

It will be a hard decision to take because all habit is against it. Many persons of consequence and their entourages of experts would have to think fresh thoughts. They would have to risk losing friends and not influencing people. For example, so far as they involve nuclear warfare, our commitments to Nato, Seato and the rest, and our obligations to the Commonwealth, would have to be sharply adjusted. Anywhere from Brussels to Brisbane, reproaches would be hurled, backs would be turned. But what else have these countries to suggest, what way out, what hope for man? And if, to save our souls and this planet, we are willing to remain here and take certain risks, why should we falter because we might have complaints from Rhodesia and reproaches from Christchurch, NZ? And it might not be a bad idea if the Nato peoples armed themselves to defend themselves, taking their rifles to the ranges at the week-end, like the Swiss.

American official and service opinion would be dead against us, naturally. The unsinkable (but expendable) aircraft carrier would have gone. Certain Soviet bases allotted to British nuclear attack would have to be included among the targets of the American Strategic Air Service. And so on and so forth. But though service chiefs and their staffs go on examining and marking the maps and planning their logistics, having no alternative but resignation, they are as fantastic and unreal in their way as their political and diplomatic colleagues are in theirs. What is fantastic and unreal is their assumption that they are traditionally occupied with their professional duties, attending in advance to the next war, Number Three in the world series. But what will happen – and one wrong report by a sleepy observer might start it off – will not be anything recognizable as a war, an affair of victories and defeats, something that one side can win or that you can call off when you have had enough. It will be universal catastrophe and apocalypse, the crack of doom into which Communism, western democracy, their way of life and our way of life, may disappear for ever. And it is not hard to believe that this is what some of our contemporaries really desire, that behind their photogenic smiles and cheerful patter nothing exists but the death wish.

We live in the thought of this prospect as if we existed in a permanent smog. All sensible men and women – and this excludes most of those who are in the *VIP-Highest-Priority-Top-Secret-Top-People Class*, men now so conditioned by this atmosphere of power politics, intrigue, secrecy, insane invention, that they are more than half-barmy – have no illusions about what is happening to us, and know that those responsible have made two bad miscalculations. First, they have prostituted so much science in their preparations for war that they have completely changed the character of what they are doing, without any equivalent change in the policies of and relations between states. Foreign affairs, still conducted as if the mobilization of a few divisions might settle something, are now backed with push-button arrangements to let loose earthquakes and pestilences and pronounce the death sentences of continents. This leaves us all in a worse dilemma than the sorcerer's apprentice. The second miscalculation assumed that if the odds were only multiplied fast enough, your side would break through because the other side would break down. And because this has not happened, a third illusion is being welcomed, namely, that now, with everything piling up, poker chips flung on the table by the handful, the tension obviously increasing, now at last we are arriving at an acknowledged drawn game, a not-too-stalemate, a cosy balance of power. This could well be the last of our illusions.

The risk of our rejecting nuclear warfare, totally and in all circumstances, is quite clear, all too easy to understand. We lose such bargaining power as we now possess. We have no deterrent to a nuclear threat. We deliberately exchange 'security' for insecurity. (And the fact that some such exchange is recommended by the major religions, in their earlier and non-establishment phases, need not detain us here.) But the risk is clear and the arguments against running it quite irrefutable, only if we refuse, as from the first too many of us here have refused, to take anything but short-term conventional views, only if we will not follow any thought to its conclusion. Our 'hard-headed realism' is neither hard-headed nor realistic just because it insists on our behaving in a new world as if we were still living in an old world, the one that has been replaced.

Britain runs the greatest risk by just mumbling and muddling along, never speaking out, avoiding any decisive creative act. For a world in which our deliberate 'insecurity' would prove to be our undoing is not a world in which real security could be found. As the game gets faster, the competition keener, the unthinkable will turn into the inevitable, the weapons will take command, and the deterrents will not deter. Our bargaining power is slight; the force of our example might be great. The catastrophic antics of our time have behind them men hag-ridden by fear, which explains the neurotic irrationality of it all, the crazy disproportion between means and ends. If we openly challenge this fear, then we might break the wicked spell that all but a few uncertified lunatics desperately wish to see broken, we could begin to restore the world to sanity and lift this nation from its recent ignominy to its former grandeur. Alone, we defied Hitler; and alone we can defy this nuclear madness into which the spirit of Hitler seems to have passed, to poison the world. There may be other chain-reactions besides those leading to destruction; and we might start one. The British of these times, so frequently hiding their decent, kind faces behind masks of sullen apathy or sour, cheap cynicism, often seem to be waiting for something better than party squabbles and appeals to their narrowest self-interest, something great and noble in its intention that would make them feel good again. And this might well be a declaration to the world that after a certain date one power able to engage in nuclear warfare will reject the evil thing for ever.

2 November 1957

Of the active leaders of CND the greatest was Bertrand Russell. Before he began to play the part which led to his imprisonment at the age of 89, he used the New Statesman, *for which he had been writing during four decades, to appeal directly to the two most powerful men in the world to save us from the danger which he had long foreseen: for, in his first contribution to the*

New Statesman, *more than thirty years before, Lord Russell had described the division of the creative minority into what Sir Charles Snow, also writing in the* New Statesman, *was to call the Two Cultures. Moreover he had seen that this separation of the sciences and the arts would entail the very danger which the advances of physics have, in fact, created.*

Open Letter to Eisenhower and Krushchev   Bertrand Russell

Most Potent Sirs,

I am addressing you as the respective heads of the two most powerful countries in the world. Those who direct the policies of these countries have a power for good or evil exceeding anything ever possessed before by any man or group of men. Public opinion in your respective countries has been focused upon the points in which your national interests are thought to diverge, but I am convinced that you, as far-seeing and intelligent men, must be aware that the matters in which the interests of Russia and America coincide are much more important than the matters in which they are thought to diverge. I believe that if you two eminent men were jointly to proclaim this fact and to bend the policies of your great countries to agreement with such proclamation, there would be throughout the world, and not least in your own countries, a shout of joyful agreement which would raise you both to a pinnacle of fame surpassing anything achieved by other statesmen of the past or present. Although you are, of course, both well aware of the points in which the interests of Russia and America are identical, I will, for the sake of explicitness, enumerate some of them.

1. The supreme concern of men of all ways of thought at the present time must be to ensure the continued existence of the human race. This is already in jeopardy from the hostility between East and West and will, if many minor nations acquire nuclear weapons, be in very much greater jeopardy within a few years from the possibility of irresponsible action by thoughtless fanatics.

Some ignorant militarists, both in the East and in the West, have apparently thought that the danger could be averted by a world war giving victory to their own side. The progress of science and technology has made this an idle dream. A world war would not result in the victory of either side, but in the extermination of both. Neither side can desire such a cataclysm.

The hope of world dominion, either military or ideological, is one which

Bertrand Russell [*18 May 1962*]

has hovered before many men in the past and has led invariably to disaster. Philip II of Spain made the attempt and reduced his country to the status of a minor power. Louis XIV of France made the attempt and, by exhausting his country, led the way to the French Revolution, which he would have profoundly deplored. Hitler, in our own day, fought for the world-wide supremacy of the Nazi philosophy, and perished miserably. Two great men propounded ideologies which have not yet run their course: I mean the authors of the Declaration of Independence and the Communist Manifesto. There is no reason to expect that either of these ideologies will be more successful in conquering the world than their predecessors, Buddhist, Christian, Moslem, or Nazi. What is new in the present situation is not the impossibility of success, but the magnitude of the disaster which must result from the attempt. We must, therefore, hope that each side will abandon the futile strife and agree to allow to each a sphere proportionate to its present power.

2. The international anarchy which will inevitably result from the unrestricted diffusion of nuclear weapons is not to the interest of either Russia or America. There was a time when only America had nuclear weapons. This was followed by a time when only Russia and America had such weapons. And now only Russia, America and Britain possess them. It is obvious that, unless steps are taken, France and Germany will shortly manufacture these weapons. It is not likely that China will lag far behind. We must expect that during the next few years the manufacture of engines of mass destruction will become cheaper and easier. No doubt Egypt and Israel will then be able to follow the example set by the great powers. So will the states of South America. There is no end to this process until every sovereign state is in a position to say to the whole world: 'You must yield to my demands or you shall die.' If all sovereign states were governed by rulers possessed of even the rudiments of sanity, they would be restrained from such blackmail by the fear that their citizens also would perish. But experience shows that from time to time power in this or that country falls into the hands of rulers who are not sane. Can anyone doubt that Hitler, if he had been able to do so, would have chosen to involve all mankind in his own ruin? For such reasons, it is imperative to put a stop to the diffusion of nuclear weapons. This can easily be done by agreement between Russia and America, since they can jointly refuse military or economic assistance to any country other than themselves which persists in the manufacture of such weapons. But it cannot be achieved without agreement between the two dominant powers, for, without such agreement, each new force of nuclear weapons will be

welcomed by one side or the other as an increase to its own strength. This helter-skelter race towards ruin must be stopped if anything that anybody could desire is to be effected.

3. So long as the fear of world war dominates policy and the only deterrent is the threat of universal death, so long there can be no limit to the diversion of expenditure of funds and human energy into channels of destruction. It is clear that both Russia and America could save nine-tenths of their present expenditure if they concluded an alliance and devoted themselves jointly to the preservation of peace throughout the world. If they do not find means of lessening their present hostility, reciprocal fear will drive them further and further, until, apart from immense armaments, nothing beyond a bare subsistence will be left to the populations of either country. In order to promote efficiency in the preparation of death, education will have to be distorted and stunted. Everything in human achievement that is not inspired by hatred and fear will be squeezed out of the curriculum in schools and universities. Any attempts to preserve the vision of Man as the triumph (so far) of the long ages of evolution, will come to be viewed as treachery, since it will be thought not to minister to the victory of this group or that. Such a prospect is death to the hopes of all who share the aspirations which have inspired human progress since the dawn of history.

4. I cannot but think that you would both rejoice if a way could be found to disperse the pall of fear which at present dims the hopes of mankind. Never before, since our remote ancestors descended from the trees, has there been valid reason for such fear. Never before has such a sense of futility blighted the visions of youth. Never before has there been reason to feel that the human race was travelling along a road ending only in a bottomless precipice. Individual death we must all face, but collective death has never, hitherto, been a grim possibility.

And all this fear, all this despair, all this waste is utterly unnecessary. One thing only is required to dispel the darkness and enable the world to live again in a noon-day brightness of hope. The one thing necessary is that East and West should recognize their respective rights, admit that each must learn to live with the other and substitute argument for force in the attempt to spread their respective ideologies. It is not necessary that either side should abandon belief in its own creed. It is only necessary that it should abandon the attempt to spread its own creed by force of arms.

I suggest, Sirs, that you should meet in a frank discussion of the conditions of co-existence, endeavouring no longer to secure this or that more or less surreptitious advantage for your own side, but seeking rather for such agreements and such adjustments in the world as will diminish future occasions of strife. I believe that if you were to do this the world would acclaim your action, and the forces of sanity, released from their long bondage, would ensure for the years to come a life of vigour and achievement and joy surpassing anything known in even the happiest eras of the past.

23 November 1957

As a result of Lord Russell's 'Open Letter' the ruler of one-sixth of the world became a contributor to the New Statesman. *His style was gratifyingly new statesmanly.*

Nikita Krushchev Replies to Bertrand Russell

Dear Lord Russell,

I was extremely interested to read your open letter addressed to the President of the United States and to myself. In your letter you touched on the most essential questions of the present international situation, which have for a long time been a matter of deep concern to people throughout the world. We, Soviet people, understand and hold dear the main idea expressed in your letter – to protect mankind from the threat of a war which would be waged with the most terrible weapons of destruction ever known to the world; to safeguard universal peace and prosperity, on the basis of peaceful co-existence between states with different social systems; and, above all, through the normalization of relations between the Soviet Union and the United States.

Everyone is agreed that if a new world war should break out, it would bring untold suffering to the people. For this reason the chief concern of all people, whatsoever their way of thinking, should be to prevent such a tragic turn of events. Man's reason and conscience cannot be reconciled to such a danger, cannot but rise up against the propaganda churned out day after day, propaganda which is accustoming the nations to the idea of the inevitability of atomic war.

The government and Communist Party of the Soviet Union, expressing the wishes of the peoples of our country, are doing and will do everything possible to prevent the outbreak of a new war. We are convinced that, in the present situation, war is not fatally inevitable, that war can be prevented, if everyone who wants to preserve peace will struggle for it actively and in an organized way.

We were pleased to notice that you support the ending of the arms race which only brings nearer the catastrophe of war. You appeal for an end to the distribution of nuclear weapons, so that the armies of those states which at the present time do not yet possess such weapons will not receive them. Of course, this would be a step forward, especially if you take into account the fact that there exist plans for handing over nuclear weapons to – for example – Western Germany, whose government openly states its territorial claims in Europe; and the fact that nuclear weapons, brought in from across the ocean, are being deployed on the territories of West European member states of Nato. These weapons are imposed on these states under the guise of defence against aggression. In reality, the deployment of nuclear weapons on the territories of those countries is a mortal blow to their security, since, if an aggressor breaks the peace, then, in accordance with the inexorable logic of war, shattering retaliatory attacks on the territories of those countries in which atomic weapon bases are situated will be inevitable.

You certainly know that the Soviet Union has frequently come out with a proposal that nuclear weapons should not be deployed beyond the state frontiers of those countries which possess them already; and that, in particular, it has also proposed that the US, Britain and the USSR should reach an agreement not to deploy their nuclear weapons in either Western or Eastern Germany. For its part, the government of the German Democratic Republic has proposed to the government of the Federal Republic of Germany that they act together so that there shall be neither German nor foreign nuclear weapons on German territory. The Polish and Czechoslovak governments have announced that if agreement is reached between the Federal Republic of Germany and the German Democratic Republic, then, similarly, neither Poland nor Czechoslovakia would produce nuclear weapons or deploy them on their territory. As you can see, the Socialist states are doing everything in their power to prevent further distribution of nuclear weapons. Unfortunately, this has not yet met with a response from the western powers. On the contrary, the two other powers in possession of nuclear weapons – the USA and Britain – are taking every possible step to involve their North American bloc partners still more deeply in the preparations for atomic war.

However, even if we succeeded in preventing the further distribution of nuclear weapons in the world, all this would by no means remove the danger of nuclear war. For, even now, when only three powers have nuclear weapons, this danger is very great. The Soviet Union considers that the danger of atomic war will only be removed finally and completely when the manufacture and use of atomic and hydrogen weapons will have been completely prohibited and the stockpiles destroyed. For almost twelve years now the Soviet government has been demanding such a solution of this question and has made quite a few concrete proposals in the UN in support of these aims. If the western powers would express a sincere desire to end the danger of atomic war, then it would be possible – tomorrow, even – to advance along this path, taking, for a start, such steps as the immediate ending of nuclear weapon tests and renunciation of the use of such weapons. But it must be said straight out that, up to the present, unfortunately, we have not had evidence of any such desire by the American, British or French governments. The fact is that those quarters which formulate the policies of those countries wish to preserve war in their arsenal as a means of securing the aims of their foreign policy.

We, Soviet people, engaged in building Communist society – a social system in which, alongside the achievement of material abundance for all, there will for the first time be the free development of man's spiritual wealth, in all its diversity – we understand particularly well your concern over the criminal policy of militarism, which absurdly wastes society's material resources, which corrupts man morally and which leads to people being brought up in the spirit of fear and hate. It is impossible to be reconciled to such a prospect – all the more so when today the wonderful discoveries of science have given man such immense power over the forces of Nature. Now there really are no limits to the possibilities of transforming Nature's destructive forces, or of using natural resources to ensure the prosperity of all peoples, on the basis of friendly co-operation among the nations.

As a philosopher and humanist, deeply concerned at the abnormality of the present international situation, you understand very well along what lines solution of the present situation must be sought. 'The one thing necessary,' you write, 'is that East and West should recognize their respective rights, admit that each must learn to live with the other and substitute argument for force in the attempt to spread their respective ideologies. It is not necessary that either side should abandon belief in its own creed. It is only necessary that it should abandon the attempt to spread its own creed by force of arms.'

I am ready to lend my name to those words, since they correspond fully to the conception of peaceful co-existence between states with different social systems, upon which our state has based its foreign policy since the first day of the establishment of Soviet power. There is no need to say how glad I would be to hear that your words had met with similar support from the US government.

In order to 'live with the other' – that is in order to ensure peaceful co-existence – both sides must recognize what politicians call the *status quo*, must recognize the existing state of affairs. The right of each country to develop as the people of that country desire must be recognized. The conduct of 'cold war', engaging in threats, aiming at changing state frontiers and interfering in other countries' domestic affairs with the aim of changing their social structure – these things must not be permitted. 'Cold war' and the arms drive will lead to a new and very bloody war.

You are completely right, of course, when you say that one of the chief reasons for the present state of tension in international relations, and for all that is meant by 'cold war', is the abnormal character of the relations between the Soviet Union and the United States of America. The normalization of these relations, on the rational basis of peaceful co-existence and respect for one another's rights and interests, would beyond a doubt lead to a general improvement in the international situation. The Soviet Union has always tried for just such a normalization of relations with the United States, and it will continue to do so. We have taken quite a few definite steps in this direction. You will probably remember, for example, that in January 1956 the Soviet government proposed to the government of the USA that a treaty of friendship and co-operation be concluded between our two countries. Our proposal still holds good. We have tried and will continue to try to re-establish Soviet-American trade relations, which were broken off by the government of the US, and we want to open up cultural, scientific and technical exchanges with the United States. Negotiations are now, incidentally, taking place in Washington on Soviet initiative for the widening of cultural relations between our two countries.

The Soviet leaders have always believed, and still do believe, that personal contacts with government leaders of other countries are of very great importance, as one of the most effective ways of improving international relations. We readily took part in the Geneva four-power conference of heads of government, and, as you are no doubt aware, we have also met the government leaders of many other countries. Such meetings, and the Geneva conference in particular, definitely helped bring about an improvement in the international situation.

I fully support your proposal, Lord Russell, that the leaders of the

Soviet Union and the United States should meet and frankly discuss conditions of co-existence. Like you, we are convinced that there are far more questions on which the interests of the Soviet Union and the United States coincide than there are questions on which our interests differ. This, precisely, is why on the Soviet side the opinion has been repeatedly expressed that a high-level meeting between representatives of the USSR and the United States would be most useful for both our countries, as well as for peace among all nations.

We have, of course, no intention or wish whatsoever to reach agreement with the United States at the expense of the interests of any other state, of West or East, large or small, or at the cost of a deterioration in the United States' relations with any other country. On the contrary, we consider that an improvement in Soviet-American relations could only be of use, and that no one would lose by it.

We favour a meeting between the leaders of the United States and the Soviet Union. It depends, therefore, on the leaders of the United States whether or not such a meeting will take place. We know that there are forces, both in the United States itself and outside it, which fear improvement in relations between the US and the USSR, and which actively oppose any step in that direction. Those forces base their policy on exploiting the distrust and differences existing at present between the two biggest powers, and they are doing everything they can to exacerbate these differences and to use them for their own selfish purposes. Is there any need to point out that this policy is against the interests of strengthening peace, against the interests of all peoples?

There can be no doubt that the easing of tension in international relations does not depend on the USSR and the United States alone. Other countries too, including, of course, Great Britain, must make their contribution to it. Unfortunately, it cannot be said that the present policy of the British government has been helpful in solving this most important task. It can hardly be denied that the transformation of Britain into an American base for nuclear and rocket weapons will bring no good either to world peace or to Britain's own security. In the relatively small area of the British Isles many United States military bases, bases at which stocks of atomic and hydrogen bombs are stored, are already deployed, and a proposal is now being made to build launching sites for American rockets there. All the indications are that Britain is being more or less given the role in Europe of the main American medium-range rocket base. I may be permitted to ask – what assurance can anyone have that the latest weapons, deployed on American bases in Britain, will not be used at the discretion of the military command, without the knowledge of the British people, parliament or even government?

Isn't a situation being created whereby Britain may become the spring-board for the unleashing of war against the Soviet Union and other peace-loving countries? Just suppose that, by the merest chance – say, for instance, as the result of an incorrectly understood order – death-dealing weapons of war are used from American military bases in your country against the peace-loving countries. A crushing retaliatory blow would follow immediately. In such an event, the British people might find them-selves suddenly in a situation of atomic war, a situation in which Britain's very existence would be threatened. Believe me I am not saying this with the object of frightening your fellow-countrymen. We have a great respect for your people, and would like to strengthen the friendliest relations with your country. I say this because I know the power of modern means of warfare. No wonder millions of British people feel legitimate anxiety and disquiet over the establishment of such bases on the territory of their country.

As far as the Soviet Union is concerned, it advocates joint efforts by countries to ease international tension. This object could be served both by a meeting of representatives of the two powers, the USSR and the United States, and by a wider meeting of representatives of the capitalist and the Socialist countries.

The situation in the world today is so serious that anyone who can do anything to ease the war danger, to remove the threat of war, must do what he can. The British people, who displayed such courage in the struggle against our common enemy during the Second World War, could make a substantial contribution to the preservation and strengthening of peace. The louder the voice of the peoples is raised in the struggle for peace, the smaller will be the chance the adherents of military adventures have to unleash a new war.

I am confident that your call for united efforts by the USSR and the United States to strengthen peace, on the basis of peaceful co-existence, will meet with sympathetic response and support from all who cherish peace.

Your letter is a call to action in the struggle for peace. I permit myself the liberty of expressing the hope that this call will multiply the number of fighters for peace in Britain and in other countries of the world.

I fully support this call; my colleagues and I would like to express the hope that your ardent desire for improved relations between states will meet with support also from the leaders of other countries.

Today the struggle for peace, for the ending of the cold war, which sharpens international tension and which could lead mankind to immense disasters; the struggle for the peaceful co-existence of states, is the vital concern of all peoples of the world, of all men of good will. What we advocate is that the superiority of any particular system be proved, not on the field of battle but in peaceful competition for progress, for improved living standards of the people.

21 December 1957

President Eisenhower's violon d'Ingres being golf, it fell to his éminence grise, *the effective master of US foreign policy, John Foster Dulles, to follow N. S. Krushchev into the pages of the* New Statesman. *He revealed himself as either more candid or more fanatical than the Russian.*

John Foster Dulles Replies to Russell and Krushchev

Sir,

On behalf of the President I am replying to Lord Russell's letter to him and to Mr Krushchev published in the 23 November issue of the *New Statesman.* I have also read Mr Krushchev's reply thereto, which you sent the President under cover of your letter of 18 December. As you know, Chairman Bulganin wrote to President Eisenhower on 10 December setting forth certain views of the Soviet Union on the international situation. I thought it best to defer a reply to your letter until the President replied to Mr Bulganin, which he did on 12 January. His letter substantially answers many of the points raised in Lord Russell's letter and Mr Krushchev's reply.

Surely if we lived in a world of words, we could relax to the melody of Mr Krushchev's lullaby. The world in which we live is, however, made of stuff sterner than mere words. It is necessary now, as it has always been necessary, to look behind words of individuals to find from their actions what their true purpose is.

I note that Mr Krushchev directs himself to Lord Russell's statement that as between the East and West, 'It is not necessary that either side should abandon belief in its own creed. It is only necessary that it should abandon the attempt to spread its own creed by the force of arms.'

The creed of the United States is based on the tenets of moral law.

That creed, as well as the universal conviction of the United States, rejects war except in self-defence. This abhorrence of war, this determination to substitute peaceful negotiation for force in the settlement of international disputes, is solidly founded on the religious convictions that guided our forefathers in writing the documents that marked the birth of America's independence. Indeed, there are important elements in our religious groups who even decry the use of force for self-defence. I do not think that it is possible to find in the history of the United States any occasion when an effort has been made to spread its creed by force of arms. There is, therefore, no need on our side to 'abandon' what Lord Russell condemns. On the contrary, it would be abhorrent and unthinkable that there should be introduced into our creed the concept of its maintenance or extension by methods of violence and compulsion.

Unhappily, it is otherwise with the creed of Communism, or at least that variety of Communism which is espoused by the Soviet Communist Party. Marx, Lenin, and Stalin have all consistently taught the use of force and violence. Marx said 'the proletariat, by means of revolution, makes itself the ruling class.' Lenin taught that the dictatorship of the proletariat means 'unlimited power based on force and not on law'; and Stalin said that the ruling bourgeois classes can 'only be removed by the conscious action of the new classes, by forcible acts of these classes by revolution.' These teachings of Marx, Lenin, and Stalin have never been disavowed by the Soviet Communist Party of which Mr Krushchev is now the First Secretary. On the contrary, as recently as 16 November last, the Communist Parties rededicated themselves in the Moscow declaration to the cause of world revolution directed by the Soviet Communist Party. There are indeed multiple examples of the continuing use of force by the Soviet Communist Party and by other Communists of the same school. A recent illustration is Hungary where, at the behest of the Hungarian Communist Party, the Soviet Communist Party requested the Soviet government to invade with massive military force to repress the people and to assure that they would continue to be subject to a rule dictated by the Hungarian Communist Party.

It is indeed quite improbable that the Soviet Communist Party should now abjure the use of force and violence to maintain the supremacy of its creed where that party, directly or through satellite Communist Parties, is today dominant. The Soviet Communist Party seized power by violence of an intensity and extent that shocked the civilized world. It has extended its power by violence, absorbing one nation after another by force or the threat of force. Within the Soviet Union it has perpetuated its power only by force and violence, the nature of which is usually kept hidden but which is occasionally revealed, as when Mr Krushchev in his speech to the 20th Congress – a speech sought to be kept secret – portrayed the cruel practices employed by Stalin through Beria to maintain his despotism.

Nowhere in the world today does the Communist Party maintain its rule except by forcibly imposing that rule upon the great majority of the people as against their wishes. Although Communist Parties today rule nearly a thousand million people, comprising what at one time were nearly twenty independent nations, never anywhere have these Communist Parties been willing to have free elections or to limit their rule to peoples whom they persuade by peaceful means. The fact of the matter is, and this I believe is a fact which no one can realistically dispute, that the Communist Parties depend upon force and violence and could not exercise power anywhere in the world today if they should relinquish that. It is equally true that they could not achieve ultimately their announced goal of world domination without involving the same forcible methods which they have consistently used to gain and retain rule where they have it.

That, I feel, is the heart of the problem. That is why those who have freedom must be organized to preserve it. If, indeed, Lord Russell could persuade the Communist Parties of the world to renounce dependence upon force and violence and to exercise power only when this reflected the freely given consent of the governed, then indeed the world would become a happier and safer place in which to live.

I earnestly hope that the idealism and persuasiveness of Lord Russell may move the Communist Parties in this direction.

I note that Mr Krushchev's letter deals primarily with a world war which would be a nuclear war. I do not doubt that the Soviet rulers, like all other people who want to go on living, reject that concept. The United States not only rejects that concept, but strives earnestly to do something to remove the danger of nuclear war.

A decade ago, when the United States had a monopoly of atomic weapons and of the knowledge of how to make them, we proposed that we and all others should forgo such destructive weapons and assure that the power of the atom should be used for peaceful purposes. We proposed an international agency to control all use of atomic energy everywhere. That proposal was rejected by the Soviet Union, with the consequence that nuclear weapons today exist in vast and growing quantities.

In a further effort to stem the increase of nuclear weapons stockpiles and their irresponsible spread throughout the world, the United States joined in proposals that fissionable material should no longer be produced for weapons purposes and that existing nuclear weapons stockpiles should be steadily diminished by agreed contributions to peaceful purposes internationally controlled. This proposal, too, has been rejected by the Soviet Union.

Now a new source of danger to humanity looms in the use of outer space for weapons purposes. Both the Soviet Union and the United States are beginning to make such use of outer space. But the United States, in pursuance of its peaceful purposes, proposed that we should not repeat the mistake of ten years ago but should quickly take steps to assure that outer space shall be used only for peaceful purposes. President Eisenhower eloquently pleaded for this peaceful step in his letter of 12 January to Chairman Bulganin. Thus, the Soviet is afforded, now for the third time, a chance to demonstrate that its words of peace mean something more than a mere effort to lull the non-Communist world into a mood of illusory security.

At the moment its propaganda efforts are primarily directed, as was Mr Krushchev's letter, to trying to assure that western Europe shall be armed only with weapons of the pre-atomic age, while the Soviet Union uninterruptedly develops the most modern weapons of the nuclear age and of the age of outer space. At the recent North Atlantic Council meeting, the heads of the fifteen member governments had this to say:

'The Soviet leaders, while preventing a general disarmament agreement, have made it clear that the most modern and destructive weapons, including missiles of all kinds, are being introduced in the Soviet armed forces. In the Soviet view, all European nations except the USSR should, without waiting for general disarmament, renounce nuclear weapons and missiles and rely on arms of the pre-atomic age.'

As long as the Soviet Union persists in this attitude, we have no alternative but to remain vigilant and to look to our defences.

But also they said:

'We are also prepared to examine any proposal, from whatever source, for general or partial disarmament, and any proposal enabling agreement to be reached on the controlled reduction of armaments of all types.'

While, of course, nuclear war is the form of war most to be dreaded, particularly if, to nuclear power, is added the use of outer space, the essential is to avoid war of any kind, nuclear or non-nuclear, and to renounce all use of force as a means of subjecting human beings to a rule to which they do not freely consent. That, I take it, is the heart of what Lord Russell seeks. I can assure you it is also what is sought by the government of the United States, by every element in government, and also by all of our people who adhere to the creed of America as it is expressed in the words of the American Declaration of Independence: 'We hold these truths to be self-evident, that all men are created equal, that they are endowed by their Creator with certain inalienable rights, that among these are life, liberty and the pursuit of happiness; that to secure these rights governments are instituted among men, deriving their just powers from the consent of the governed.'

That, I assure you, is the creed of America. It is the creed by which we live and in defence of which many Americans have laid down their lives – in France, in the Philippines, in Korea, and many other foreign lands – in a supreme act of fellowship with those of other lands who believe in the dignity of men and men's right to have governments not imposed upon them but chosen by them. Such a creed cannot be imposed by force because to use force to impose a creed would of itself be a violation of our creed.

I revert again to Lord Russell's statement that 'it is not necessary that either side should abandon belief in its own creed.' Certainly that is true of the United States, where creed comprehends the renunciation of force and violence to spread its creed. The same, unhappily, cannot be said of Soviet Communism, whose creed comprehends the use of force and violence. Therefore, I believe that it is necessary that at least that part of the Soviet Communist creed should be abandoned in order to achieve the peaceful result which is sought by Lord Russell and all other peace-loving people.

It is the steadfast determination of the United States – you may call it a creed if you will – to work in a spirit of conciliation for peaceful solutions based on freedom and justice of the great problems facing the world today.

8 February 1958

Of the poets, Richard Church – like Robert Graves – has contributed to the New Statesman *over most of its first fifty years.*

A Parting   Richard Church

If to lose all, is gain;
If the experience of grief
Brings solace after pain,
Then you and I may find relief
In this present anguish.
Parting, we may learn to prove
Faith is wiser than to languish
After an impossible love.

Now that you are out of reach,
Surrendered to harsh circumstance,
Death itself has less to teach
Than I discover by this chance.
That which lust could not reveal,
I have found in our farewell.

22 February 1958

By the age of thirty Paul Johnson had become a master journalist, a well-known performer on television, and an assistant editor of the New Statesman. *He is at his best when angry. In that mood his writing is 'typically' new statesmanly: mostly there is a strong link between his analytical method and the old Fabian technique.*

Sex, Snobbery and Sadism   Paul Johnson

I have just finished what is, without doubt, the nastiest book I have ever read. It is a new novel entitled *Dr No* and the author is Mr Ian Fleming. Echoes of Mr Fleming's fame had reached me before, and I had been repeatedly urged to read his books by literary friends whose judgment I normally respect. When his new novel appeared, therefore, I obtained a copy and started to read. By the time I was a third of the way through, I had to suppress a strong impulse to throw the thing away, and only continued reading because I realized that here was a social phenomenon of some importance.

There are three basic ingredients in *Dr No*, all unhealthy, all thoroughly English: the sadism of a schoolboy bully, the mechanical, two-dimensional sex-longings of a frustrated adolescent, and the crude, snob-cravings of a suburban adult. Mr Fleming has no literary skill, the construction of the book is chaotic, and entire incidents and situations are inserted, and then forgotten, in a haphazard manner. But the three ingredients are manufactured and blended with deliberate, professional precision; Mr Fleming dishes up his recipe with all the calculated accountancy of a Lyons Corner House.

The plot can be briefly described. James Bond, an upper-class Secret Service Agent, is sent by his sadistic superior, M., to Jamaica, to investigate strange incidents on a nearby island. By Page 53, Bond's bodyguard, a faithful and brutal Negro called Quarrel, is already at work, twisting the arms of a Chinese girl to breaking point. She gouges his face with a broken flash-bulb, and in return, he smilingly squeezes the fleshy part of her thumb (described by Fleming as 'the Mount of Venus', because if it is well-developed then the girl is 'good in bed') until she screams. ('She's Love Moun' be sore long after ma face done get healed,' chortles Quarrel.) Next, Bond's mysterious enemies attempt to poison him with cyanide-loaded fruit, and then insert a six-inch long venomous centipede in his bed ('Bond could feel it nuzzling at his skin. It was drinking! Drinking the beads of salt sweat!').

Bond visits the island, falls asleep, and on waking sees a beautiful girl, wearing only a leather belt round her waist ('The belt made her nakedness extraordinarily erotic'). Her behind, Bond notices, 'was almost as firm and rounded as a boy's.' The girl tells Bond she was raped at the age of 15 by a savage overseer, who then broke her nose. She revenged herself by dropping a Black Widow spider on his naked stomach while he slept ('He took a week to die'). Bond rejects her urgent invitation to share her sleeping bag. Then the enemy arrives – huge, inhuman Negro-Chinese half-castes, known as Chingroes, under the diabolical direction of Dr No. Quarrel is scorched to death by a flame-thrower, and Bond and the girl are captured.

There follows a vague series of incidents in a sort of luxury hotel, built into the mountain, where Dr No entertains his captives before torturing them. This gives Fleming an opportunity to insert his snob ingredient. A lubricious bathroom scene, in which the girl again attempts to seduce Bond, involves Floris Lime bath-essence, Guerlain bathcubes and 'Guerlain's Sapoceti, *Fleur des Alpes*'. Bond, offered a drink, demands 'a medium vodka dry Martini' ('I would prefer Russian or Polish vodka'). A third attempt by the girl is frustrated only by Bond's succumbing to drugs inserted in his breakfast. At last Dr No appears, 6 ft. 6 in. tall, and looking like 'a giant venomous worm wrapped in grey tin-foil'. Some years before, his hands had been cut off, but he is equipped with 'articulated steel pincers', which he has a habit of tapping against his contact-lenses, making a metallic noise. He has a polished skull, no eyelashes, and his heart is on the wrong side of his body; he is, needless to say, Chinese (with a German mother). His chief amusement is to subject his captives to prolonged, scientific tortures. ('I am interested in pain. I am also interested in finding out how much the human body can endure.')

Bond contemplates stabbing No's jugular vein with the jagged stem of a broken wine-glass, but reluctantly abandons the idea. The girl is taken off, to be strapped, naked, to the ground and nibbled to death by giant crabs. Bond is put through an ingenious, and fantastically complicated, obstacle course of tortures, devised by No. First come electric shocks. Then an agonizing climb up a steel chimney. Then a crawl along a red-hot zinc tube, to face twenty giant Tarantula spiders 'three or four inches long'. Finally Bond is hurled into the sea, where he is met by a 50-foot giant squid (everything is giant in *Dr No* – insects, breasts and gin-and-tonics). Having survived all these, Bond buries No alive under a mountain of bird-dung, rescues the girl and at last has a shot at a jugular vein, this time with a table-knife. He also shoots three Chingroes, one in the head, one in the stomach and one in the neck. The girl's feet get cut up, but they tramp to safety, 'leaving bloody footsteps on the ground'. The story ends with Bond biting the girl in an erotic embrace, which takes place in a special giant sleeping bag.

I have summarized the plot, perhaps at wearisome length, because a bare recital of its details describes, better than I can, how Fleming deliberately and systematically excites and then satisfies the very worst instincts of his readers. This seems to me far more dangerous than straight pornography. In 1944, George Orwell took issue with a book which in some ways resembles Fleming's novels – *No Orchids for Miss Blandish*. He saw the success of *No Orchids*, published in 1940, as part of a discernible psychological climate, whose other products were Fascism, the Gestapo, mass-bombing and war. But in condemning *No Orchids*, Orwell made two reservations. First, he conceded that it was brilliantly written, and that the acts of cruelty it described sprang from a subtle and integrated, though perverse, view of human nature. Secondly, in contrasting *No Orchids* with *Raffles* – which he judged a healthy and harmless book – he pointed out that *No Orchids* was evil precisely because it lacked the restraint of conventional upper-class values; and this led him to the astonishing but intelligible conclusion that perhaps, after all, snobbery, like hypocrisy, was occasionally useful to society.

What, I wonder, would he have said of *Dr No*? For this novel is badly written to the point of incoherence and none of the 500,000 people who, I am told, are expected to buy it, could conceivably be giving Cape 13*s*. 6*d*. to savour its literary merits. Moreover, both its hero and its author are unquestionably members of the Establishment. Bond is an ex-Royal Navy Commander and belongs to Blades, a sort of super-White's. Mr Fleming was educated at Eton and Sandhurst, and is married to a prominent society hostess, the ex-wife of Lord Rothermere. He is the foreign manager of that austere and respectable newspaper, the *Sunday Times*, owned by the elderly Lord Kemsley, who once tried to sell a popular tabloid with the slogan (or rather his wife's slogan) of 'clean and clever'. Fleming belongs to the Turf and Boodle's and lists among his hobbies the collection of first editions. He is also the owner of Goldeneye, a house made famous by Sir Anthony Eden's Retreat from Suez. Eden's uneasy slumbers, it will be remembered, were disturbed by (characteristically) giant rats which, after they had been disposed of by his detectives, turned out to be specially tamed ones kept by Mr Fleming.

Orwell, in fact, was wrong. Snobbery is no protection: on the contrary, the social appeal of the dual Bond-Fleming personality has added an additional flavour to his brew of sex and sadism. Fleming's novels are not only successful, like *No Orchids*; they are also smart. The *Daily Express*, pursuing its task of bringing glamour and sophistication to the masses, has serialized the last three. Our curious post-war society, with its obsessive interest in debutantes, its cult of U and non-U, its working-class graduates educated into snobbery by the welfare state, is a soft market for Mr Fleming's poison. Bond's warmest admirers are among the Top People. Of his last adventure, *From Russia, With Love*, his publishers claim, with reason, that it 'won approval from the sternest critics in the world of letters.' *The Times Literary Supplement* found it 'most brilliant', the *Sunday Times* 'highly polished', the *Observer* 'stupendous', the *Spectator* 'rather pleasant'. And this journal, most susceptible of all, described it as 'irresistible'. It has become easier than it was in Orwell's day to make cruelty attractive. We have gone just that much farther down the slope. Recently I read Henri Alleg's horrifying account of his tortures in an Algiers prison; and I have on my desk a documented study of how we treat our prisoners in Cyprus. I am no longer astonished that these things can happen. Indeed, after reflecting on the Fleming phenomenon, they seem to me almost inevitable.

5 April 1958

The Farmer's Concern   Bertolt Brecht

> The farmer's concern is with his field,
> He looks after his cattle, pays taxes,
> Produces children, to save himself labourers and
> Depends on the price of milk.
> The townspeople speak of love for the soil
> Of healthy peasant stock
> And call farmers the pillars of the nation.
>
> The townspeople speak of love for the soil
> Of healthy peasant stock
> And call farmers the pillars of the nation.
> The farmer's concern is with his field,
> He looks after his cattle, pays taxes,
> Produces children, to save himself labourers and
> Depends on the price of milk.
>
> *12 September 1959*

Another new star since risen towards the zenith:

The Bike   Alan Sillitoe

The Easter I was 15 I sat at the table for supper and mam said to me: 'I'm glad you've left school: now you can go to wok.'

'I don't want to go to wok,' I said in a big voice.

'Well, you've got to,' she said. 'I can't afford to keep a pit-prop like yo' on nowt.'

I sulked, pushed my toasted cheese away as if it was the worst kind of slop. 'I thought I could 'ave a break before startin'.'

'Well you thought wrong. You'll be out of 'arm's way at wok.' She took my plate and emptied it on John's, my younger brother's, knowing the right way to get me mad. That's the trouble with me: I'm not clever. I could have bashed our John's face in and snatched it back, except the little bastard had gobbled it up, and dad was sitting by the fire, behind his

264

paper with one tab lifted. 'You can't get me out to wok quick enough, can you?' was all I could say at mam.

Dad chipped in, put down his paper. 'Listen: no wok, no grub. So gerrout an' look for a job tomorrer, and don't come back till you've got one.'

Going to the bike factory to ask for a job meant getting up early, just as if I was back at school; there didn't seem any point in getting older. My old man was a good worker though, and I knew in my bones and brains that I took after him. At the school garden the teacher used to say: 'Colin, you're the best worker I've got, and you'll get on when you leave' – after I'd spent a couple of hours digging spuds out while all the others had been larking about trying to run each other over with the lawnrollers. Then the teacher would sell the spuds off at three-pence a pound and what did I get out of it? Bogger-all. Yet I liked the work because it wore me out; and I always feel pretty good when I'm worn out.

I knew you had to go to work though, and that rough work was best. I saw a picture once about a revolution in Russia, about the workers taking over everything (like dad wants to) and they lined everybody up and made them hold their hands out and the working blokes went up and down looking at them. Anybody whose hands was lily-white was taken away and shot. The others was O.K. Well, if ever that happened, *I'd* be O.K., and that made me feel better when a few days later I was walking down the street in overalls at half-past seven in the morning with the rest of them. One side of my face felt lively and interested in what I was in for, but the other side was crooked and very sorry for itself, so that a neighbour got a front view of my whole clock and called with a wide laugh, a gap I'd liked to have seen a few inches lower down in her neck: 'Ne' mind, Colin, it ain't all that bad.'

The man on the gate took me to the turnery. The noise hit me like a boxing glove as I went in, but I kept on walking straight into it without flinching, feeling it reach right into my guts as if to wrench them out and use them as garters. I was handed over to the foreman; then the foreman passed me on to the toolsetter; and the toolsetter took me to another youth – so that I began to feel like a hot wallet.

The youth led me to a cupboard, opened it, and gave me a sweeping brush. 'Yo' do that gangway,' he said, 'and I'll do this one.' My gangway was wider, but I didn't bother to mention it. 'Mike,' he said, holding out his hand, 'that's me. I go on a machine next week, a drill.'

'How long you bin on this sweeping?' I wanted to know, bored already.

'Three months. Every lad gets put on sweeping first, just to get 'em used to the place.' Mike was small and thin, older than me. We took to each other. He had round bright eyes and dark wavy hair, and spoke in a quick way as if he'd stayed at school longer than he had. He was idle, and I thought him sharp and clever, maybe because his mam and dad had died when he was three. He'd been brought up by an asthmatic auntie who'd not only spoiled him but let him run wild as well, he told me later when we sat supping from our tea-mugs. He'd quietened down now though, and butter wouldn't melt in his mouth, he said with a wink. I couldn't think why this was, after all his stories about him being a madhead – which put me off him at first, though after a bit he was my mate, and that was that.

We was talking one day, and Mike said the thing he wanted to buy most in the world was a gram and lots of jazz records – New Orleans style. He was saving up and had already got ten quid. 'Me,' I said, 'I want a bike, to get out at weekends up Trent. A shop on Arkwright Street sells good 'uns second-'and.'

I went back to my sweeping. It was a fact I'd always wanted a bike. Speed gave me a thrill. Malcolm Campbell was my bigshot – but I'd settle for a two-wheeled pushbike. I'd once borrowed my cousin's and gone down Balloon House Hill so quick I passed a bus. I'd often thought how easy it would be to pinch a bike: look in a shop window until a bloke leaves his bike to go into the same shop, then nip in just before him and ask for something you knew they hadn't got; then walk out whistling to the bike at the kerb and ride off as if it's yours while the bloke's still in the shop. I'd brood for hours: fly home on it, enamel it, file off the numbers, turn the handlebars round, change the pedals, take lamps off or put them on . . . only no, I thought, I'll be honest and save up for one when I get forced out to work, worse luck.

But work turned out to be a better life than school. I kept as hard at it as I could, and got on well with the blokes because I used to spout about how rotten the wages was and how hard the bosses slaved us – which made me popular you can bet. Like my old man always says, I told 'em: At 'ome, when you've got a headache, mash; at work, when you've got a headache, strike. Which brought a good few laughs.

Mike was put on his drill, and one Friday while he was cleaning it down I stood waiting to cart his rammel off. 'Are you still saving up for a bike then?' he asked me, pushing steel dust away with a handbrush.

'Course I am. But I'm a way off getting one yet. They rush you a fiver at that shop. Guaranteed though.'

He worked on for a minute or two, then without turning said, as if he'd got a birthday present or was trying to spring a good surprise on me: 'I've made up my mind to sell *my* bike.'

'I didn't know you'd got one,' I said.

'Well' – a look on his face as if there was a good few things I don't know – 'I bus it to work: it's easier.' Then in a pallier voice: 'I got it last Christmas, from my auntie. But I want a record player now.'

My heart was bumping. I knew I hadn't got enough, but: 'How much do you want for it?'

He smiled: 'It ain't how much I want for the bike, it's how much more dough I need to get the gram and a couple o' discs.'

I saw Trent Valley spread out below me from the top of Carlton Hill – fields and villages, and the river like a white silk scarf dropped from a giant's neck. 'How much do you need, then?'

He took his time about it, as if still having to reckon up. 'Fifty bob.' I'd only got two quid – so the giant snatched his scarf away and vanished. Then Mike seemed in a hurry to finish the deal: 'Look, I don't want to mess about, I'll let it go for two pounds five. You can borrow the other five bob.'

'I'll do it then,' I said, and Mike shook my hand like he was going away in the army: 'It's a deal. Bring the dough in the morning, and I'll bike it to wok.'

Dad was already in when I got home, filling the kettle at the scullery tap. I don't think he felt safe without there was a kettle on the gas. 'What would you do if the world suddenly ended, dad?' I once asked when he was in a good mood. 'Mash some tea and watch it,' he said. He poured me a cup.

'Lend's five bob dad, till Friday.'

He slipped the cosy on. 'What do *yo'* want to borrow money for?' I told him. 'Who from?' he asked.

'My mate at wok.'

He passed me the money. 'Is it a good 'un?'

'I ain't seen it yet. He's bringing it in t'morning.'

'Mek sure the brakes is safe.'

Mike came in half an hour late, so I wasn't able to see the bike till dinnertime. I kept thinking he'd took bad and wouldn't come at all, but suddenly he was stooping at the door to take his clips off – so's I'd know he'd got his – my – bike. He looked paler than usual, as if he'd been up the canal-bank all night with a piece of skirt. I paid him at dinnertime. 'Do you want a receipt for it?' he laughed. It was no time to lark about: I gave it a short test around the factory, then rode it home.

The next three evenings, for it was well in to summer, I rode a dozen miles out into the country, where fresh air smelt like cowdung and the land was coloured different, was wide open and windier than in streets: marvellous. It was like a new life starting up, as if till then I'd been tied by a mile-long rope round the ankle to home. Whistling along lanes I planned trips to Skeggy, wondering how many miles I could make in a whole day. If I pedalled like mad, bursting my lungs for fifteen hours I'd reach London where I'd never been: it was like sawing through the bars in clink. It was a good bike as well, a few years old, but a smart racer with lamps and saddlebag and a pump that went. I thought Mike was a bit loony parting with it at that price, but I supposed that that's how blokes are when they get dead set on a gram and discs. They'd sell their own mother, I thought, enjoying a mad dash down from Canning Circus, weaving between cars for kicks.

'What's it like having a bike?' Mike asked, stopping to slap me on the back – as jolly as I'd ever seen him, yet in a kind of way that don't happen between pals.

'You should know,' I said. 'Why? It's all right, ain't it? The wheels are good, aren't they?'

An insulted look came into his eyes. 'You can give it me back if you like. I'll give you your money.'

'I don't want it,' I said. I could no more part with it than my right arm, and he knew it. 'Got the gram yet?' And he told me about it for the next half-hour; it had got so many dials for this-and-that he made it sound like a space ship. We was both satisfied, which was the main thing.

That same Saturday I went to the barber's for a hair-cut and when I came out I saw a bloke getting on my bike to ride it away. I tapped him on the shoulder, my fist flashing red for danger.

'Off,' I said, sharp, ready to smash the thieving bastard. He turned to me: a funny sort of thief, I couldn't help thinking, a respectable-looking bloke of about 40 wearing glasses and shiny shoes, smaller than me, with a moustache. Still, the swivel-eyed sinner was taking my bike.

'I'm boggered if I will,' he said, in a quiet way so that I thought he was a bit touched. 'It's my bike, anyway.'

'It bleddy-well ain't,' I swore, 'and if you don't get off I'll crack you one.'

A few people gawked at us. The bloke didn't mess about, and I can understand it now. 'Missis,' he called, 'just go down the road to that copper-box and ask a policeman to come up 'ere, will you? This is my bike, and this young bogger nicked it.'

I was strong for my age. 'You soddin' fibber,' I cried, pulling him clean off the bike so's it clattered to the pavement. I picked it up to ride away,

268

but the bloke got me round the waist, and it was more than I could do to take him off up the road as well, even if I wanted to. Which I didn't.

'Fancy robbin' a working-man of his bike,' somebody called out from the crowd of idle bastards now collected. I could have mowed them down. But I didn't get the chance. A copper came, and the man was soon flicking out his wallet, showing a bill with the number of the bike on it: proof right enough. But I still thought he'd made a mistake. 'You can tell us all about that at the Guildhall,' the copper said to me.

I don't know why – I suppose I want my brains testing – but I stuck to a story that I found the bike dumped at the end of the yard that morning and was on my way to give it in at a copshop, and had called for a hair-cut first. I think the magistrate half believed me, because the bloke knew to the minute when it was pinched, and at that time I had a perfect alibi – I was in work, proved by my clocking-in card. I knew some rat who hadn't been in work though when he should have been.

All the same, being found with a pinched bike, I got put on probation, and am still doing it. I hate old Mike's guts for playing a trick like that on me, his mate; but it was lucky for him I hated the coppers more and wouldn't nark on anybody, not even a dog. Dad would have killed me if ever I had, though he didn't need to tell me. I could only thank God a story came to me as quick as it did; though in one way I still sometimes reckon I was barmy not to have told them how I got that bike.

There's one thing I do know; I'm waiting for Mike to come out of Borstal. He got picked up, the day after I was copped with the bike, for robbing his auntie's gas meter to buy more discs. I've got a big bone to pick with him, because he owes me 45 bob. I don't care where he gets it – even if he goes out and robs another meter – but I'll get it out of him, I swear blind I will. I'll pulverize him.

Another thing about him though that makes me laugh is that, if ever there's a revolution and everybody's lined-up with their hands out, Mike's will still be lily-white, because he's a bone-idle thieving bastard – and then we'll see how he goes on; because mine won't be lily-white, I can tell you that now. And you never know, I might even be one of the blokes picking 'em out.

26 December 1959

Many people have forgotten that Mao Tse-tung is also a poet. This was written in 1920.

269

Midstream   Mao Tse-tung

    Alone in a cold autumn I stood
    Where Hsiang-Chiang flows north
    Past the point of Orange-Grove Isle.
    The ten thousand hills were crimson,
    In crimson tiers the forest.
    Up the great hyaline river
    Struggled a hundred vessels.
    Eagles in the vast air posed to strike;
    Fish in the shallows hovered.
    Each living form under the frosty heaven
    Fought with another for freedom.
    I stared from a desolate tower
    And asked the immense earth –
    Who decrees the rise, the fall?

    With a hundred friends now, returning
    I range back over the rainbow days,
    The crowded risky years.
    O schoolmates, in youth blossoming and tall with talents,
    We must now in the arrogance of our knowledge
    Uproot our scented careers.
    Fingering mountains only, and rivers,
    To hold poetry alive in our minds,
    We will use for manure
    Those bygone dreams of ten-thousand-household fiefdoms.
    Don't you remember, once it has reached midstream
    Your craft shoots past
    As the rapids take flight?

(Adapted by Earle Birney from the literal translation of Ping-ti Ho.)

24 September 1960

John Freeman was not a journalist when he resigned his post in the Labour Government in 1951 and accepted Kingsley Martin's invitation to join the New Statesman. When Martin resigned at the end of 1960, Freeman became Editor;

having, by that time, become a very widely known television personality for his method of getting at the truth in the BBC's Face to Face *programme. He used the* New Statesman *to deal with some criticisms of his methods – methods which have their new statesmanly side.*

Face to Face   John Freeman

Twice this year disquiet has been widely and responsibly expressed about methods of TV interviewing. Phrases such as 'third degree', 'brain-washing' and 'amateur psychiatry' have been bandied about in the Press and accepted without much examination. Since in both cases – Mr Frank Foulkes last February and Mr Gilbert Harding last month – I was the interviewer called in question, and since some of these criticisms seem to me to raise a real issue of freedom of speech, perhaps I may be permitted to put a different point of view.

The case of Mr Foulkes was straightforward enough and might never have led to controversy outside the ranks of the Communists and their apologists if a group of Labour MPs had not written to *The Times* complaining that my questions to Mr Foulkes, in the BBC programme *Panorama*, about specific and widely-publicized allegations of mal-practice in his union amounted to public trial by television: I was described as 'a self-appointed public prosecutor . . . coercing him by challenge to prove his innocence'. In the ensuing correspondence the MPs were seen off so effectively by such varied champions of journalistic freedom as Malcolm Muggeridge, Francis Williams, Woodrow Wyatt, Christopher Chataway and Lord Boothby that on that occasion I did not reply to them.

It is perhaps relevant in discussing the subsequent criticism of my handling, in very different circumstances, of Mr Gilbert Harding to say now that I did not – and do not on reflection – accept the judgment that the Foulkes interview was an abuse. Mr Foulkes was one of the central figures in a series of events which concerned the public interest and gave rise to widespread scandal. *Panorama* is a review of current affairs, and its purpose is to illuminate such matters for its viewers. My duty on that occasion, not as a 'self-appointed prosecutor', but as the professional journalist assigned to the job of interviewing Mr Foulkes, was to question him as stringently as I could on the viewers' behalf about the matters of public concern for which he was responsible. My questions were strictly relevant to his responsibilities, courteously put – and as sharp as I could make them. In so far as they implied criticism of Mr Foulkes' conduct, they went no further than the already existing allegations of malpractice which he was there – incidentally at his own request – to answer. Even the much publicized 'challenge' to him to bring an action for libel against those journals (including the *New Statesman*) responsible for publishing the allegations, was no more than a public expression of the question which was already being asked inside every newspaper office.

It is not for me to say whether Mr Foulkes answered these questions well or badly; but what is certain is that, if he stood in any serious sense. condemned by public opinion after his interview, he was condemned by his answers and not by my questions – which were those which must have been put to him by any competent journalist who had taken the trouble to unravel the complicated network of allegation and counter-allegation about the affairs of the ETU. To deny to the TV interviewer the right of questioning which, subject to the laws of libel and contempt, is conceded almost without query to the newspaper journalist, is unnaturally to limit the freedom of television to serve the public, whether as a purveyor of news and ideas or as a watchdog.

Of course television techniques can be abused – as can the printed word. My point is that in this case they were not; that the complaints indicated an unreasonable touchiness about the legitimate probing of responsible public inquiry. So high, indeed, is the sense of public duty in the editorial control of BBC news and current affairs that the likelihood of any significant abuse in this specialized field of television interviewing is very much smaller than in the daily Press. In any case, few responsible critics of the Press, disgusted by the intrusion and impertinence of some of the gossip writers, would suggest that the cause of freedom would be helped by limiting the right of serious journalists to ask embarrassing questions about matters of public concern.

The Harding case is a different, and far more debatable, matter. The BBC's interview programme *Face to Face*, with which I have been associated, subjects selected public figures to sustained personal questioning before the cameras – without necessarily any particular topical news-peg. People appear on this programme by their own choice: nobody has ever been subjected to any sort of improper pressure; the names of those who, being invited, have preferred the haven of discreet obscurity have never been divulged – nor yet those of that more sanguine company who hopefully press their claims to public exposure. From time to time during the series it has seemed profitable to spend the time digging for what can loosely be called a 'news' story. For instance, I do not regret persuading Lord Shawcross, on the morrow of his appointment to the Monckton

Commission, to define with valuable, if embarrassing, precision his personal view of its terms of reference; or inviting Herbert Morrison, in reply to Lord Attlee and others, to give his version of some of the more controversial episodes in his public career. But usually and basically the purpose of *Face to Face* has been to try, by question and answer, to induce public figures to remove the mask which they habitually present to the world, to peel off the layers of protective covering and let the viewers see what lies beneath.

Given that objective, there is at once a problem of taste and judgment for the interviewer. How much protective covering can be removed without indecency? Very often in practice the question will not arise: it can easily take twenty minutes of the keenest questioning to induce most public figures to surrender, metaphorically, the hat and gloves in which they choose to confront the world. And if you are going to penetrate the outer wrapping at all, the questions must be, within the bounds of courtesy, sharp, intrusive and persistent. The problem arises because, once you do get underneath the wrappings, you can never be quite sure what you are going to find.

Take, for instance, two recent examples: many people thought that the interrogation of Gilbert Harding had transgressed the bounds of taste. An earlier interview with Stirling Moss was, as far as I can find out, equally widely held to be both acceptable and successful. Yet the two sets of questions ran closely in parallel. In both cases I judged that the key to character might lie behind superficial inconsistencies in their known behaviour; Harding, the rough-tongued curmudgeon *versus* Harding, the kindly sentimentalist; and Moss, the playboy *versus* Moss, the iron-willed self-disciplinarian. In both cases it occurred to me that their attitude to fear and death might serve as a catalyst of the real human personality. Thus I asked them many of the same questions – questions which bounced off the extravert Moss and cut far deeper than many people thought seemly into the more complicated, and perhaps less integrated, Harding. The fact that, through a clumsy misunderstanding, I maladroitly asked Harding one question which upset both him and the viewers, does not alter the point. In each instance the public got a clear and genuine glimpse of the real man behind the mask. Indeed, in Harding's case, that one moment of poignancy – fortuitous though it was – illuminated for millions of viewers the private decency and sensibility of a public figure who had previously been stereotyped as something of an ogre.

It seems to me that those who object to these programmes, on the ground that they are in some way 'indecent' or 'intrusive', ought to face the central

273

question: Is it desirable to remove the wrappings from our public figures ? I think it is. I think that, in an age which is perhaps contributing more to the art of packaging than to any of the deeper-seated virtues, responsible public opinion is strengthened by the ability to meet public figures without their masks. So far, mass communications have been used far more to spread the siren-call of the public-relations man than to project the uncomfortable angularities of truth. As public idols become superficially more and more widely known, an ever greater investment is made in the image. Who is Gaitskell? Is Supermac a myth? What bones does Harding grind? Nobody knows: hardly anyone bothers to inquire. *Face to Face* has set out, not only by its methods of questioning, but also by the unwinking scrutiny of its cameras, to enable the viewer in his home to meet the famous with an immediacy and intimacy possible in no other medium and to pass his own judgments on them.

If it is thought that this is desirable, then one or two other considerations follow. The first is that the process of unwrapping can be accomplished only by the keenest and most concentrated questioning (involving, of course, the risk of an ocasional error of judgment or lapse of taste). The second is that there is no formula which can ensure success: for each Carl Gustav Jung there will be a von Senger, for each Sitwell a Gulbenkian; every subject presents a new and individual problem which must be solved for the first time. The third is that occasionally the process of unwrapping will reveal a private reality shocking to those who value cosiness above all else in their viewing; but that risk is inseparable from the process itself.

Whether it is worth taking is ultimately for the viewer to judge. I should like to suggest, however, that the judgment has implications which go far wider than liking or disliking a single not very important television programme or one particular interviewer's style. It would seem to me a pity if the most potent medium of communication since Caxton were to be wrapped up for ever in a cocoon of panel games and polite evasions in order to avoid shocking those who find it more comfortable to live with the image than the reality.

15 October 1960

In its third epoch the New Statesman *is becoming much tougher, harder-minded in its handling of criticism; also broader in range, so that under the 'Arts and Entertainment' heading anything from cigarette-packet design to poetry-reading may be included. Here John Coleman, of the new generation of new statesmen, dissipates complacency on the subject of contemporary poetry, and Reyner Banham deals with Coventry Cathedral in an essay worthy of being joined to the very small body of critical writing which is of permanent rather than ephemeral value.*

Centres and Ceremonies   John Coleman

Eight days of poetry at the Mermaid Theatre drew to a close last Sunday night. We had heard poets reading their own works on record and in person, seen them on film and seen films made by them, witnessed performances of their plays and listened to them discussing, most amiably, their craft or sullen art. We had also jostled glasses and bandied words with them during the intervals for refreshment. Poetry was in our lips and eyes, not forgetting our hair, and I must be forgiven it if gets into my prose, too, here and there. The whole amazing jamboree originated in the executive committee of the Poetry Book Society and was helped financially by the Arts Council and by Mr Norman Collins of ATV. The unflagging master of ceremonies was John Wain.

Chatting to a full house on the first night, he set a fine informal key for subsequent proceedings. The simple aim was to bring together like-minded people who enjoyed good poetry and to give them some good poetry to listen to. There were so many good poets today that he could easily have filled the bill at three or four festivals like this one, using different poets all the time; we would understand if our own favourites weren't on the programme. Inevitably, things had gone wrong. 'One of our poets was hit by a discus.' The idea this evening was to enjoy ourselves; we were going to have an *enormous* interval, with wine and cheese, during which we could mingle with the many poets present. He hadn't meant to strike a sombre note, but a picture in that morning's *Observer* of a baby starving to death had made him wonder whether all the energy and money being devoted to this festival shouldn't be going rather to confront such problems. He thought not. Against the prevalent 'anti-human' tendency, poetry kept on saying that people matter more than things or organizations. We must cure the sickness from the inside out and not from the outside in – that was his *personal* justification for us all being there.

We would hear all sorts of poets: meditative, exuberant, hard to follow and easy to follow; but they would all be poets of quality. Mr Wain was against dilution and had an ungentle word for poetry-and-jazz. He read a Yeats poem ('he's put my thoughts for me') and we scattered for the foyer-party.

275

Sipping *rosé* with Lee, my thoughts went back to an afternoon of poetry-and-jazz held at the Festival Hall some five weeks before, in turn the offshoot of a hugely attended occasion at the Hampstead Town Hall in February. The Festival Hall was packed, the acoustics bad, the poets with three exceptions worse, and the only thing to pierce the deep, dazed glow of self-satisfaction rising from the youngish, hip audience was when Laurie Lee, feeling the moment unpropitious, quietly tore in two a poem he had intended to read about the Spanish Civil War and dropped it to the floor. It was an act as impulsive as making a poem, and a memorable achievement in the lethargic hug of that great auditorium, something human in the stale rant about H-bombs and the whimpering bad jazz. If that afternoon had witnessed a momentous breakthrough for poetry ('one of the few remaining social consciences in this country' – see programme note), then poetry was something we could well do without.

But, back at the Mermaid, an enthusiastic lady had addressed me. 'Are you a poet?' she said. (I have a beard and was clutching a glass. Most of the better poets are clean-shaven.) I disabused her, pointed to one who looked like a bank manager, and went and talked to a critic.

After the interval, six poets from Oxford and Cambridge read some verses, too many of which leant heavily on the public significance of their recent sexual experiences. Nothing happened, no spark flew, and not even Mr Wain, at his most manful, could convince me otherwise: 'How good this new generation of poets is – how strong they are, aren't they?' No, one wanted to shout, no, they're not, and it's getting awfully late and they read abominably, anyway. Why haven't we got a broadsheet so that we can *see* what they're saying.

The night's encounters were not over. On the platform at Blackfriars underground station I was approached by a very young man who introduced himself as a poet and asked if I had enjoyed myself. He waved his programme at me: 'I went round getting signatures,' he said. 'This may be worth a bit in a few years' time.' We shared a compartment and he told me he had been to Russia, reciting his works to the accompaniment of an electric guitar and being pelted with flowers. He was to perform on the last, gala night of the Mermaid festival. Mr Wain's intimations of 'quality' began to seem unduly starry-eyed.

Convinced that I enjoy poetry, I am obviously not a poetry-'lover', not in the way necessary to get the most out of these gatherings. There were some twenty-two different programmes during the week, of which I sampled a reasonable proportion, going – it is perhaps proper to add – in no hostile spirit. It proved a baffling experience. A poem by Mr Ray Mathew, an Australian, which made wonderful play with the image of a bowl (and drew spontaneous applause); a harsh reading by Ted Hughes of his poem, 'My Uncle's Wound', one of twelve commissioned especially for the Festival by Messrs Guinness Son & Co.; Miss Carolyn Kizer from America – *these* fragments I should shore against my ruins? Even Miss Kizer, a stunningly glamorous adornment of the second half of Wednesday night's programme ('Five American Poets') and a lucid, relentless reader of some of the funniest verse of the week – from her projected marathon 'Four Women', a sort of anti-Juvenal – even that piled golden head and scrupulous diction have to war in one's memories against the long hours of boredom and despair.

I was not there on the final night when Ursula Vaughan Williams came on with a great box from which she plucked a laurel wreath to crown the director. (Nor were a lot of the contributing poets, apparently. Their seats had been sold by an over-eager management.) But I had soldiered through dustier country. There was the incredible evening of translations ('Our furthest piece of audacity,' as Wain rightly said), when George Seferis must have needed all his diplomacy to sit so still through poems read in a Serbo-Croatian monotone, a Glaswegian version of Apollinaire, and the interminable susurrations of Rafael Pineda from Venezuela. This was downright bad planning. By the time Mr Seferis rose to deliver the *bonne bouche*, appetite had fled.

The next night, there was a discussion between poets young and old of 'the problems and opportunities for poetry in the new oral culture.' Intended as a half-way point of the Festival, at which audience and platform might fruitfully interact, it never got off the ground. Short stump-speeches from the platform (Sir George Rostrevor Hamilton, Anthony Thwaite, V.C. Clinton-Baddeley and others) were followed by a tepid anecdotal conversation between the panel-members and a couple of unprofitable questions from the house. A third question – 'what about some more poetry' – ended it.

It was about there that I began to think myself of some private reward for Mr Wain. One didn't always like what he was doing (after all, he was presumably responsible for some of the programming), but one had to admire his unquenchable verve and, even, gall. He marvellously offered and acted out responses for the audience. Robert Gittings read a short – I thought undistinguished – poem by a 13-year-old schoolgirl to illustrate something or other. Mr Wain was up there in a second: 'Well, that was a bomb-shell, wasn't it? I never thought we'd get anything like that.' The audience, as it were, purred its luck.

We had all sorts of poets – great ones, small ones, lean ones, brawny ones black ones, grey ones and tawny ones, grave old plodders and gay young friskers, and presumably quite a few fathers, mothers, uncles and cousins as well – for Mr Wain to play the piper to; poets we had and, if anyone wants to know, most of them look disconcertingly like you or me these days, exception made for Miss Kizer and Mr Empson: but what about the *audience*? On the weeknights I went the house was three-quarters full (the Mermaid seats 499) and attendance at the day-time poetry-on-record sessions and talks was variable but quite impressive. One caught the odd rancorous post-mortem going on at the bar, but generally the impression was one of almost churchy docility. Nobody booed, though I heard some jazz was barracked one lunch-time, and nobody stood up and cheered either. There should have been some catcalls and there might have been a pelting with flowers (for the professional readers on the Ezra Pound evening, whose excellence underlined the absurdity of letting most poets read their own works). The audience was decorous, unexigent, and here and there – one felt – a bit pleased with itself for having turned up in a good cause.

This is the crowning fallacy. 'Poetry' doesn't matter, since it doesn't mean anything: good poems do and of these there were all too few. There may have been more than I have allowed, for part of the trouble was the sheer aural difficulty of dealing with poems of extreme congestion supinely delivered. Another part was that a good number of the poems seemed *unnecessarily* congested, working out their small destinies in a welter of private references.

It was odd and enlivening after this to go to Arnold Wesker's house on Monday evening to meet the management committee of the group known as Centre 42. They take their name from the pious resolution passed by the TUC last September (first fore-shadowed by Wesker in this journal), urging a closer participation by the trade union movement in cultural activities. Wesker and others, among them Doris Lessing and the lady Mayor of Greenwich, are out to combat what they see as a class stranglehold on the arts in Britain today. They want to take art *to* the people, aiming to raise enough money to open a centre in London, which can be used as a theatre, dance hall, art gallery and concert hall, from which regional projects can take strength and guidance. This was an interim gathering designed to allow the committee to show their hand before they proceed to the sharpening of their ultimate objectives.

Wouldn't going after this larger audience have an effect on the *content* of the art offered? asked someone. What, anyway, *was* the art that the 'working classes' (the phrase rang, undefined, throughout the discussion) were going to draw new life from? Examples, please? Early days for that, said some of the committee; the thing was to get things moving, to explore, not to dogmatise.

'Artists,' claims the manifesto of Centre 42, 'no matter what their background, have been forced to produce work for . . . minority taste in order to earn a living.' Poets rarely earn their bread by their poems, and most of the poems read at the Mermaid were presumably written without an eye cocked to the main, 'minority' chance. But that the audience there represented some sort of minority taste today is beyond question, and Centre 42 might do well to attempt, for their own ends, a diagnosis of the strained and permissive values that can make such an occasion a success.

28 July 1961

Coventry Cathedral   Reyner Banham

There can be little doubt that Coventry Cathedral is the worst set-back to English church architecture for a very long time. Its influence, unless sternly resisted, can only be confusing and diversionary. This is not a snap judgment: I have known the cathedral since it was a concrete foundation-slab, and followed all Sir Basil Spence's long series of modifications and revisions since the competition results were first published, and my conviction that something was fundamentally wrong with the whole operation has grown in parallel with my increasing admiration for the skill and astuteness with which Sir Basil has done what he set out to do.

In other words, it is the basic proposition that is adrift, not the architectural execution – there is only one fundamental point on which the architect is to be blamed, which is that (like every other architect in Britain fit enough, at the time, to lift a pencil) he accepted the competition conditions. It is important, among all the rock-n-roll-crucifixion jazz currently being trumpeted up about 'a modern cathedral for a modern age', to remember that Coventry's original intention after the war was not to have a modern cathedral at all, but a Gothic-revival one, and that when this was abandoned after public outcry (largely from the architectural profession), the assessors chosen to judge the competition were about as square as could be found without going grave-robbing. The cards were effectively stacked to make a modern cathedral impossible: what was wanted, and what was got, was a traditional cathedral restyled. Not modern, because no radical reassessment of cathedral functions was undertaken before the conditions were issued.

Stories go round of heavy cerebration in the diocese during the preliminary stages of drawing up the conditions, but that must have been like the 'thinking' which goes on in the Conservative Central Office – mountains are in travail, and bring forth the status quo. Like the Tories, Coventry is trad, Dad, but has tried to give itself a new image – a medieval long plan with aisles and off-lying polygonal or circular chapels, but executed in non-medieval materials (in part) and adorned with devotional art-work in various non-medieval styles. A true modernist, a radical functionalist, would have rejected this basic proposition, seeing his obligation as Richard Llewelyn Davies sees it: 'To read carefully the client's statement of his needs, and to understand it fully – and then tear it up and find out what he really wants!' To accept the conditions of a competition is to by-pass this obligation, and, in spite of the very drastic modifications to some parts of the fabric, Sir Basil has still built something very close to his original sketch-plan.

This is not to object to that sketch because it does not exhibit the kind of centralized plan that has become fashionable, despite Peter Hammond's better intentions, since he published *Liturgy and Architecture*. To impose such a plan, as Archbishop (The Cruel See) Heenan did in the competition for Liverpool RC cathedral – again without radical analysis of cathedral functions – is worse, because merely fashionable. What was needed in both cases, and given in neither, was a fundamental and imaginative enquiry into those functions, engendered by the rites and responsibilities of episcopacy, that distinguish cathedrals from other churches. At Coventry, the emergence of certain genuinely new and progressive relationships between cathedral and town, cathedral and overseas Christendom, has resulted in no radical innovations, merely two clip-on chapels, one rejected by the guilds for whom it was intended, the other – the Chapel of Unity – a dramatic polygonal volume for which no one has yet devised a ritual function, other than lectures and readings for which its plan-form is unsuited.

Given then, that Sir Basil may be blamed for not embarrassing the diocese into genuine thought by shock tactics after he had won the competition (such things have been done), what sort of job has he made of executing this brief that he ought not to have accepted? A real whizz! A ring-a-ding God-box that will go over big with the flat-bottomed latitudinarians who can't stand the quiet austerities of St Paul's, Bow Common (which remains the *pons asinorum* of genuinely modern church architecture in England). The sheer quality, and quantity, of detailing at Coventry, the mastery of dramatic effects, the richness of the art-work, the resplendent sonority with which the note of absolutely conventional piety has been struck, all combine in an image that will have to be fought to the death by everyone who believes, like Peter Hammond (and myself), that church architecture is part of the mainstream of the Modern Movement, not a picturesque backwater.

Only two things have gone wrong with Spence's scheme. The Sutherland tapestry is wrong in colour and in the scale of its elements – it dominates the east end, but chiefly because it *is* the east end; it fails to achieve the commanding presence of a Byzantine pantocrator, which is the nearest term of comparison. Clearly, in attempting this unprecedented scale in tapestry, architect and artist were biting off more than the artist could chew, and while failure was doubtless foreseen by professional told-you-sos, the detailed grounds of failure could not have been. But it is difficult to understand why the detailed grounds for the failure of the west window were not foreseen. Strictly, it is a screen of clear glass occupying the entire liturgical west wall of the cathedral, some of the panes engraved by John Hutton with life-sized figures of saints and angels in a forced and arty style that one associates automatically with the Royal College of Art. However, the style of the applied art matters less than the amount of light that enters through it.

It was intended that the crowning moment of the entire design should be that when the communicant rises from the altar rail and turns to go back to his place, he sees, for the first time, the glowing ranks of stained-glass windows down either side of the nave. As it is, he is simply half-blinded by the glare of hard white light from the west. There are three reasons for this: liturgical west is, in fact, south, so that the window receives all day a level of illumination that a genuine west window does not begin to receive until evensong; the glass is clear, not stained, and therefore transmits vastly more light than, say, the west window at Norwich; and the successive raisings of the roof of the porch in search of a more monumental entrance since the first version of the design have lifted it to the point where it does not shade the window at all.

So, after the first blast of light, and the first disappointment with the tapestry, one avoids looking at either. The rest exhibits a level of sheer professionalism in the creation of visual effects and the manipulation of spaces that is rare in Britain (because the opportunities are rare, perhaps). The porch in particular, avowedly modelled on the exposed aisles of the unfinished nave at Siena, is masterly, creating with great economy of means the sense of soaring monumentality that has eluded both Scott at Liverpool and Maufe at Guildford. The general grouping of the exterior, with the two off-lying chapels seen against the long flank of the main building, is one of the few designs which preserves anything worth having of the South Bank aesthetics of 1951, but Spence has mated it with a manner of handling details that looks very like the smart modern churches of Western Germany – which seems fair enough: what's good for Mercedesdorf should be good for Jaguarsville also.

The main ranks of stained-glass windows are so much at home with the whole conception that one is surprised to remember that they are not by Spence himself, but by Keith New and Geoffrey Clarke and Lawrence Lee. Similarly, Stephen Sykes's mosaic relief in the Gethsemane chapel, irrespective of its merits in its own right, is the perfect work of devotional art to catch and draw the eye at the end of the south aisle. This exact conjunction of architectural and artistic intentions becomes most obvious, but also most resoundingly successful, in John Piper's glass for the tall curved wall of the baptistery on the liturgical south side. The area covered is large, and largely, darkly glowing, but centrally placed and high up is a huge circular patch in much lighter golden colour. Seen unexpectedly, on emerging from the Chapel of Unity opposite, it startlingly creates the impression of the Holy Ghost descending on the font in a ball of atomic fire.

Time after time, Sir Basil gives us, in this sense, masterstrokes of architectural religious drama. The pity is that the play itself should be by Eliot at his most Establishment, not Osborne at his most probing.

25 May 1962

Among the young novelists and poets working for the New Statesman *as it takes its new shape and place under John Freeman, Colin MacInnes has come nearest to giving expression to the mind and face of the teenagers and those in their early twenties who seem to have detached themselves from the body of our society. In a 'Books in General' essay he seems to try, with that warmth which characterizes all his work, to equate the new 'outlawry' with an old and noble one.*

Eve's Children   Colin MacInnes

Some months ago the BBC, falling into its habitual error of supposing enlightenment will arise from throwing together in a studio persons of diametrically different political views, conducted a symposium on anarchism. Mr Colin Ward, an architect and editor of the monthly *Anarchy*, confronted a liberal socialist and a Roman Catholic Tory. Both the non-anarchists ran gay rings round their courteous opponent; scarcely giving him a chance to tell his listeners what anarchism might be – which was presumably the object of the programme. What struck me most about the performance was not so much Colin Ward's sly, patient Socratic dignity, but the condescending disdain of his interlocutors. Clearly, for them, anarchism was a movement of no past, present or possibly future significance whatever.

If they did think this, Mr George Woodcock's *Anarchism*, penetrating, scholarly, and as immensely detailed as it is entirely readable, must prove them wrong. Indeed, his text shows, among so many other things, why this theme is vital to political thinkers in our country. The forefathers of anarchism, from Winstanley to Godwin, were English, most of the chief anarchist agitators lived and worked in England (Peter Kropotkin for over 30 years), and while the great strength of the movement lay in continental Europe, it was germinal to socialism in our land. And though Mr Woodcock's study ends with the fall of the Spanish republic, I would myself go on to suggest that anarchist ideas are more influential today than is usually supposed. His method is to examine the 'Family Tree' of anarchism, with its roots in Lao-Tse, Zeno and the Essenes (though he does not claim an ancestress, as many nimble anarchist genealogists do, in Eve), and with flowerings in the thought and agitation of the main anarchist worthies and precursors – Godwin, Stirner, Proudhon, Bakunin, Kropotkin and Tolstoy. Then, in a second part, there is an account of international anarchism in action, mostly during the 19th century, in the countries of Europe and the Americas where its influence was most enduring.

To seek the consistent core that survives through all personal and theoretical anarchist contradictions, one may first try to say what anarchism is not. The terrorism of popular supposition has always been marginal, and existed chiefly in countries of endemic governmental violence as Spain and Russia, though in France of the 1890s there were sensational explosions of individual anarchist rage. There is also a popular confusion with nihilism and, at the other extreme, with Utopian mysticism, all of which anarchism rejects, since it holds men must intervene positively ('direct action') in the social sphere, is resolutely non-religious as well as anti-clerical, and scorns Utopias, for it holds this static concept to deny the imperative of perpetually evolving nature and human society. Being anti-authoritarian it is violently anti-Marxist, as the quarrels and final split in the First International bore ferocious witness. Yet since it is opposed to all government whatsover, it is equally hostile to democracy ('the deciding upon truth by the casting up of numbers is an intolerable insult upon all reason and justice,' said William Godwin).

To define the positive aspects of anarchism, I can only offer a highly personal interpretation which will no doubt be unacceptable to many of the faithful. To be an anarchist I think one must hold that these propositions are true:

'Man, if not distorted by an authoritarian education, religion, or social order, is fundamentally good; or, if not good, at any rate perfectible in favourable social conditions.

Men fulfil themselves most when they voluntarily associate in co-operative endeavours; and they are most stunted when subjected, or when they subject themselves, to any external authority, and especially those of an organized

284

church and state. Society stems from nature and is instinctive to mankind; government of any sort is a perversion of the natural order.

"Property is theft" (Proudhon). This, with anti-clericalism, is I think the only point of agreement between anarchists and Marxists – though the means proposed for restoring the booty to the community are of course totally at variance.

To alter the social order, all forms of centralized political action (as in orthodox parties) or of industrial action imposed from on high (as with monumental trade unions) must be rejected absolutely. Only spontaneous "direct action" in the social and political fields can alter society without transforming one tyranny into another. No majority ever has the right to rule any minority. The hope lies not in mass revolution led from above, but in rebellion by a mass of sovereign individuals acting in co-operation.'

One can see at once how, in the more fluid political conditions that preceded the October revolution, these doctrines won millions of fanatically devoted adherents – and continued, indeed, to win them in our own day in the special conditions of republican Spain. To begin with, for anyone with respect and feeling for his fellow creatures these ideas are, in human terms, immensely attractive: if man does not seem like that or, when put to the test, behave like that, one feels he ought to. And if anarchist doctrine may initially appear engagingly cranky, one may reflect that all political ideas are this in some measure – and often not engagingly so at all; and that the political paradox of yesterday has often become the commonsensical commonplace of today. One may also consider the astonishing successes of these 'impractical' notions in the testing years of the Spanish republic, and ponder on the unparalleled disasters which 'practical' governments, both democratic and authoritarian, have inflicted on mankind since the decline of anarchism in our era. Yet one may equally see – and here the fates of the CNT and FAI in Spain are once again an illustration – how hard it is for anarchists to reconcile their dogma of spontaneity, and the rejection of centralized organization, with any durable political success.

Mr Woodcock suggests that 'the ideal of anarchism, far from being democracy carried to its logical end, is much nearer to aristocracy universalized and purified.' One may notice how many of the anarchist or near-anarchist prophets were in fact displaced aristocrats (as Kropotkin, Bakunin, Tolstoy), or of an intellectual élite (as Coleridge, Hazlitt, Courbet, Mallarmé, Wilde), or of the artisan 'aristocracy' (as Proudhon the printer or Malatesta the self-taught electrician), or else belonged, like the exalted peasantry of Andalusia, to a class wherein the highest sense of personal dignity accompanied abject poverty. The bourgeoisie and petty-bourgeoisie were never enthusiastic (not surprisingly), which may well account for the relative failure of the movement in Victorian England by comparison with its passing triumphs on the continent. Nor, with exceptions, was the rapidly growing industrial proletariat persuaded in great numbers; reformist socialism won most of their loyalty, and this defeat – coupled with the magnetic attraction, after October, of anarchist militants to communism – seems the chief reason for anarchist decline.

For anyone who, like myself, has anarchist sympathies, the historical portion of the book makes gloomy reading. When the anarchist worthies were not in jail, they lived mostly in exiled destitution. The co-operative factories, farms, colonies and banks they founded usually floundered in the capitalist or Marxist oceans, the non-party 'parties' and decentralized trade unions which they built up rose to amazing strength, then quarrelled, failed to connect internationally, and were soon eroded by reformist or totalitarian rivals. 'Lost causes may be the best causes – they usually are – but once lost they are never won again,' is Mr Woodcock's dispiriting conclusion. In our own day, as phantom anarchist survivals, he sees only the village communities of India (and, of course, the earlier successful use of anarchist-inspired political techniques by Gandhi) and the near-anarchism of the Israeli kibbutzim. One might conclude of anarchism, as has been said of religion, that it is only for good people, and there are never enough of these.

Yet Mr Woodcock also believes that 'the theoretical core of anarchism may still have the power to give life to a new form under changed historical circumstances.' And so fervent, intuitive, prophetic, and often startlingly practical in their apparent simplicity are the doctrines of the anarchist thinkers, that one cannot believe so many men, in so many centuries and countries, could have arrived, often quite independently, at these diagnoses of the human predicament without their thoughts corresponding to some ultimate reality.

They were also, in the main, unusually attractive human beings: as political thinkers generally are not. Godwin's ideas on education, government, the distinction between justice and mere law, on 'accumulated property' (in which he anticipates Marx), on crime (which he believed arose from destitution), and on marriage ('the worst of properties') seem hardly to belong to 1793, when his *Political Justice* appeared. Proudhon was the first to call himself specifically an anarchist with pride – it had been hitherto, as it is still mostly now, a term of abuse (as when a Cromwellian pamphleteer denounced the Levellers as 'Switzerizing anarchists'). A political activist as well as a voluminously self-taught writer, his *What Is Property?* won Marx's grudging approval ('a penetrating work') and his vigorous prose the praises of Baudelaire, Flaubert and of Leo Tolstoy, who met him and read with profit his *La Guerre et la Paix*. He took part in the revolution of 1848, went in and out of prisons, founded innumerable newspapers (*Le Représentant du Peuple* of that year was the first anarchist journal), started a People's Bank (it failed), stood for the Constituent Assembly, was elected and soon repented.

The anarchist saint is, of course, Prince Peter Kropotkin – though myself I must confess that, while admiring enormously his courage, benevolence and massive erudition, I find him almost too good to be true. (I think it is the modest exclusion of sex from his anthropological writing that embarrasses me – a reticence certainly not shared by contemporary young anarchists my acquaintance.) After serving in the Imperial army, he came under the influence of Proudhon, and went to live among the proto-anarchist of watchmaking villagers of the Jura. Returning to Russia to spread the good news he was arrested, dramatically escaped, and eventually settled in various London suburbs where he became the chief polemical philosopher of anarchism, while also addressing English learned societies and contributing to *The Times*.

Among his most striking ideas are the doctrine of 'free distribution' (anticipated by Sir Thomas More) by which he declared that society owes a debt to every man, whether he earns his keep or not; and his refutation of neo-Darwinian and Malthusian ideas in *Mutual Aid*, in which he deployed his formidable scientific armoury to show that primitive societies – and even animals – are organized on a basis of self-help, not self-destruction. With fellow exiles and English Fabians he founded *Freedom* (whose 75th birthday party I attended last autumn at the Fulham Town Hall). When he supported the Allies in World War I he was momentarily estranged from his anarchist comrades, but after he returned to Russia at the revolution, and defied Lenin (or tried to), he was restored to the anarchist pantheon.

Freedom, I would say, is about the only authentically polemical weekly surviving in our country (their headline on Dr Verwoerd's accident was 'Too Bad He Missed'); and *Anarchy* the most original monthly that I know of in its perceptions of shifting trends in our society. Such anarchists as I have met are not of the late-1940s ex-bourgeois eccentric variety, but sane, humorous, and remarkably consistent, in their private lives, to their anarchist principles of patient co-operation and determined persuasion. Their chief activities are in education, particularly of children, as in their

287

libertarian 'Adventure Playgrounds' – much frowned on by asphalt-minded municipal fathers. Their industrial influence seems less, and this is their weakness, as it always has been.

In a larger way, it seems to me anarchist ideas have spread considerably in the past decade, even if those who hold them may be unaware of their anarchist origins. The direct action of the CND, and especially of the Committee of 100, have a largely anarchist inspiration and technique, and the whole spirit, among the young of all classes, of 'contracting out' of adult social and political obsessions appears to be a form of anarchism, if only negatively so. And this tendency would seem to be international: so that one can see it in the West, and easily imagine, in Marxist countries, the existence of an unconscious anarchist underground. The profound appeal of anarchism is in its concern for each human person; and I believe most of the young have sensed – rightly – that all governments today regard them as expendable.

My own chief reservations about anarchist thinking are that there does exist a pharisaical fringe, such as Orwell noticed when he criticized the near-anarchist social order of the Houyhnhnms:

'In a Society where there is no law, and in theory no compulsion, the only arbiter of behaviour is public opinion . . . less tolerant than any system of law.'

In the anarchist detestation of a vulgarized commercial society, and its hideous fruits, there is perhaps still some hankering not just for the smaller humanly manageable industrial and urban unit, but also that backward-looking tendency which led Marx to place anarchists among the reactionaries in his demonology. Nor do I think that anarchists have quite admitted to themselves the degree to which anarchism, however fervently and sincerely it rejects organized churches, is in fact, by its faith and doctrine, a religion without a God.

To disdain a perennial human ideal because it has hitherto failed in proof, and now seems in following numerically insignificant, may turn out to be unrealistic, and is certainly philistine. And I reflected, as I heard the socialist and the Roman Catholic patronizing the editor of *Anarchy*, how the might of Marxism grew out of the musings of two exiled Germans in a Dean Street tenement, and the Christian church out of a nucleus of twelve. Anarchism has survived in our consciousness for centuries and yet it has not, save on a small scale and for brief periods, ever been put into application. And of those political systems which, in my own lifetime, have (during which we Europeans alone have killed 30 millions of one another, and look like murdering many millions more), it is hard to think with enthusiasm or affection.

7 September 1962

'*Yeah, I know it's mine, but I ain't marryin' no bird wot ain't a virgin.*' by Trog [*4 Jan. 1963*]

The placing of Colin MacInnes' essay last in this anthology is not simply fortuitous, nor is it a mere matter of chronology. As I have tried to show in my The New Statesman: The History of the First Fifty Years 1913-1963 (*Longmans Green, London, 1963*), *the* New Statesman *has striven weekly for half a century to express the principles of a society which, while enabling the individual to retain a substantial measure of freedom, of 'protestant' responsibility for his own thoughts and acts, would give us a social order rationally planned and humanely administered. But time after time the same difficulty recurs: scientifically planned socialist order is not immediately and readily compatible with the old liberal freedom which is also in the* New Statesman'*s traditions. New statesmanship has enjoyed a remarkable measure of success in the last fifty years: an important number of its ideas have been accepted by nations all over the world; in law, if not always in practice, new statesmanly principles have become the rules by which peoples govern themselves. But it cannot be denied that, in the process of ensuring that more people shall live more nearly under economic and social justice, some of the old freedoms, some of the qualities of individualism and the kind of happiness derived from it, have been mislaid. I will not say 'lost' because they are recoverable and it is possible that the* New Statesman'*s task in the next fifty years will be, in part, to try to get the balance restored; and therefore to give expression to the kind of 'anarchism' implied in Mr MacInnes' essay. Even Marxists (I do not mean National Communists) have no use for the State excepting as a temporary and expedient device; it is destined by their founder to 'wither away'. Before it can do so, however, we have to find out how to behave, voluntarily and of our own will, as if we were under law; to behave well out of the goodness of our hearts and the good sense of our minds, and not simply under threat of the policemen's truncheons. The* New Statesman'*s task until now has been to try to lay down the principles of social institutions so just that it is reasonable to compel us to respect them. This task is far from completed; but while it is being completed it will also be as well to find out how we can remove the compulsion and so restore full freedom to men, while being sure that they will continue to behave 'socially'. What Mr MacInnes is seeking, and what many of the writers whose work composes this anthology have been seeking less obviously, is a law derived from our own goodwill towards each other, not a law imposed by social contract. It is possible that that will also be what the* New Statesman, *and for that matter any decent, humane, honest form of new statesmanship by whatever name, will find itself trying to devise.*